Praise for
The Mystic Heart of Justice

The Mystic Heart of Justice is a clarion call for a radical examination of our legal system whose very design promotes conflict and inhibits healing. Crime and divisiveness are the natural by-products of the American criminal justice system. While the retributive model for addressing harm (the real "bad apple") should be plucked from our midst and incarcerated—thereby protecting the populace from "judiciogenic misery" — victims and offenders ought to be more involved in healing processes that build community connectedness. Breton and Lehman describe a growing revolution that is moving us away from our adversarial system of codified courtroom "justice" and toward an internally derived therapeutic justice grounded in cherished personal values. Restorative justice offers a forward-looking return to ancient (but never outdated) aboriginal methods for repairing fractured relationships. By reconnecting with our selves and our communities, we can, and will, feel safer and more whole. *The Mystic Heart of Justice* offers a true crime prevention plan that will ennoble everyone who participates in it.

Geral Blanchard, Author, *Sexual Abuse in America*

I loved the book. I am so pleased to see these authors take esoteric truths usually delegated to spirituality or theology and explain the fundamental essence of justice. What society has delegated to an intellectual science is really a matter of the heart.

William van Zyverden, Esq.
President, International Alliance of Holistic Lawyers

Many of us working in restorative justice have found that the deep inner work on self is as important as the outer work on public justice. *The Mystic Heart of Justice*, in probing deeply into the meaning of justice and the foundations of our current cultural framework around justice, illuminates possible pathways for the inner work and makes clear why we feel that pull to inner work so profoundly.

Kay Pranis, Restorative Justice Planner
Minnesota Department of Corrections

Reading this book was like going back to college and confronting once more all those wonderful, idealistic thoughts from ancient philosophers about who we are and why we are here. The authors are right—as individuals we don't often connect with the noblest impulses of our inner selves . . . and, therefore, we fail to react to such glaring examples of injustice as our court and prison systems. We can only hope that this book gives a shot of growth hormone to today's slowly growing movement toward restorative justice in America. The personal stories of redemption validate the authors' thesis in dramatic form.

Maralys Wills, Author, *Save My Son*

Finally, a book on justice that focuses on true healing rather than retribution! *The Mystic Heart of Justice* is elegantly infused with a living and loving wisdom. Breton and Lehman are sharing from the pulse of evolution's most creative positivism. A highly recommended spiritual masterpiece!

Michael Picucci, Ph.D., M.A.C.
The Institute for Authentic Process Healing <www.theinstitute.org>

Denise Breton and Stephen Lehman brilliantly and convincingly reimagine justice as a friend of our soul that brings in its surge healing, connectedness, unity, and well-being. Their vision of restorative justice is deep, wide, and eminently down-to-earth.

Frederic and Mary Ann Brussat
Co-authors, *Spiritual Literacy* and *Spiritual Rx*

I hope every lawyer and judge and teacher in the world reads this book. It has a perspective on justice that transcends the trap of the petty reductionistic mind of our culture's archaic, sick-at-heart institutions of justice. *The Mystic Heart of Justice* is a deeper view of justice than, for example, the current criminal justice system, whose only virtue is that it is aptly named. The authors take on the task of healing justice. My God! What brass! What courage! What presumptiveness! What foolhardy venturing into the jaws of the dragon! And, talk about hubris, listen to this: "We write as philosophers who take a spiritual approach, which means we think about meaning and purpose within a larger scope of life. . . . We want a concept that affirms soul and meaning—that doesn't crush our spirits in the name of justice." This book could heal justice.

Brad Blanton, Ph.D.
Author, *Radical Honesty* and *Radical Parenting: How to Raise Creators*

THE MYSTIC HEART OF JUSTICE

The Mystic Heart of Justice

*Restoring Wholeness in a
Broken World*

Denise Breton

Stephen Lehman

Foreword by Vine Deloria Jr.

CHRYSALIS BOOKS

WEST CHESTER, PENNSYLVANIA

Library of Congress Cataloging-in-Publication Data
Breton, Denise.
    The mystic heart of justice : restoring wholeness in a broken world / Denise Breton, Stephen Lehman.
        p.   cm.
    Includes bibliographical references and index.
    ISBN 0-87785-300-2
    1. Justice.   2. Restorative justice.
        I. Lehman, Stephen.   II. Title.

JC578 .B684 2001   2001037256
172'.2–dc21

Credits: See page viii

Edited by Mary Lou Bertucci
Designed by Gopa Design and Ted2
Set in Janson and Poetica by Gopa Design
Printed in the United States of America.

Chrysalis Books is an imprint of the
Swedenborg Foundation, Inc. For more information,
contact: Swedenborg Foundation Publishers
320 North Church Street, West Chester, PA 19380
or
http://www.swedenborg.com.

To Sara Picone

& Christopher Largent

Credits

Original images of dove with scales on cover and part pages, courtesy of ©Photodisc

Pages 7–8: "Sir Penny" from George F. Whicher, *The Goliard Poets*, copyright © 1949 by George F. Whicher, is reprinted by permission of New Directions Publishing Corp., New York.

Pages 12–13; 57–60: Excerpts from *Satisfying Justice* are reprinted by permission of The Church Council on Justice and Corrections, Ottawa, Ontario, Canada.

Pages 39–40 and 140; Extracts from Rumi, "The One Thing You Must Do," from *Say I Am You* and from *Delicious Laughter*, are reprinted by permission of Coleman Barks.

Pages 61–64: Excerpt from "Restorative Justice," *Yes! A Journal of Positive Futures*, is reprinted by permission of the author, Tag Evers.

All excerpts from *Returning to the Teachings: Exploring Aboriginal Justice* by Rupert Ross, copyright © 1996 by University of Saskatchewan, are reprinted by permission of Penguin Books Canada Limited.

All excerpts from *The Sacred Tree* are reprinted by permission of The Four Worlds International Institute for Human and Community Development, 347 Fairmont Blvd., Lethbridge, Alberta T1K 7J8, Canada

Contents

❧ *Foreword*
by Vine Deloria Jr.

T HE RECENT TURMOIL over the execution of Timothy McVeigh brought to the surface many abstract concepts that have not been examined for decades, if not centuries. We demanded justice for the victims of McVeigh's twisted act of violence, but we also made arrangements to televise his execution to an increasingly large group of people, vainly suggesting that watching him expire would somehow bring "closure" to the pain and suffering generated by his actions. Justice, in an industrial society that is evolving toward feudalism, seems to be a thinly disguised demand for vengeance. For all our technology and sophistication, we reveal ourselves as barbarians of the first order, far below the tribal peoples who considered and rejected the retributive sense of law and order.

Why does the most complex industrial and technological society on the planet adopt a crude "eye-for-an-eye" system of justice—with exemptions for wealth, class, and political connections? Denise Breton and Stephen Lehman set out to explore this thicket of inconsistencies. In many ways, they are charged with rounding up the cattle of our minds, those elusive, ill-considered emotional responses to the unexpected that appear to us as common-sense solutions to the problem of violence. Offering restorative justice as a substitute for the present tendency to punish by class and stereotype, they seek to invoke a vision of a society in which the personhood of the individual becomes important. Their proposal makes perfect sense, and the examples they give of instances where restorative justice was the operating principle demonstrate the existence of a viable alternative to our present system.

Identifying the theoretical roots of our present system is difficult because so many strands of ancient tradition, religious beliefs, folk customs, family loyalties, and philosophical speculations are woven together and inseparable. Breaking any of these highly charged topics loose from their emotional moorings in Western culture and using them to create leverage for reform of the justice system are mighty tasks, not lightly undertaken. We need critiques of each subject that can be reasonably isolated from the others and an analysis of the bonds that attach the respective subjects to each other. Restorative justice depends on our emotional confidence in creating the complex of persons who can resolve the injuries suffered by the participants in activities crying for resolution. And we need to examine the confidence that gives many people reasons to vest their loyalties in the present system.

From the beginning of Western thought, there has been an avowed tie to the idea of objectivity. We seek to create and maintain justice by lauding impartiality, knowing, nevertheless, that our objectivity is simply the alignment of our emotions with the external facts of the situation as our culture has taught us to see them. In seeking objectivity, we discard any facts or attributes that do not fit into preconceived categories. Hence, our explanations of phenomena are increasingly generalized, while it is the particularization of data that enables us to live in the physical world. We are thus often brought into a hard collision with the realities of life, and we respond with abstract generalizations.

Since justice is, we believe, administered by our political institutions, we must look to efforts to give those institutions intellectual respectability. John Locke and John Rawls are two of many good examples of thinkers who have tried to provide a mechanism for distributing justice within a social contract and have sought to ground their offerings in terms of fairness, a close relative of justice. Locke believed that citizens within the social contract would make rational, objective choices in their political affairs, a notion touchingly naive. Since reason was the mortar holding the social contract together, Locke made no mention of age, gender, degree of education, place of residence, adherence to local custom, or, most importantly, family as influences that would eliminate any semblance of reason.

John Rawls proposed that a society could be constructed in which all positions would be equally good choices for anyone from outside to entice them to join. Rawls' articulation of the framework of this society is pleasurable reading, but it makes no sense at all if we try to take real people and expect them to make theoretical choices that do not involve the same influences as those that tumbled Lockean philosophy. Yet Rawls titles his book *A Theory of Justice* with the expectation that, having created a perfectly logical social machine, justice would be served by the impartial functioning of institutional procedures. Both Locke and Rawls see humans as another phenomenon of nature, subject to the manipulations of the coercive power of institutions.

Americans should replace the eagle as a symbol and install the sheep. Not only are we led around by continuous political bleating, but we say "Baa" to every progressive idea that is suggested. If we but look at the manner in which we presently administer the law, we can see that not even retributive justice is achieved. One is reminded of the revelations of the wrongdoings of Spiro Agnew and the argument that he had suffered enough by being exposed so that we need not punish him. Contrary to our beliefs in justice or the admonition of Amos the prophet to let righteousness roll down like the waters, our current system of justice is simply the arbitrary use of plea bargaining and deals. Solutions emerge depending on the economic and political influence of the defendant and often the race of the parties. Thus, we have a system of laws, not of justice. Indeed, there is an old apocryphal anecdote that, once in oral arguments before the Supreme Court, Oliver Wendell Holmes admonished a party that the court was there to determine the law, not to do justice.

The basis of Western political institutions is the belief that, at some remote time in the past, all individuals were free agents and that they banded together, each ceding his or her sovereign right to kill and do violence, to form a society. We cherish this fantasy because we began the United States under similar circumstances. We have, therefore, built our society on the idea of rights, and these rights are always *against* the state or our fellow human beings. Rights in themselves suggest a society built on the principle of conflict; each member of the society is in a potential adversarial relationship with every other member. Given this, we cannot help but live in a society that inflicts pain and injury, even though it may only be our feelings that are hurt.

Restorative justice must have deep roots that extend farther than the simple notion of rights. They must reside in the idea that we are responsible for making a positive contribution to the society in which we live. Prior to the assertion or exercise of rights, we must have an alert citizenry that has sought to make a contribution to the peace and harmony of our community. People must take on the duty of assisting those who have difficulty living by the customs and codes we cherish. It is only as we act responsibly toward others and live in the expectation that they will act in a similar manner toward us that we can have restorative justice.

Each society eventually settles on a number of virtues, strangely, often four virtues. Breton and Lehman remind us of Plato's four virtues: wisdom, courage, moderation, and justice as recounted in *The Republic*. I did an informal survey of Sioux Indian people to see what our four virtues were. I got as many answers as there were people queried, and not often did the four virtues appear to be the same. Curiously, however, every person mentioned generosity first and bravery second. The last two virtues varied considerably. We do not often see generosity suggested as a civic virtue; we keep it carefully closeted within our private lives. How refreshing, then, to find a virtue that does not look to feats of individual actions but emphasizes sharing one's time, energy, and concern with others.

Generosity, of course, is the light side of what Breton and Lehman describe as competitive selfishness, which is encouraged in our society. One need only remember the temper tantrums of John McEnroe and Jimmy Connors to see that establishing the individual's relationship to others on ego-driven competition precludes the one neutral posture that must be present if there is to be a society worth joining. The posture is that of civility—the self-discipline and sense of good manners that seek to promote the atmosphere of decency, whether the society possesses it or not. Civility fills the spaces between individuals with sufficient concern that people are encouraged to act respectfully toward others, thus ensuring that the social contract is actually social—or has a vision of it. The lack of civility encourages the injustice that Breton and Lehman chronicle because we do not bother to show respect for other human beings simply because they are human beings.

Indian tribes built a social contract on premises exactly the opposite from those of Europeans. Recognizing that blood and friendship were more influential than reasoned thought, they established rules whereby people had responsibilities toward family members and the means of including nonfamily members and even strangers within the network of concern. Foremost in this society was the necessity of calling family members by their genetic relationship—that is, mother, brother, cousin, grandmother, and so forth. While people had names that were used in social discourse in the larger society, one had to call relatives by the kinship term. This practice was to remind people of their responsibility to each other.

The identification of family roles meant an allocation of the kinds of behavior that one could expect within the family. Thus recognizing that children need both love and discipline, the Indians charged the father's brothers, the uncles, with the training and discipline of the boys. The mother's sisters, the aunts, had charge of the education and training of the girls. The parents were thus not placed in a position where they would be disciplinarians with their own children. To avoid overzealous training by aunts and uncles, the father's sisters and the mother's brothers provided secondary comfort for the children so that having been chastised by one set of uncles and aunts, a child could find some encouragement from another set. Over this pyramid of relationships were the grandparents. Basically, the grandfather decided what the rules of the family were. He acted as a lawgiver for the younger relatives. The grandmother's role was to decide whether a course of action was appropriate in any particular case. Thus, both law and equity were found within the family of clan structure. Society was simply sets of families who were compatible with each other.

Breton and Lehman stress throughout their examination of justice that we have a task, mystical almost in its origin, to "do what's ours to do." By this admonition, they suggest that we each have a higher calling that, if followed, builds integrity within us and allows for the functioning of restorative justice. How do we find ourselves and our niche in the larger society? How can we join with others in reconciling the hurts and injuries that others have inflicted on us? We can measure ourselves by acknowledging the existence of a path that we must take to remain consistent with ourselves. For most societies, this path is a religious journey in which we have levels of comprehension followed by

long periods of routine daily life. Our task is to remain true to our perception of our life and destiny between the episodes of awareness and
the revelation of the larger cosmic processes.

Doing our unique tasks must certainly involve some vision of the
larger cosmic process to which we accommodate ourselves. Whether
we like it or not, and if only on size alone, we must admit that there are
greater powers than ourselves. The Western tradition has made much
of its belief in "God." But belief and actions are far distant from each
other in reality. Against the accusation that we worship money is the
practical admission that we simply practice the accumulation of money;
it really means very little to those who have it. There is nothing in modern American society before which we bow in reverence. So we have no
ultimate power that we admit or that in relation to which we seek to
guide our lives. Perhaps doing what we were intended to do is a solution
to the problem of justice. But discovering our vocation as persons, not
employees, is almost unheard of today.

When people stand before the many institutions that direct their
lives, they must establish an ethical relationship to them, so that the
work they do and the activities they undertake have some meaning.
Because we believe so devoutly in the equality of people, we tend to
believe that a proper relationship with institutions guarantees that we
live a reasonably moral life, a life in which we could institute a process
of restorative justice. We must recognize, however, that every relationship has within it the outline of a personal ethic and functions automatically according to the nature of the experience. Unfortunately,
equality projects the sense that we all function in the same way and
should therefore share the same ethical decision-making process. In an
industrial society, we then become part of the machine and dehuman-
ize ourselves.

The present practical ethic that most of us share relieves us of any
responsibility for ourselves and for others. It is a two-step logical process
and covers every conceivable situation we can encounter. How often
have we heard the following words spoken by the people who operate
the big machines and administer the massive social programs? "If I don't
do it, someone else will," and "Don't blame me—I'm just doing my job."
Obviously we have accepted the proposition that the temporal process

in which we are engaged requires the logical next step; it is inevitable. Once a pattern of behavior is regarded as inevitable, no one is to blame. Everyone does his or her job and lets the responsibility fall on shoulders that do not exist, for everyone has segregated his or her portion of the job from everything else. If there is no one at the controls, we can hardly accept blame for the overall disaster.

Thus it is that we stand at a crossroads that is always before us. We seek to transform retributive justice into restorative justice, but to do so, we must visualize replacing the intellectual edifice that has brought us to this point of decision. The task of transformation is not difficult, but it involves gathering enough people together to begin to force change in our institutional life. Today when we execute people, the chances are great that we are killing innocent men and women. We seem satisfied that, since the procedural rules appear to be reasonably followed, justice will be done. Our popular word now is *closure*—once a person is executed, we seek to forget as quickly as possible what has happened. It is very sad to see dozens of people who consider themselves upright and moral Christians screaming for Timothy McVeigh's blood.

A mass society depends on statistical realities. We pass laws with the full expectation that only a small percentage of people will violate them. When the percentage of violators becomes too large, we either stop enforcing the law or, with sudden political pressure, seek to reform or abolish the law that has offended the majority of us. A mass society can be easily manipulated, because all efforts to communicate must be phrased in the most general terms so that we can communicate with as many people as possible. Thus, ideas that would not make sense to a small society become logical and even common sense to people in a larger society. That is how lynch mobs set their goals. The importance of *The Mystic Heart of Justice* is that it does not depend on the invention of new vocabulary to develop its thesis. On the contrary, the authors hammer relentlessly with everyday examples and reasoning, revealing to us why we think the way we do and what we can do to change that kind of thinking.

Since the 1960s, we have adopted a strange kind of belief that, if we make people aware of problems, solutions will be found. Thus, we have all kinds of stunts performed by utterly sincere people trying to get their cause elevated in the minds of others with the belief that awareness is sufficient to deal with conditions we have been reluctant to confront. We believe the squeaky wheel will get the grease. Yet we do not offer reasonable alternatives to many of our problems, and as a result, old solutions are put forward that we know will not work. Further testing in schools will not produce good readers. Nor will it improve penmanship.

If local people begin to take up the responsibilities they have as members of society and insist that we treat everyone with respect, if people will become more generous, and if people will seek to heal injuries instead of evening the balance of violence, then we can move toward restorative justice. In the meantime, we are stuck with retribution, as it seems that the vengeful God of the Old Testament is always ready and willing to demand sacrifices in place of healing.

ℛ *Preface*

P HILOSOPHY IS NOT like news reporting. It's not a matter of giving information but of walking around a subject, considering the same issues from many angles. Philosophy is more like art than science, more like exploring recurring themes in music than deciding on one right answer and then moving on to the next question. No subject is ever "finished," and the more fundamental the issue, the more it warrants rethinking.

Philosophy's art explores implications: what are the implications if we define *justice* one way, and what are the implications if we shift to a different core definition? Implications are like ripples on water: they keep spreading out. Consequently, the philosophic endeavor is approximate, not final. It is open and exploratory. But it is also passionate. When we walk around a concept and feel waves of suffering coming from it, it's in the tradition of philosophy to say so.

The themes we "walk around" in this book cut to the core of our cultural philosophy, affecting just about every aspect of life. To start the process, we'll be thinking about the following:

Punishment

• Does punishment create justice among us?

• Does punishment make us better people?

• Does punishment heal our wounds?

• Does punishment help us understand each other better or clarify what went wrong, so we can correct it?

• Does punishment either build good relationships or help us mend them when they've broken down?

Rewards

• Do rewards make us happy, or does the pursuit of them yield a satisfying life?

• Does competing for rewards build honest, open, trusting, or cooperative relationships?

• Do the judgments and comparisons that reward-allocation requires benefit our self-esteem or support peace of mind? Do they do us justice for who we uniquely are?

• Do rewards enhance motivation and enthusiasm for what we are doing?

• Does organizing our lives around obtaining rewards bring freedom, or do we become slaves to chasing carrots?

Justice

• Can punishments and rewards offer a good model of justice, and do the worlds created from them feel just?

• What if justice isn't about blaming and hurting but about restoring and healing?

• Can we envision a justice that works for us, helping us instead of accusing us?

• Can we imagine a justice that calls us to do what is ours to do in life and supports us all along the way, encouraging us to live from our center and essence?

• If this feels more like justice—if true justice is about coming home to who we are and doing what is ours to do, personally and together—how might this change our entire philosophy as well as our practice of justice?

In writing this book, we are operating from a philosophy that says we as humans are beings of soul and meaning, possessed of hearts and feelings. We are seeking models of justice that better fit our nature—that help us express more of who we are, rather than less. We want to walk around models of justice that draw life from us: from our human capacities to care, feel pain, understand each other, heal, transcend, love, experience compassion, and be creative together. As it turns out, such models are possible. Not only do they exist, but they work—and have worked for millennia.

⌘ *Acknowledgments*

B EYOND THE WRITING, books are about birthing ideas, and that involves a team effort that keeps spreading out.

At Chrysalis Books, former acquisitions editor Susan Poole was the first to move this book toward published form. We are grateful to her for her enthusiasm during the early writing period. Deborah Forman, executive director of the Swedenborg Foundation, supported the project with careful attention to every detail. To our cover and interior designer as well as typesetter, Gopa, we are indebted for her sensitivity to the subject and her ability to translate intangible ideas into beauty. George Dole, the consummate scholar and translator of Emanuel Swedenborg's works, was a reader for us and made exceedingly helpful suggestions, as did Don Rose, the assistant pastor of Bryn Athyn Cathedral. Betsy Smailer helped us get what we needed when we needed it. Cathy Broberg, the freelance copyeditor who worked wonders on our previous books, juggled her tight schedule to help us with this one as well. To Mary Lou Bertucci, our editor, we owe profound gratitude. Like a sculptor, Mary Lou knew what to cut and what to leave. She made our work infinitely better, and not only that, she moved us to a different place in writing, a place we needed to be.

In personal encouragement, Mary Joy Breton made the writing possible on many levels: support, research, proofing, as well as vision. She also stepped in to help with indexing. Ernie Breton and Ruth Newman, both diligent readers of drafts, offered valuable feedback. When a writer's refuge was needed, Jeannine and Mike Baden provided it, along with their wise counsel. To Loretta Draths, we are grateful for her nurturing presence and her astute comments and critiques of the manuscript. And we are grateful to Clark Erickson, who helped us "ground our high-mindedness" in our lives.

On an individual basis, I, Denise, want to express gratitude to Christopher Largent, my former husband of twenty-four years. He is an avid researcher with a mind that won't quit, a friend always in my corner believing in what I do, and the person who has encouraged me over decades to find my voice in writing. We have graduated from the life we had together, and our paths are unfolding in different directions, though we remain close friends. Because we talked ideas, philosophy, spirituality, recovery, social issues, and everything else nonstop for all those years, his ideas and perspectives will always be a part of what I write. And the man has a knack for picking titles: "The Mystic Heart of Justice" was his idea.

We also feel profound gratitude for the abiding vision, courage, and open-hearted forgiveness of indigenous and First Nation people for sharing their wisdom and healing ways with all people. Without their philosophy and practice, this book never would have happened. Of course, we wouldn't have known about their current work in reforging a healing approach to justice had it not been for Geral Blanchard's passion for restorative justice and Pat Carne's enthusiasm for sharing his findings.

That Professor Vine Deloria Jr. was willing to write a foreword for this book is a huge gift. He brings together in his life all the perspectives that we call upon for help in rethinking what justice may mean—law, spirituality, history. But most of all, as a Lakota Sioux, he comes from an indigenous philosophy and life. We are honored that he would lend his time, thought, and energies to our quest to rethink justice.

We also want to thank our commentators, people whose time is always in great demand, for giving their thought, reflection, and support. And we want to thank in advance reviewers of the work, who play such an important role in disseminating the ideas brought forth through independent publishing.

And finally, we want to thank you the reader for going on this idea journey with us. Philosophy is its own creature. It's about engaging in thought and dialogue, and for that, we need each other.

⅋ Introduction
Can We Do Justice Greater Justice?

THIS BOOK IS ABOUT changing how we think about justice, not just in formal, legal ways but in the ways justice affects every aspect of life. Justice isn't only about laws, courts, police, and prisons. It's about creating what's right, good, and principled in all our relationships. Justice is about all of us everyday, because it has to do with how we harmonize our ways of being together—how we create peace and happiness among us. Ideally, our concept of justice guides us in managing our personal relations, so that they feel right to everyone involved. Sometimes we experience this happy balance, but often we don't. In trying to be fair to one person or group, we end up being unfair to another. It's no small job that justice has, nor an easy one.

Etymologically, the word *justice* comes from root-meanings that have to do with "law" and "righteousness"—what's right, good, and principled—and how these values operate in our dealings with each other. What is it to live a good life and to be a person of integrity? The models of justice that we use both personally and as a society guide us in how we organize our lives together, so that we treat each other well and fairly.

Since everything we do happens in a context of relationships that require a harmonious, sustainable balance to work, justice is central to virtually everything we do. How we interact with our spouse, children, coworkers, fellow motorists, neighbors, animal companions, or the earth is all shaped by how we conceive of justice.

Consider, for instance, business life: fairness or the lack of it plays a key role in what goes on. How does a business treat its employees, customers, and clients? How does it deal with other businesses? Without minimum standards of justice in financial and market exchanges, we could never trust each other enough to do business at all. Certainly, we don't do return business with companies that treat us badly. In the larger sphere, what responsibility does a business take for its waste? How responsibly does it use resources in relation to communities, ecosystems, and future generations? The ways we address these everyday business issues depend on our actual, lived concept of justice.

Justice or the lack of it also shapes how governments govern and how they interact with other governments, peoples, and cultures. We expect governments to uphold justice in human affairs; that's presumably why we have them. And yet governments don't always do this. Native Americans, for instance, find justice sorely lacking in the ways the United States government has dealt with the First Nations since its inception, and African Americans have struggled against injustices since they first arrived. The struggles of both these races, not to mention the struggles of women and children, raise the issue: if a government fails to treat those in positions of lesser power justly, is anyone safe? Can anyone feel assured of fair treatment under such a government? Moreover, how just can that government claim to be? If it's not just, what is its authority for ruling?

When people are unhappy with how a government treats them, they try to find ways either to remedy the problem or to get rid of the unjust policies and regimes, whether it takes days or centuries to do this. In the Philippines in 1986, for instance, "people power" overthrew Ferdinand Marcos. In Romania in 1989, the people toppled Nicolae Ceausescu, and in Yugoslavia in October 2000, citizens, including some of the police, rose up against the electorally defeated president Slobodan Milosevic, who tried to stay in power nonetheless. When the model of justice underlying a government violates the model of justice held by its people, the people can prevail.

But justice struggles aren't limited to the public stage. Even deciding what to eat involves issues of what's right and good. For vegetarians, eating meat isn't fair to either animals or the earth. More broadly, we face the issue of which foods grown by which methods do justice to the natural world and fellow species. Coffee lovers, for instance, can choose to drink shade-grown coffee, which preserves the habitats of wintering songbirds. Tuna lovers can choose suppliers whose fishing methods don't trap dolphins.

Then there's the issue of how we nourish our bodies fairly—what's right to put in them. Out-of-control health insurance costs are at least partly attributable to our treating our bodies without respect, subjecting them to overprocessed diets, sugar, tobacco smoke, alcohol, and other addictive products.

What about the practices of the company that produces a food? How does it treat its workers? If it raises animals, how does it treat them? What is its commitment to safe, nutritious products? Does it bribe congresspeople to achieve unfair market advantages?

Clearly, issues of justice are alive and well every time we sit down to eat. This may seem trivial; but considering the size of the food industry and its impact on the lives of millions of farmers, workers, and animals, on the earth, not to mention on our health, questions about what's fair and balanced around food take on great import.

But how we think about justice isn't all outwardly focused. It has a voice inside us as well, shaping how we think and feel about ourselves. How should we allow ourselves to be treated by others, and how should we treat ourselves? What will we tolerate without and within? Where do we put our energies? What do we allow ourselves to dream? Our concepts of justice guide how we answer these questions.

Unfortunately, our relationship with ourselves is fraught with injustices. Thanks to unhealthy models we've internalized from parents, teachers, and peers, we often judge ourselves unfairly and maintain self-concepts that don't value who we are. We think we're not good enough, that we're unworthy of happiness, or that we deserve instead punishment for some inchoate sense of wrongdoing, inadequacy, or failure. We scold and blame ourselves, instead of celebrating what's good. As to dreams, either we don't allow ourselves to have them, or we try to tell ourselves that dreaming inside the box is the same as dreaming new worlds into being.

If we're serious about justice, we have to apply it to ourselves too. What does it mean to hold ourselves in fair regard and then to treat ourselves justly? Do the standards that we apply to ourselves—however effective they may be at pleasing others and meeting social expectations—grant us the freedom to live from our souls? Some self-messages honor our inner being and call it forth, while others say that who we are is unacceptable and that we should become instead what others expect us to be. If we've internalized the latter sort of messages, we become our own abusers. We think we're not much good, so it's only right for us to try to become other than who we are. In the name of justice—or our model of it—we do injustice to ourselves.

Whatever model of justice we use, it affects our larger philosophy of life—our sense of meaning and purpose. The ways we think about justice shape our views of the world, where we see ourselves fitting in, and what we can best do with our lives. If being a certain way seems right and good, then that way of being has meaning for us. We believe in it, because it fits our sense of justice, which in turn is tied to our sense of an order to things. Through our philosophies of justice, we find a road to harmony based on our models of what's good and what ultimately works.

Finding a road to harmony is relatively easy when the world seems just, but it can also be found when the world seems riddled with injustices. Injustices make life hell, and that doesn't work in the long run. It's not sustainable. Sooner or later, the jig is up on injustice: people get so angry that they rebel, or the model of injustice comes home to roost and makes life hell for the perpetrators, or the system—whether interpersonal, social, economic, biological, or ecological—gets so out of balance that it breaks down. One way or another, patterns of injustice fail.

Assuming that unjust systems fall on their own, Gandhi and his followers worked to reveal injustice. They aimed not to destroy social or political systems but rather to expose their true character. By practicing nonviolent noncooperation with the colonialism of British rule, even though it involved suffering and imprisonment, Gandhi and his followers found a meaningful response based on a deeper understanding of justice. Surrounded by injustices, they found a path to meaning and inner harmony.

For most of us, though, our model of justice falls short of showing us how to cut a path through injustice. We feel overwhelmed by a world full of wrongs. When life seems more unfair than fair, values lose meaning, and our concepts of justice go into crisis. We wonder what meaning there is in our being principled if people around us seem to be getting ahead by being exploitative and irresponsible. With our concepts of justice pulled out from under us, we lose our road to harmony.

For example, if we're treated poorly on the job, we wonder why we should make the effort. What meaning can we find in giving our best to people who give us their worst—who behave unfairly or who institute policies that convey the message that we're inferior and that it's acceptable to treat us as such? Worker apathy and low quality output directly reflect workers' perception of workplace injustice, precisely because the situation leads to a loss of meaning.

However, when a sense of justice balances workplace relationships, our work is validated. The more justice is practiced top to bottom— until there is no top or bottom but simply differing responsibilities in an equal and cooperative effort to do a good job—the greater everyone's enthusiasm and the better his or her performance, as many companies have discovered. Employee ownership and nonhierarchical flow charts are gaining acceptance because the equity they represent fires motivation.

This makes sense. Relationships based on honesty, fairness, freedom, and a deep honoring of each other inspire us to be creative. We feel that what we do matters, and we're confident that we'll be treated well. When justice lives both in our hearts and in our relationships, we get out of bed with purpose, because we feel that we fit in a larger order of things that's good, that's worth fitting into, and that affirms our worth.

In other words, our concepts of justice lie at the heart of virtually everything we do. It affects our quality of life on every level, within and without, personal, collective, and global. When a model of justice rules that does justice to justice—i.e., that creates worlds that feel good and right to everyone in them—we have harmony. We value ourselves, we value others, they value themselves, and they value us. And we all value our shared environments, the earth and fellow life-forms. With loved ones, communities, businesses, animals, nature, and the earth, justice serves as the backbone of personal, family, social, and planetary well-being.

But there's a problem: justice as we now experience it doesn't work this way, not consistently at least. Many people on the planet don't experience much justice in their lives at all. Children often don't; neither do many employees. Many races don't; neither do many cultures and subcultures. The poor seldom do, but the middle and wealthy classes experience injustices as well. Even lawyers—no, especially lawyers—see injustice prevailing every day, and it takes a toll on them. That's because not all models of justice create the kinds of worlds that we experience as just.

Some models of justice call for hierarchies of power that dictate who gets what according to criteria of deservability. It's easy to imagine how injustices follow: what are valid criteria for deciding who gets what? And if more than external, quantifiable factors are involved, how do we judge these intangibles?

Some models of justice fall short because they draw the spheres to which they apply too narrowly—e.g., only to humans, only to certain races, only to certain economic or social groups, only to certain ages, or only to one gender. Theoretically at least, this isn't such a hard problem to solve. Once we acknowledge the hurt inflicted by narrow ways of applying justice, we realize that we can't afford to let the hurt go on, because it damages the systems on which we too depend. In social dialogue, we're moving in the direction of thinking about justice more inclusively, so that our worlds can be more harmonious and balanced.

But expanding the scope of justice won't create justice if our core concept of it is inadequate or even wrongly skewed. That's the deeper challenge: to sort out what justice itself means. What creates justice among us? Can power hierarchies do it? What is right, good, fair and equitable? When we talk about justice, what do we mean, and how do we live it?

The debate over justice takes many forms. In election years, for instance, we debate what counts as fair taxation. Who should be taxed more, and who less, or would it be fairer to have a flat tax—a fixed rate for everyone over a minimum income? Or maybe income tax isn't the best way at all, and sales tax or corporate and business taxes are more equitable methods. Everyone who debates these issues has a different concept of justice behind his or her reasoning.

So, too, on personal levels, we wrestle with what justice means. We've raised the issue of applying justice to ourselves. The next question is, how do we create harmony, balance, and happiness in our intimate, family, and professional relationships, especially when these relations undergo restructuring? As we'll discuss in the following chapters, change is inescapable. That's life. To remain static is death. We all know this in theory, and yet when our relationships change—as they must to stay real and alive—we often hurt each other, not knowing how to handle change better. It's not fair, good, or right to ask that relationships remain "as is" forever, and yet what is the best way to make transitions, especially when everyone has a different vision of what the new forms should be? We need good, workable models of justice to guide us through such difficult personal experiences.

In all areas of life, then, what justice means remains an open question. There's an unspoken crisis in collective thought around this issue. Too often one senses despair about justice existing in the world at all—we've gone there ourselves. This painful questioning isn't a bad thing, though, since it spurs us to evolve how we think about justice. Like ever-changing reality, our models of justice must evolve. Too-tight models must expand, and sometimes we have to rethink justice from the ground up. That's where we as a culture are right now, we believe, and that's why we're writing this book.

Not that we're proposing absolute definitions of justice or seeking final answers about how to create it. Rather, we're exploring what justice has meant in the past and what it could mean in the future. We're critiquing old views shaped by culture, religion, and history, and we're contributing our voices to a dialogue on how we as individuals, as nations, and as a species can move toward a fairer life, a more just world, and a greater humanity by evolving our philosophy of justice.

PART I

What Do We Have—
Justice or Its Shadow?

ONE

The Quest for True Justice

L ET'S BEGIN by examining some models of justice that were
accepted in the past and some that we live with today.
We form models of justice to deal with public and private concerns:
concerns that arise in our functioning as groups (how we form rules
and laws; how we run businesses; how we build communities, states, or
nations; and how we manage land and resources) and concerns that arise
in how we function as individuals (how we can best interact and how we
can settle disputes when differences arise). Yet there's more than one
possible model for dealing with these concerns. Some models of justice
help us achieve what we seek in terms of social harmony—"Life, Liberty, and the pursuit of Happiness"—while others make happiness more
elusive.

Feudal societies, for instance, used hierarchies of power to define
justice. Those in power by virtue of owning the most land decided what
was just and when and how to apply it. As a culture, we've long since
realized that this model doesn't create happiness, and so we've officially
moved beyond the feudal model—at least, that's our story about modern forms of government. Ending a feudal model of state justice was
what the Magna Carta, the institution of parliamentary, representational
governments, Thomas Paine's *The Rights of Man*, the Declaration of
Independence, the Constitution, and the Bill of Rights, for instance,
were all about. Unfortunately, how governments actually work is often
another story.

But as we suggested in our introduction, models of justice aren't
limited to governments, and that's true of the feudal model as well.
When John Milton argued for divorce in the 1600s, he was attempting

to challenge the feudal model in the family. Challenging a feudal model of justice is a theme in many of Shakespeare's plays, *Romeo and Juliet*, for example, or *As You Like It*, both of which suggest that feudal models in the family lead to feudal models in society and government. Today, what are the *Dilbert* cartoons but a critique of the feudal model in business and corporate life? As a model of justice, feudalism has a history of shooting itself in the foot, because it devalues too many people in the social system. The very people it dismisses as inferior hold the key to its life and regeneration.

Faced with such a model, what do we do? Over time, we shift models. As we realize that a particular model of justice isn't creating happiness, we challenge it everywhere. That's the story of civilization, namely, a process spanning generations of adopting models, critiquing them, and eventually rejecting them as we explore new models.

In the spirit of this evolutionary process, we'll start by taking a hard look at the prevailing model and then in the following chapters explore an alternative—one that grows from ancient spiritual wisdom and is currently transforming many people's experiences of what justice can be.

The Reward-Punishment Model

We're critiquing the dominant model of justice—a reward-punishment model—because as far as we're concerned, like feudalism, it's not creating happiness and therefore isn't convincing as valid justice. It does not yield the goods in terms of creating harmony, balance, and a sense of meaning within or without. Granted, when it works flawlessly, it's more democratic than feudal justice; but, at its worst, it's feudalism revisited. Whoever controls the flow of rewards and punishments functions as the feudal tyrant.

The reward-punishment model fails to create a sense of harmony and happiness in basic systemic ways. It burdens all our relations with a constant calculation of who gets what and whether it is deserved. We become preoccupied with judgments, fears of punishment, envy of rewards, calculations about how to avoid punishments and increase rewards, and the attendant emotions of guilt, shame, and anxiety. We become obsessed with our status in the reward-punishment hierarchy.

Not that we find obsession with status fun; it's a nightmare. It creates heart attacks and high blood pressure, depression and chronic stress. By imposing reward-punishment categories on every aspect of life, the model makes obsessive fear and insecurity hard for us to keep at bay.

Worn down from living in a world run by this model, many people doubt that justice exists. Resigning ourselves to an unfair world, we stop believing that justice as we imagine and long for it to be is attainable.

But even though our model disappoints us repeatedly, we keep trying to make it work. We know something is wrong, so we go back to the reward-punishment system and strive to make it better, not thinking that the model itself may be the problem.

We try harder, for instance, to make our courts effective or to make our reward systems less prone to imbalance and unfairness. In schools, we institute multiple-choice tests instead of essays to eliminate the subjective element of evaluation. In the workplace, we try to find quantifiable output and performance measures to which we can attach objectively calculated merits and rewards.

On the punishment side, we're confused. On one hand, we want to make punishment humane, but on the other hand, the model claims that we establish justice by inflicting pain, especially in the form of loss—loss of money, resources, and possessions, loss of freedom, of identity and individuality, even loss of life. How much pain is called for? If hurt creates justice, wouldn't it follow that the more brutal our methods of punishing, the more justice we'd have?

When we grow sufficiently frustrated with the model and the systems it creates, we start wondering whether the threat of loss really balances our relations and makes us happier. Does it even deter? Not uncommonly, for instance, the rate of murders and crimes increases when capital punishment is instituted. Government statistics and a survey done by *The New York Times* question the deterrence theory:

10 of the 12 states without capital punishment have homicide rates below the national average, FBI data shows, while half the states with the death penalty have homicide rates above the national average. The analysis found that during the past 20 years, the homicide rate in states with the death penalty has been

48 percent to 101 percent higher than in states without the death penalty. . . . "It is difficult to make the case for any deterrent effect from these numbers," said Steven Mesner, a criminologist at the State University of New York at Albany.[1]

But the problem with the retributive model of justice goes beyond specific methods of judicial punishment. Since, as we have suggested, justice extends beyond the legal system into everyday life, the constant threat of retribution affects our emotional patterns, making us habitually defensive. We jump to "It's not my fault!" rather than asking, "What broke down in our shared system?" "How might I have contributed to whatever went wrong?" "How can we work together to make things right or better?"

In the worlds created by the reward-punishment model, cynicism and despair about the system become inevitable. The paradigm takes a heavy toll on all of us. No wonder: it calls not only for judgments and threats of condemnation but also for competitive struggles for rewards: win-lose. By its very nature, the model is divisive, hence antithetical to human peace, joy, and happiness.

For all these reasons, many of us don't actually embrace the model as much as we think we do. Despite the cultural conditioning, we sense something seriously amiss. Indeed, we personally suspect that the current model of justice sets up "counterfeit justice," because it doesn't yield justice's true value. We don't experience the "justice" it creates as the genuine article. Plato would say that what we experience as justice in the world represents a dim shadow of what justice really is and can be. There's some truth in what we have, but it's lost the inner essence that makes justice a living, active force for good in our lives.

Worse, the model's shadowy quality creates inequities, spreading injustices among us. When imposed on every human difference or conflict, the "win-lose" model guarantees that one party will go away feeling badly treated and unsatisfied. And that's when the model works

1. Raymond Banner and Ford Fessenden, "States with no death penalty share lower homicide rates," *The New York Times*, September 22, 2000, A1. See also: Ford Fessenden, "Deadly statistics in survey with crime and punishment," *The New York Times*, September 22, 2000, A23.

well. When it doesn't, even unintentionally, the wrong child is punished, an innocent person is imprisoned or put to death, or rewards go to the most aggressive and cutthroat—hence least deserving—people.

At its worst, the systems of shadow justice become pawns, tools of the influential and powerful, as the reward–punishment model gets carried to its cynical extreme. Justice for those with money to buy it is no news to the poor who dominate prison populations, nor is this a recent phenomenon. Medieval Goliard monks, a rambunctious, irreverent lot, sang of "Sir Penny" and his influence in matters of justice:

> The hand that holds a heavy purse
> Makes right of wrong, better of worse.
> Sir Penny binds all bargains fast;
> Rough is smooth when he has passed.
> Who but Sir Penny settles wars?
> He is the prince of counselors.
>
> > Sir Penny's law no man can budge
> > in courts ecclesiastic;
> > Make room for Penny, ye who judge
> > With consciences elastic.
>
> Where Sir Penny's voice is heard
> The sense of right is sadly blurred.
> The poor man seldom finds redress
> Whose one hope is his righteousness;
> But pampered Dives needs no pull
> Beyond the name of bountiful;
>
> > Whate'er he asks, the judge concedes,
> > And thanks his condescension.
> > The man for whom Sir Penny pleads
> > Makes good his whole intention.
>
> While Penny vaunts, the wise man grieves
> For justice fallen among thieves:

For courts that hear, to line their pockets,
The lamest suits that shame their dockets.
Wherever money's power is found
The poor man gets the run-around;

    The best of pleas is brushed aside
        That has no cash to back it,
    And lawful judgments are denied
        By those who own the racket.

Here's a case, let none deny it,
Fixed before the court can try it;
But when poor Codrus starts a suit,
Case dismissed—he's destitute.[2]

In all of this, it's not the ideal of justice that has failed us, but the particular model we're using: the reward-punishment system. Instead of despairing of justice altogether, we need to change our model. To this end, our job in this new century is to distinguish the true from the counterfeit, the real from the shadow. We're called to evolve models that come closer to fulfilling our ideals of what justice can be.

A Philosophical Basis

We raise these issues not as lawyers, judges, or people connected with the legal or court systems. Neither do we write from an analytic, academic perspective. We write as philosophers who take a spiritual approach, which means we think about meaning and purpose within a larger perspective—more than only physical and psychological, although these are obviously important too. This "more" involves the view that life unfolds in relation to a higher power or force for wholeness, something beyond us that supports our highest good. Accordingly, we want to think about justice in ways that include this larger perspec-

---

2. George F. Whicher, trans., *The Goliard Poets: Medieval Latin Songs and Satires* (Westport, Conn.: Greenwood Press, Publishers, 1949, 1979), 147.

tive without being religiously dogmatic. We want a concept that affirms soul and meaning—that doesn't crush our spirits in the name of justice.

We also believe that inner healing—reclaiming our souls and who we are—is a life's work and that it cannot be done alone. We need to heal personally; but our families, communities, social systems, cultures, and worlds need to heal with us. Because we're participants in these systems, we have the opportunity to prompt larger healing processes. As we do this—as we create more just communities, workplaces, and societies—they return the favor by helping us heal.

We want to think about justice's philosophical foundations, therefore, not as an intellectual exercise but for practical, transformative purposes, starting with ourselves and moving out. Shifting our models of thought—an act of revolution that's in the power of each of us to do—can effect profound personal and social change.

Why is working from a philosophical basis so powerful? First, because philosophy gets at the root of things. It investigates the formative categories that then shape everything that follows: our assumptions, principles, values, systems, methods—all the invisible equipment that we use to give form to the visible and interact with it.

Second, contrary to its popular image, philosophy is practical. It makes us think about what really works, not just today but in the long run, not just as quick fixes but as addressing the deeper causal and systemic issues. In the case of justice, philosophy makes us ask: Is the paradigm we're using to define justice serving us well? Does it give us the justice we want and need? What alternative paradigm might unlock a greater experience of justice among us?

And third, philosophy does this—gets at the root of things and makes us think about what's practical—because it invites us to ponder life in the big picture. Philosophy calls us to sniff out unifying orders, patterns, and ideas that aren't apparent from looking at parts in isolation. The more we narrow our focus, the more we're in danger of having one-sided and distorted perceptions. Exploring the big picture protects us against this myopia, deepening our insight and lending balance and perspective. In fact, what makes something shadowy or counterfeit is the opposite of a big-picture perspective, namely, its incompleteness or one-sidedness.

This is exactly the problem with defining justice as rewards and punishments. The model gives an incomplete, hence shadowy view, because it deals exclusively with the outer forms of our lives, not with our inner processes. Yet we're both inner and outer beings.

The outer side of us is what we see of each other: our physical appearances shaped by gender, race, culture, and clothes; our families and children; our work lives; our personal hobbies and schedules; and our possessions. Even our personalities, educational histories, religions, and politics have an outer orientation, since these represent how we've adapted what's inside of us to the external worlds we move through.

The inner, by contrast, gives meaning to all of this—or rebels when the outer lacks meaning for us. The inner is our unseen side, the part that we ourselves may not notice, unless we make a conscious effort to do so. In an outwardly focused culture, inner awareness is not a priority. Making money and meeting external expectations come first.

That's a shame, since the inner dimension gives meaning to how we make money and enhances the kind of person we can be with our families, on the job, or in communities. Our inner being stands as our compass and touchstone in life, connecting us with our souls and life purposes. Through our inner side, we tap the rich, deep resources of who we are beyond our outer forms, and this whole perspective keeps us focused on what matters in the big picture. From our inner side, we feel the energy and enthusiasm—the life force—flowing through us, giving us the vision and strength to pursue our life's callings.

Whereas true justice engages both our inner and outer experiences, shadow or counterfeit justice is limited to the external side alone. It's a shadow, because the whole form is missing.

This one-sidedness radically limits what shadow justice can accomplish. Outer facts are fixed—"what's done is done." We can't undo an act of harm. It's out there in the world, and we can't take it back. We're stuck with it.

Our inner lives, by contrast, are dynamic and changing. From our inner transformation, we can change how we treat ourselves and interact with others. For example, we can become more aware of how and why harm happens; we can feel regret, sorrow, forgiveness, understanding, and compassion; and, by sharing these feelings, we can work together to heal pain and mend broken trust.

In other words, our powers of inner transformation offer possibilities for working things out that aren't apparent from a one-sided, outer perspective. No wonder shadow justice so often paints a picture of impasse and hopelessness, and no wonder it so often leaves us in despair. Given its limits, it offers no way out. Its "solutions" extend pain rather than heal it, because healing is an inner process, and that's what external justice excludes.

As we'll see, whole, big-picture justice works quite differently. By including both the inner and outer dimensions of who we are, it opens unlimited opportunities for exploring meaning, transformation, and healing.

Nor is this an unrealistic ideal. The more we've journeyed into the heart of justice, the more justice has proven full of hope, promise, and liberation. Big-picture justice is about righting wrongs, inspiring hope in our potentials to change, and restoring harmony and happiness to everyone involved. True justice is amazing. It's amazing in its ability to spur deep transformation, amazing in its skill to mend what's broken in human affairs, amazing in its power to spur social reform, and, closest to home, amazing in its power to liberate us, both to be who we are and to do whatever calls us. True justice offers a sense of security, happiness, and meaning in life as nothing else can.

The promise is there, but only if we engage our philosophical powers and think beyond the shadow model.

Healing Justice

This is precisely what is happening. Utter frustration with the modern justice system and with the damage it does to individuals and communities has spurred a worldwide "restorative justice" movement. This diverse movement now offers a potent alternative to retributive justice. Although we'll discuss this alternative approach at length in the following chapters, we'd like to give you a glimpse of justice's healing power.

Keep in mind that the reward-punishment model of justice is not concerned with healing or transformation. These processes simply do not fall within its domain. Although it uses terms like "correctional institutions" or "rehabilitation facilities," its model is one of punishment: who did what to whom and who pays—who deserves a kick and how hard.

Restorative justice has a different aim. Its purpose is to understand what has happened as a basis for change. Accordingly, it considers the whole person in webs of relationships that go back generations. When relationships break down, this model considers everyone involved, what's going on inside each of them, and what experiences led each to think, feel, and act as he or she did. By seeking the larger picture—one that weds outer events to inner processes—this paradigm instills an understanding and compassion that can restore badly broken relationships.

The following case illustrates the healing power of a restorative approach. Terry O'Connell of Australia, a pioneer in what is known as "family group conferencing," was called upon to help a case in which two seventeen-year-old Asian youths, reacting to a racial slur, firebombed a house, trapping four family members who had to jump out the windows to escape, the mother breaking her back in her fall. The youths were sentenced to two years in prison, but the family could not recover. After many struggles with lawyers, the police, probation personnel, and victim-support people, O'Connell was finally able to arrange a conference of everyone involved:

> "I have not experienced a more pitiful sight," recalled O'Connell, "meeting a family that was so highly regarded, which contained two champion basketball players, and the local regional basketball coach, who had completely lost it as a result of the trauma from the crime. Both boys were constantly frightened, had hardly slept since the incident, had completely lost interest in school and basketball. Their mother, who was clad in a large brace, needed a steel walking frame to get around. The father cried constantly and had gone from being a very popular outgoing teacher to a stage where 'nothing mattered any more.' They agreed to participate although they had some reservations."
>
> After negotiating in the local prison with the two offenders and their families, O'Connell held a family group conference in the county hall (above the police station) on a Sunday afternoon. The conference lasted three hours and involved 30 participants (which comprised victims, offenders, families, friends, and

neighbors). In describing the conference as the most emotional conference he had coordinated, O'Connell said:

"Listening to the anguish of the victims for about 90 minutes was extremely difficult for everyone. This had a significant impact on the offenders and others. However, by the end of the conference there was a complete transformation in the victims' emotional states and general outlook. It was an amazing experience to see the two young victims smiling and hugging people, where two hours earlier they virtually could not look at anyone."

The conference was an outstanding success, as it gave the victims the opportunity to address some of their emotional needs. The victims felt the conference gave them some hope for the future, something that the court had failed to provide. As for the offenders, it gave them and their families an insight and an opportunity to rebuild some trust between themselves and the broader community.[3]

As this case suggests, restorative justice involves far more than punishing wrongdoers. It preserves what's meaningful in life, starting with issues of safety, self-worth, self-respect, and mutual understanding. Instead of being reactive to events, this model uses events as opportunities for everyone to feel heard, to share hurts from injustices, to rebuild trust in ourselves and each other, and thereby to restore relationships. More than restoring even, healing justice uses instances of hurt to enhance bonds between people and to build communities. The process of working through pain creates an understanding of each other that inspires compassion for our shared human condition.

In other words, justice isn't about abstract standards of legality but about serving human well-being and making our relationships work well—effortlessly, peacefully, even joyfully in calling forth the growth of

---

3. The Church Council on Justice and Corrections, *Satisfying Justice: Safe Community Options That Attempt to Repair Harm from Crime and Reduce the Use or Length of Imprisonment* (Ottawa, Ontario, Canada: Church Council on Justice and Corrections, 1996), 29–30. This book is available by contacting the Church Council on Justice and Corrections, 507 Bank Street, Ottawa, Ontario, K2P 1Z5, Canada. Reprinted by permission of The Church Council on Justice and Corrections.

which we're capable. Through the process, we come out of our boxes of pain and discover potentials we didn't know we had. This not only brings healing but also builds self-esteem. Instead of the judging that makes us feel condemned and rejected, restorative justice opens our hearts to self-acceptance and the forgiveness that flows from this, both of others and of ourselves.

In this sense, the quest to find true justice is the quest to find meaning and happiness. With justice as our base, we work together easily, we soar in creativity, and the joy that flows among us knows no bounds, no longer shadowed by competitive comparisons and system-engendered fears and insecurities. Justice is a treasure whose riches we have yet to mine. It's a healing elixir whose balm, ancient as it is, we're just learning to apply.

Without justice's healing processes, things go from bad to worse. When no healing or transformation occurs, pain becomes chronic. As amazingly positive as restorative justice can be in unlocking our resources for happiness, it's equally amazing how miserable we become when our model of justice excludes these resources and leaves us locked in "the facts of a case," the outer side only.

Again, that's because, from a one-sided, outer-shell perspective, counterfeit justice can't do what real justice requires. In the case just cited, the Asian boys must have felt black-hole misery about racial inequities to do such a terrible, potentially murderous thing. And the victim family obviously felt black-hole misery from the bombing that proved completely debilitating, even after court action. Punitive verdicts did nothing to heal the anguish of either victims or offenders.

We don't have to suffer such trauma to know injustice, however, or to feel the depth of misery that outer-focused justice causes. To adapt the medical term "iatrogenic diseases" (diseases caused by medical practices), we can talk about "judiciogenic misery," that is, pain caused not merely by bad lawyers or biased court decisions but by a skewed model of justice, and hence by our wrongheaded efforts to practice such a model, one-sided that it is.

Because justice issues are everywhere in life, judiciogenic misery goes everywhere too. For example, a major part of our current model of justice involves authorities, powers over us, who, we're led to believe, always act fairly on our behalf. They're the ones who allocate rewards and punishments, and we're supposed to trust that they do this fairly. How do we feel, then, when this doesn't happen, which it often doesn't? Every child has been subjected at one time or another to unfair power relations, and every adult has had to deal with powerful people and institutions—bosses, politicians, religious leaders—who claim to be just but aren't. Trusting the authorities who judge us and who hand out rewards and punishments is essential for maintaining belief in the model and a faith that it will work as it's supposed to—that the good be rewarded and the bad punished—yet there's no category of authority that doesn't regularly behave unjustly.

Even with all good intentions, for instance, parents and teachers frequently fail to treat children fairly. Realistically, a parent would have to have the wisdom, patience, and compassion of God to be perfectly fair all the time. Why then do we have a model that asks those in positions of authority to be something they cannot possibly be? The reality is that we have fallible, imperfect, inescapably partial people judging and blaming each other all the time—or equally imperfect institutions doing this for us. Why not design our model of justice to use our human capacities differently—to build on our powers to understand, heal, and forgive each other, for example, rather than on our potentials to accuse, blame, and judge each other?

Clearly, the intangible called justice, invisible and elusive as it may be when it's present, creates a festering sore when it's missing. The blatant sores could fill books: horrific injustices imposed on Africans and African Americans; on Native Americans and all indigenous cultures and communities; on the poor; on working people; on women, children, and ethnic minorities, as well as on animals and the earth.

These gross wrongs have been perpetrated at one time or another in the name of justice—cosmic, religious, social, racial, biological, developmental, economic, Darwinian—or even to "the white man's burden." Our current model of justice has its own version of feudalism: the most powerful, the most aggressive, the richest, the best educated, the most "cultured," the "best" religion, the "whitest," the head of the family, the top of the food chain, or the higher rungs on the "Great Chain of Being" dictate what counts as justice for everyone else, creating wounds that take generations to heal.

Suffice it to say, justice is worth thinking about, both for the amazing happiness it can foster and for the amazing suffering we can either avoid or seek to heal. And justice is worth thinking about in new ways because prevailing notions of justice aren't doing the trick. Even so, as disillusioned as we become with the old model, not knowing any other, we try to convince ourselves that it works—that tit for tat, kick for kick creates justice among us.

This isn't a rational response but one stemming from childhood programming: "If we're good [whatever others expect of us], good things happen to us [no kicks]; if we're bad [doing our own thing], bad things happen [we get kicked]." This correlation is drilled into us by parents and teachers for the simple purpose of controlling our behavior. It's a technique of child-rearing, not a philosophy of justice. Yet we carry it into adulthood as our model of justice. When bad things happen, we assume we or someone else must have been bad in some way.

Social psychologist Melvin Lerner during the 1960s and 1970s confirmed this response through his studies. When confronted with blatant acts of injustice by authorities, people would excuse cruelties and do mental gymnastics to preserve the illusion of justice. In Lerner's studies, a consenting assistant was treated badly by the experimenter for no reason, and the observing "subjects" (Lerner's students) consistently "blamed the victim" ("something must be wrong with her" or "he must have deserved it") rather than conclude that the authority (the experimenter) was behaving unjustly or that the situation was unjust by its very structure. Lerner came to believe that we'd rather blame innocent victims than confront the possibility that we're dealing with injustice in our world.[4] Justice is that important to us.

Yes, justice *is* that important. It's just more important as the real thing, the big-picture, healing, restoring experience of justice. Child-

4. Melvin J. Lerner, *The Belief in a Just World: A Fundamental Delusion* (New York and London: Plenum Press, 1980). It may be that some of the reactions of people defending authorities and blaming victims that Lerner observed are due to the authoritarian schooling and cultural upbringing. We're trained to assume that the

hood illusions of justice, however culturally instilled, don't cut it. The obvious next question is, what is justice really?

Our Current Paradigm

We approach this question from philosophy, because how we experience justice depends on how we look at it, the paradigm we use. For that matter, how we experience anything depends on our perspective, the lens through which we see things and the models by which we interpret them.

Our point of view isn't just personal, though. It's influenced by many factors. Physicist David Bohm came to believe that no thought is entirely individual. How we perceive life draws heavily on the culture—how we've been raised and trained, even systematically programmed to think by family, religion, and schooling as well as by our peers and the media.

This collective component is especially forceful when it comes to considering models of justice. Different cultures conceive of justice differently, using different rules, principles, and standards to create it. Environmental justice, for example, is a central concern for most indigenous cultures, as it would be. Living close to nature, they realize that we must maintain a harmonious balance with it. These and other cultures also tend to emphasize maintaining just relations with the unseen world—Spirit, the Creator, as well as with guides, angels, and other unseen presences. They also work hard to heal broken relations as a process that engages the entire community.

In other words, not everyone looks at justice the way we do in the West. How we think about justice is both a personal and a shared model. Philosophy is about sifting and sorting ideas—about naming which views come from where and critiquing them. As we engage in this process, we clean our philosophical house and create space for new perspectives to come in.

The first job, then, is to tackle the shadowy, counterfeit version of

---

authorities are right and those under them prone to be wrong. Is Lerner observing an intrinsically human or a culturally created tendency to "blame the victim" in order to keep the perception of justice in place?

justice, the reward-punishment model. What's its deep reasoning? Where did it get started? And how did justice become a source of misery and disillusionment?

Knowing what we now know about trauma, our guess is that this dark, fear-ridden paradigm formed in response to pain, of which European and American history offers innumerable examples. From this collective, multigenerational trauma, we've adopted a paradigm designed to guide us through what is perceived as a violent, predatory, meaningless world. The way to endure such a life, the model tells us, is to be that way too—violent, predatory, and without higher meaning—not noticing that our coping mechanism perpetuates the very pain we seek to escape.

In his classic story *A Christmas Carol*, Charles Dickens sketched this mindset in the character of Ebenezer Scrooge. Scrooge was cynical about human kindness and all the inner sensibilities that make life rich. He was also self-righteously committed to keeping score on external rewards and punishments, firmly believing that these mattered more than anything. Coming out ahead on external measures counted as righteousness, justice, and the good. Though today we try to soften this philosophy and not state it too baldly, it nonetheless forms the root of the originally European and now Euro-American model of justice. It lurks in the back of our psyches: the inward is expendable; what matters is establishing a good outer image, keeping our external ducks in a row.

How might we arrive at such a stern, even inhuman worldview? In the West, the philosophy grows from the assumption—supported both religiously and secularly—that we humans are a miserable, disorderly, "sinful" lot. This grim self-portrait reflects the further assumption that we have a consuming drive to control externals for competitive self-advantage. We're out for all we can get, no matter what the cost to ourselves or others. In short, we're a greedy, selfish creature.

Naturally, we have to wonder if we really are this way or whether the philosophy is teaching us how we have to behave to survive and prosper. In other words, is the grim self-portrait selectively calling forth our potential to act selfishly while suppressing our potentials to be kind and generous, or is this the bottom line of who we really are? We'll talk more about this in Part 2, since it's central to deciding which model of justice is appropriate to human beings.

For now, we can say that there are cultures, particularly indigenous and ancient ones, that don't postulate competitive selfishness as the sum total of our nature and so raise people to interact more cooperatively, assuming that cooperation is the human way. Because they don't construct societies on a competitive model, such behavior is not culturally built-in, hence not selectively taught and favored.

In the West, however, because we've accepted competitive selfishness as a virtual law of human nature, we raise people to behave this way—competition is the rule in school, sports, and business—and then we claim such behavior is an objective, paradigm-free universal for all humans: "just the facts" of grasping, selfish, greedy human nature.[5]

This Euro-American assumption about human nature raises a serious social problem. How can we ever have social order with all these greedy, selfish people? To impose law—some semblance of justice—onto the chaos created by so many desperate, grasping creatures, the Euro-American model employs force, specifically, economic force: who owns what and who has a right to control whom.

Obviously *somebody* has to control the unruly mob, and it may as well be the ones who own property or, more simply, the wealthy. Who but they have the greatest interest in security, that is, in keeping the status quo in place? They need all their economic might to either intimidate or, if need be, force the mob into shape. Their disproportionate wealth actually does the masses a favor by giving the owners the power to impose social order, which the unruly mob needs but can't achieve on its own. Or so the logic goes.

How do they exert their economic power on behalf of social order? By extending their economic control to people. Land doesn't foment revolution; people do. Hence more than money and property must fall

5. We cannot pass over this issue without mentioning Alfie Kohn's book *The Brighter Side of Human Nature*. Anyone weary of this academic, cultural dogma should treat themselves to his book. Kohn doesn't deny that we have the capacity to be as rotten as we can imagine—as both history and films depict us—but he says we have other capacities as well and which capacities get developed depend on many factors, culture and environment being not the least of them. He also includes accounts of human behavior that would surprise even Pollyanna for their altruism. The whole has not been told of human nature, but his book is an effort in this direction.

into the category of what is owned and controlled. Living beings—
humans, animals, nature—must be included in the category of own-
ables. Riane Eisler points out in *Sacred Pleasure* that, when the colonial
American South sought a legal model for the status of slaves, they bor-
rowed from the way English common law treated married women.[6]

Owning people means exercising the power to do with them what
we will, which usually means controlling their access to resources and
money. Owners create systems that maximize economic dependence,
from outright slavery to company towns to wage slavery to chronic debt-
ing. Again, systems of top-down economic control are supposedly good
for society, since economic need keeps those "owned" in line.

From this general outlook—a belief in human nature as selfish and
greedy, a consequent need to impose social order, and a belief that material force in the form of institutionalized economic neediness and
dependence is the best way to secure social order—European justice
takes form. Historically, it centers around three things: rights, rules, and
property. Rights to control go to those who own property, and rules
dictate how that control extends to everyone else. The driving concern
is not how to secure happiness, how to build good relationships, or how
to restore them when they've broken down. Instead, justice means
everyone follows the rules—rules established by the owners. It's an
objective definition, in that everyone more or less knows the rules, most
of which have to do with externals, i.e., "Don't mess with someone else's
stuff (unless you're wealthy or powerful enough to get away with it)."
Thanks to seventeenth-century philosopher John Locke's theory of the
social contract, we presumably all assent to this arrangement by virtue
of living in society. If we didn't agree, we'd move somewhere else—the
moon maybe?

To put it another way, rules attempt to contain the inevitable "war
of each against all" that seventeenth-century British social philosopher
Thomas Hobbes foresaw when everyone wants a piece of the pie—and
there's not much left after the owners dine.

The statistics on owners' appetites are hard to ignore. Eighty-three

6. Riane Eisler, *Sacred Pleasure: Sex, Myth, and the Politics of the Body—New Paths to
Power and Love* (New York: HarperCollins/HarperSanFrancisco, 1995), 210.

percent of the global income goes to the richest fifth of the population, while only one percent goes to the poorest fifth. The combined wealth of 358 of the world's richest people comes to $762 billion, a sum held by 2.4 billion of the poorest people, or $317.50 per person.[7] The owners, it seems, suffer from what Plato in *The Republic* (442a, 562b, 586b) calls *pleonexia* or insatiability, a condition he believed would inevitably cause their downfall, because they cannot think of anything but their desire for more. Today we call it addiction, and we too find it to be a "progressive, fatal disease," the phrase used to describe *addiction* by Alcoholics Anonymous.

The lopsidedness of finances—and the social fallout of this imbalance—is no surprise, though, considering a system that is developed around owners making rules that protect their advantage and then calling it justice. How could the term *justice* not lose credibility? If social order is what we are aiming for, how good is that loss of trust for securing it? How socially stable is a world polarized between haves and have-nots, those favored by the system of "justice" and those angry about having to pay its price? What incentive do angry people have for obeying rules if their gut feeling is that the game is rigged—that the system of rules called "justice" is itself unjust?

But this glitch is already covered by the Euro-American model. When people lose faith in the system and break rules, the job of justice is simple: enforce the law! Engage the power of authority to punish offenders! Crush the slave rebellion! Nip it in the bud when children exercise a will of their own! Rule infraction "deserves" punishment—a model inculcated in us first through child-rearing and then through religion, schooling, and management policies. No one likes to punish, but punishment must be done: "justice" and social order require it.

Since no one likes to receive punishment either, the arena of justice becomes a battleground, a win-lose contest to see who gets punished and who gets off. Where do we lay blame? Whose fault is it? The war of each against all is tamed into a war within the courtroom: the adversarial model.

7. Reported in *World Watch*, July/August 1996. Their source is the United Nations Research Institute for Social Development, *States of Disarray: The Social Effects of Globalization* (London: UNRISD, 1995).

The assumption of such a model, of course, is that whoever wins must be right; justice must be on their side. We don't notice that the model favors those with the means to argue the case most skillfully. In an adversarial model, might can easily make right, since the playing field is seldom level.

Offering a legal forum to "put up your dukes" sounds empowering—theoretically, we all get our day in court—but in practice, it wears us down. Turning justice into a battlefield gives us combat fatigue. William van Zyverden, a lawyer who runs the Holistic Justice Center in Middlebury, Vermont, describes our present system as "engulfed in hostility": "Adversarial disempowerment is still the prevailing relationship and conflict resolution model of our time. We accuse, we argue, we present evidence, we seek judgment, and we exact punishment. The model is taught and supported from our earliest recollections through school and into adulthood where we pass the process on to our children."[8]

The way adversarial justice frames the problem misses the actual, human-situation point. It passes over real concerns for academic sparring. The academic debate is about which rule has been broken and by whom, not what might heal the damage that has occurred or how to address the real concerns that culminated in actions that caused hurt.

Criminal-justice consultant Howard Zehr explains in his book *Changing Lenses* that, according to this paradigm, what's hurt is the abstract notion of the state—the system of social control set up by the owners-turned-rulemakers. Living, breathing humans and communities aren't the official victims, the ones in need of redress.[9] Why? Because by breaking one of the state's rules, we damage its power to control people and so diminish public security. Defending the state's power and authority is the reason behind punishment. Punishment demonstrates the fearful power of the state to enforce its rules, and it sends a message to others of what happens when a rule is broken.

Because rules are primarily concerned with the rights of owners,

8. Gail Bernice Holland, "Transforming the Legal Profession," *Connections*, no. 6 (January 1999): 5. *Connections* is published by The Institute of Noetic Sciences in Sausalito, California.

9. Howard Zehr, *Changing Lenses* (Scottdale, Pa.: Herald Press, 1990), especially 80–82.

human rights, as stated in the Magna Carta or in the Constitution's Bill of Rights, function as an afterthought. They don't change the paradigm's basic focus on rules and property rights but simply limit either punishments or the extent to which humans can be treated as property and controlled as such.

Centuries after these documents were instituted, for example, how many rights do employees or children, much less animals, have? "Wage slavery" still has meaning for millions, and the concept of paying people enough to live on—"a living wage"—still requires championing. Yes, there has been progress, especially if you happen to be born in "developed" countries to the right race and social level, not to mention the right species; but the core concept has not shifted. An employee is bought, owned, and controlled, as is a horse, who can be put in a stall for five years and made to live night and day neck deep in manure. Employees around the globe can relate to the horse's plight, some more metaphorically than others.

Adding insult to injury, such treatment gets tied with justice: it's how people and animals should be treated. It's what they deserve, given their nature, whether that nature is construed as wild and out of control or simply inferior and insignificant. Either way, external control is called for, hence the model. Rewards and punishments are straightforward mechanisms of control—a fact known long before behavioral psychologist B. F. Skinner made it official.

Still, no one likes being controlled. We like freedom. Animals go nuts in cages, and humans don't do much better. The best way to hide control, therefore, is to call it "justice." The reasoning is that a controlled people is an ordered people, so why not identify the mechanisms of control with justice? Through different systems of rewards and punishments, social systems—families, schools, businesses, religious communities, governments—control human behavior as the means for creating an ordered society.

Yet as philosopher and historian Herman Bianchi points out, the "justice" that follows is not that of free people. It's slave-law justice, and it goes back to the Romans. Whereas Roman citizens could be neither punished nor imprisoned, slaves could. In an interview with David Cayley for the radio program *Ideas*, Bianchi explains:

So what we have done, we have accepted the Roman slave law in our punitive system. It's slave law that we are using. Until about the year 1200, there is no punitive criminal law in Europe. Not really.[10]

On slave-law logic, it follows that punishment is not an illegitimate means of coercion, but rather a legitimate way to establish justice (social order) in the family, schoolroom, workplace, church, and society. And if punishment establishes justice, then so does revenge: returning hurt for hurt, settling accounts, evening the score. The only difference between revenge and retributive justice is that a person does the first and the state does the second. It's the same act, the same philosophy, the same effect: hurt for hurt, wound for wound.

Human hearts certainly have the capacity to seek revenge. Be unjustly accused at work, violated by a crime, or, God forbid, have a spouse or child molested or murdered—the burning desire for revenge is there. But should we draw our concepts of justice from the depths of emotional pain? As it turns out, seeing harm done to offenders has less healing power than we might think. Punishment wasn't designed for healing; in the classroom or the courtroom, its purpose is social control. And it has side effects. By definition, it increases the level of pain in a person and in society—pain that threatens to spill over to others. Pain is not healed but multiplied, extended.

Justice as punishments and rewards also raises the issues of who "deserves" what and the judgments that this involves. The sense of being judged infects all of life. We live feeling constantly judged by families, bosses, and associates, by God, but especially by ourselves. If we suffer, we think we must in some way deserve it. Whatever salary we make is what we deserve. Whatever happens to another raises speculation: did the person deserve it or not? Outer life becomes a tally of whether we're getting our "just deserts," and inner life an effort to account for the discrepancies.

Yet do we ever really know what's due us, much less what's due someone else? Many factors go into human thought, feeling, and action.

10. "Justice as Sanctuary," *Ideas*, October 27, November 3, and November 10, 1997, ID9743 (Canadian Broadcasting Corporation, CBC Ideas Transcripts, P.O. Box 500, Station A, Toronto, Ontario M5W 1E6 Canada), 11.

For a fair reward-punishment system, all factors should be taken into account. Yet they aren't, nor could they be. Every human judgment is inevitably based on incomplete knowledge. Even with the best research and detective skills, we're not omniscient.

In the West, the state's cohort, religion, has this objection covered. Christianity's "Last Judgment" claims that we will be judged by God for all eternity—blessed or damned—a doctrine designed to make believers stay in line. As near-death experiences suggest, it may well be true that upon death we review our lives assisted by some other being (guide, angel), but for what purpose? Is it to condemn or to heal, to punish or to promote insight, self-awareness, and growth?

Unfortunately, the Eastern notion of karma invites judging too, or at least the Western rendition of it does. With karma and reincarnation, we have more shots at getting it right, but karma's cosmic justice is still interpreted as rewards, punishments, and judgments. Tragedies, for instance, are viewed as karmic justice at work. Instead of rules of the state, we face rules of the cosmos and the nameless judges who speak through life's ups and downs. Even if we don't call it karma, the model of justice as rewards and punishments makes us react to painful experiences with self-blame and recrimination.

In *Beyond Discipline*, teacher, writer, and researcher Alfie Kohn shows how punishments and rewards teach far more than temporary social control. They imprint our mental and emotional habits by inculcating the roles, attitudes, and dynamics that go with "power-over" relations. Certain reward-punishment "facts" form the core of our mental operating system: e.g., that might makes right; that those in power can be arbitrary, condescending, and cruel; and that those on the receiving end must either accept being controlled or develop deceptive, manipulative, counter-control coping mechanisms.

In other words, punishments and rewards teach the inescapably warped relationship between the one controlling and the one controlled. The freedom to deal with situations openly and honestly—without fear in an easy partnership working together to address real issues and solve real problems—does not exist in a control model. Manipulating appearances takes precedence over dealing with realities.

Neither are punishments and rewards value-free. They teach calculating self-centeredness: "If I do this good thing, what do I get out of it?"

"If I do this bad thing, what's the cost to me—*if* I get caught?" Kohn supports with extensive research that rewards and punishments do not teach compassion, care, generosity, altruism, or even a quest for excellence.[11]

But worst of all, rewards and punishments play havoc with our motivation structure. In a reward-punishment world, instead of being inwardly guided, we become outwardly motivated. We don't learn because learning is fun and we're drawn to a subject; we learn because we'll be graded or paid—an issue we'll return to in the next chapter.

By dismissing inner experiences, the external model of justice disconnects us from our souls' promptings. It teaches us not to listen to the ways our souls speak to us. When we're organized around getting ahead in reward-punishment systems, we learn not to honor or trust the messages we get from our feelings, intuitions, longings, joys, dreams, excitements, bodies, and above all, our loves. All the rich inner resources we possess to create a meaningful life get dismissed at one stroke, with a model of justice that disregards inner values.

Challenging rewards and punishments as the meaning of cosmic justice does not mean there is no cosmic order. We personally assume there is—on physical levels as well as on moral, psychological, social, and spiritual dimensions. But we also assume that the cosmic order functions quite differently from how we conceive of it, certainly from how the reward-punishment model depicts it.

We also assume there are consequences to actions—absolutely. In a universe of connectedness, everything we do has an effect—a real effect that the contrived imposition of rewards and punishments hides or distracts us from confronting. When we think about how we're being rewarded or punished by the contrived system of social control, we tend not to think about the real-life consequences.

In business, for example, people may profit financially from environmentally damaging choices or from cutting corners on safety and quality. The system of rewards makes us focus on the profit consequences more than the real-life consequences. Tire makers, for exam-

11. Alfie Kohn, *Beyond Discipline: From Compliance to Community* (Alexandria, Va.: Association for Supervision and Curriculum Development, 1996), especially chapter 3, "Bribes and Threats," 22–36.

ple, focused on the profits to be gained by reducing quality instead of on the dangers to people from buying inferior tires. But which consequence is more important to heed: the reward one or the real one?

Children learn to think in artificial reward-punishment terms early on. They learn to seek the reward and to avoid the punishment—real-life consequences be damned—and then the adults wonder why children lie or cheat. Honesty and integrity are inward qualities. When being true to ourselves is a shared value, we're honest with each other. But when impressing those who have power over us or conforming to the demands of those who control the externals of our lives is a priority, we bend the truth; we lie. Not telling the truth is a system-created, system-reinforced behavior, whenever externals take precedence over inner values.

Children behave, therefore, exactly as the control system has trained them to behave: not to think in real terms about real consequences but rather to calculate in reward-punishment terms for reward-punishment effects. School isn't about learning; it's about grades—the artificial reward-punishment model superimposed on learning that mountains of research now indicate impedes learning.[12]

For that matter, courts exist because people have learned to think in terms of reward consequences rather than real-life consequences. Crimes occur because people have ceased to think about the real, human effects of their actions. Once caught, offenders often prefer prison sentences to meeting their victims and working for resolution or healing. The contrived punishment seems easier and less emotionally demanding than having to deal with the real-life impact of their actions, which requires a shift in how they think and feel.

To evaluate real consequences within some larger, meaningful order, we need to think in terms of real-life values, values which help us understand events and explore the meaning of consequences. Which values might we consider? For our mental and emotional well-being, we need

12. As ever, Alfie Kohn is the clearest thinker, researcher, and writer on this subject. We recommend starting with Alfie Kohn's overview given in *Beyond Discipline* and then moving to the more substantive *Punished by Rewards: The Trouble with Gold Stars, Incentive Plans, A's, Praise, and Other Bribes* (New York: Houghton Mifflin, 1993). We also recommend Kohn's book *What to Look for in a Classroom . . . and Other Essays* (San Francisco: Jossey-Bass, 1998).

to honor values of soul, spirit, learning, growth, healing, transformation, and inner evolution. For relationships, we need the values of love,
truth, honesty, intimacy, and connectedness. And for surviving in society, we need such basic values as human dignity, mutual respect, safety,
and security. These values matter in life and give it meaning. They characterize some of the most important aspects of what it is to be human.
And, according to spiritual teachings, they reflect a higher order and
align us with it.

To apply these values rather than a reward-punishment system, we
might ask how an experience relates to our growth and evolution. We
open ourselves to experiencing our inner process, whatever it is, through
the events of our lives. We investigate how we can use an experience
for healing or transformation, whether we categorize it as a positive or
a negative experience, since either one can move us along. We can also
let an experience teach us what it means to love in a deeper, purer, freer,
more open and honest way. These values, it would seem, are more helpful for thinking about the real-life meaning of consequences as well as
about a higher, cosmic order—if we're inclined to think that way—than
the artificial values of rewards and punishments.

Why? For one reason, these values are patterned in nature. Nature
is about growth and evolution. When breaks occur, natural processes
kick in for healing. Transformation and change go on constantly in the
natural world. And love is everywhere, as natural in humans as in swans
mating for life or in elephants who mourn the death of one of their own.
These aren't humanly contrived values designed for the purpose of control. They are human concepts, of course, but they describe processes
that are real and natural—processes that come with being alive.

Another reason that these values ring true is that they seem more
directly rooted in what's real and meaningful for us in everyday life. We
have real experiences of growing, healing, evolving, moving with larger
systems, being connected, going through processes, confronting our
truth, feeling meaning or suffering from the lack of it, and above all,
loving. Such values emerge naturally from within our own lives and relationships. They're not imposed from without but are intrinsic to human
experience.

If these values more closely reflect real life, then they provide the most helpful and relevant standards for evaluating our experiences, so that we have some framework for responding to them. With these values in view, we interpret wrenching experiences not as punishments but as doorways to engaging with these processes more deeply. Life may be painful—it often is—but we don't have to think that we've failed and that we're being punished. Rather, we can respond by engaging more deeply in soul-searching, inner healing, the meaning of love, or some phase of transformation.

Unfortunately, the retributive model systematically excludes these real-life values, assuming that they have no place in the justice process. Justice is supposed to be blind—blind to our differences, blind to our humanity, blind to our needs, histories, and circumstances. According to this model, justice is a "just-the-facts" matter. The less the human element comes in, the more impartial the justice done, hence the more fair and equitable it's deemed to be. A good court judge is "hard but just." Compassionate people make bad judges, this view insists, since justice on this model works best when it's unaffected by our needs and circumstances.

Writing on the history of European ideas of justice, political philosopher Alan Ryan observes, "Justice is peculiarly stringent. Its demands may not be modified. Judges and rulers must 'do justice though the heavens fall,' not allow family connections, friendship, or even personal worth to turn them aside." Later in the text, he asserts, "Justice is a chilly virtue, appropriate to the dealings of those who are strangers to each other, and who look to each other neither for intimacy nor for unrequited assistance."[13]

Does this mean that justice cannot be applied to our closest relationships? To be fair in intimate and family relations, or any other close relations for that matter, must we become "chilly" and blind to people's needs and circumstances? Close, meaningful relationships engage the inner, unseen side of us, and yet this dimension is precisely what shadow justice excludes from its model. It calls for a justice of the head that's cold and calculating instead of a justice of the heart that's compassionate and healing.

A clear expression of this chilly one-sidedness comes from Immanuel

13. Alan Ryan, ed., *Justice* (Oxford, England: Oxford University Press, 1993), 16.

Kant, the great German systematic philosopher of the eighteenth century. He had "head" powers in abundance, but his heart seemed frozen when he "claimed that courts could not let criminals off the full rigor of the law's demands, an opinion summarized in the chilling view that a society which knew it was to perish from the face of the earth in the morning must leave none of its condemned murderers unhanged."[14]

The Utilitarian philosopher Jeremy Bentham spent considerable time inventing work machines for Dickensian prisons that could punish prisoners with hard labor but achieve nothing in output, thereby depriving prisoners even of the satisfaction of doing good work. The idea was to remove any element of potential pleasure from prison punishments. Since Bentham was considered a leader in radical prison reform, we can see that Scrooge's worldview on justice was no exaggeration.

Reflecting on the Euro-American philosophical legacy, all we can think is that something highly unhealthy has been going on in Western thought around the issue of justice—something split off from normal human sensitivities, leading to an obsessive rigidity to the letter of the law no matter what the cost in suffering. In light of trauma research, this reaction is no mystery. People who have been traumatized by this model of justice as children act out their feelings of trauma on others as adults. They carry it into their professions and, in the name of justice, practice cruelty. Herman Bianchi agrees:

> There's so much cruelty, and the most cruel people are those who do not realize they're cruel. The judge, when he sends a person to prison for many years, is unbelievably cruel. He does not even realize it. Every prison sentence is life-term. You never get back your old job. People don't accept you.[15]

In short, the Western paradigm of justice is faceless, hard, unyielding, retributive, judgmental, focused more on externals than on real people, occupied with who deserves what rather than with what it might

14. H. B. Reiss, ed., *Kant's Political Writings* (Cambridge: Cambridge University Press, 1992), 156.

15. "Justice as Sanctuary," *Ideas*, 1

take to make things right again. This is the prevailing paradigm of justice in a nutshell.

We don't, however, conceive of this book as a hot-blooded critique of the prevailing model, as much fun as it is with such meaty material at hand. Nor are we slash-and-burn revolutionaries when faced with systems we don't believe are serving us well. Due to the nature of our culture, many people are suffering from trauma, traumas that they then reenact on others.

The shift to a new model of justice must happen, therefore, with compassion and vision but also safely and wisely. Conditioning toward violence over decades doesn't disappear in a day. Neither can people whose autonomy and self-determination have been blasted out since birth suddenly become responsible, competent, self-governing citizens. Some transition with a hefty focus on healing and regeneration as well as public safety is in order.

So where do we start? With consciousness and the philosophies that shape it. As consciousness shifts, we each in our own way and on our own schedule walk away from models that no longer serve us, taking with us whatever good they had to offer. For retributive justice to continue, we must embrace the paradigm behind it. When that goes—when we no longer believe in its efficacy or legitimacy—the practice of it goes too, as we forge new practices inspired by our emerging vision.

Sooner or later, institutions follow our lead. They have no choice, because they literally have no powers of choice. Consciousness carries the mind resources; institutions are but protective shells. The shells go where consciousness takes them, even though they may drag in the sand as they go.

Given the purpose of shifting consciousness, our aim is to imagine what more justice may mean—what other models might do justice greater justice, which is to say, might frame justice in ways that better serve human and planetary good.

TWO

An Ancient View
of a "New" Paradigm

THE IDEA FOR DOING THIS BOOK began while reading Plato's *Republic*, which explores the idea of justice in ways that took us completely by surprise. Socrates summarily dismisses the notion of justice that we've all taken for granted—the reward-punishment model—and then launches a fascinating journey to imagine what justice may be instead.

Socrates opens the dialogue by doing basically what we've done, namely, raising problems with defining justice as "getting one's due," what we "deserve." How can we know for sure, he asks, what someone really deserves? Are we God? Do we know all the factors that pertain to another person's deserving—or to our own?

Even if we can agree on a standard for judging who's due what—no small challenge—who applies it and how? If we go by the letter—a harsh code of getting exactly and only what we deserve—is there hope for any of us? Jesus said, "He that is without sin among you, let him first cast a stone at her" (John 8:7). Shakespeare shared these concerns about the "just deserts" model. When Polonius, the meddling advisor to the king in *Hamlet*, says he'll take care of a troop of actors "according to their desert," Hamlet replies: "God's bodikin, man, much better. Use every man after his desert, and who shall scape whipping? Use them after your own honor and dignity. The less they deserve, the more merit is in your bounty" (2.2.529).

Socrates raises another wrinkle with the "just deserts" model. Following it to the letter won't work. Someone may deserve something, and yet it may be harmful for the person to receive it, given a change in circumstances. Socrates offers the example of a friend lending us a knife and then lapsing into insanity. Do we give the knife back, even if our friend "deserves" to have it?

Socrates' concerns about the "just deserts" model pale, though, before the arguments in Alfie Kohn's *Punished by Rewards*, which blasts the notion that even the upside of the model—rewards—functions well in child-rearing, schooling, or business. We lived with this book during our investigations—a book drawing on decades of research by educators, psychologists, and management consultants—and it changed us.[1] Theory it's not. What's theoretical is the assumption that we can ignore all this research and still create healthy relationships at home, at school, or at work by using the reward, much less punishment, model.

As we've said, rewards and punishments (bribes and threats, carrots and sticks) are fraught with problems. They train people to be selfishly calculating, deceptive about difficulties, blind to real-life consequences, and either obsessively hungry for the power-over position or reactive to it in unhealthy, unhelpful ways. Why institute in families, schools, and businesses—much less religion—methods that create these patterns of behavior? The method may get a rat to push a button for food, but it won't get humans to be creative, harmonious, and happy. Frankly, even the rats get bored. Harry Levinson calls the model "the great jackass fallacy," the title of his collection of essays in which he challenges the reductionist notion that human behavior can be controlled by the use of carrots and sticks.[2]

But it's what rewards and punishments do to our motivation structure that's most devastating to creating true justice among us. Not only do rewards and punishments put the outer before the inner, but worse, they chip away at our inner connectedness, until we lose our inner guide altogether. Kohn summarizes extensive research showing that rewards and punishments erode our inner motivation. That's their prime purpose. Why would anyone want to do this?

1. Alfie Kohn, *Punished by Rewards: The Trouble with Gold Stars, Incentive Plans, A's, Praise, and Other Bribes* (New York: Houghton Mifflin, 1993).

2. Harry Levinson, *The Great Jackass Fallacy* (Boston: Harvard Graduate School of Business Administration, 1973). Quoted in Kohn, *Punished by Rewards*, 311 (n. 7).

Because inner self-guidance isn't controllable. If we want others to serve our interests and conform to our notions of order, we must replace their own inner motivation with a desire for externals—externals we control. These can be visible things such as paychecks or positions, or that most precious of invisibles, love, which in the form of approval or acceptance can be given or withheld for controlling purposes.

In other words, the model restructures our personal compass, deranging it, until we lose the ability to find our true north. Instead, we follow the norths set for us by parents, teachers, peers, bosses, or social, professional, and religious groups. What we love and what excites us we're not rewarded for, while what we find a chore to the point of drudgery is reinforced. After a while, we internalize the rule that anything that we enjoy must be suspect, while anything that seems to be a grim duty must be good, the "right" thing to do. North becomes south and south north.

Trying to follow our pole-reversed compass, we wander from ourselves and get lost. Guilt, shame, fear, obligation, and insecurity replace joy and excitement as our needle north. Instead of operating confidently from the inside out—from what's authentically us, trusting the inner guides that speak through our longings and loves—we live from the outside in. We obey duty, demand, and expectations as others have defined these for us since birth. Or we do whatever puts us ahead outwardly. Having learned to dismiss inner values, we grow hypersensitive to outer influences and adopt external values. The result is that we become easily controlled from without, cut off from our conscience, courage, or heart's longings.

That's how an apparently benign or positive practice such as rewards or even praise subverts creativity: an insatiable thirst for external rewards replaces our inner directedness. The thirst is insatiable because no quantity of external rewards can ever equal the quality of life we can have when we live from within. Yet that's what's taken from us, until we forget what it's like to live inwardly moved. Instead of learning in school simply for the joy of learning or doing a job with excellence for pure satisfaction, we do it for the grade, the perk, the bribe. The bribe becomes more important than the activity. It devalues the activity, as if it would not be worth doing without the bribe. Tests show with dead-on repeatability that rewards take all the fun out of whatever we're doing. Studies reveal that people will return to an activity of their own volition when they have not been rewarded, but will not return to that same activity of their own volition after rewards have been introduced.[3]

In other words, subjected to external control, we learn to ignore what feels right within and instead follow what external sources tell us to do. Those are the terms on which our behavior is judged and we're rewarded or not. Individual conscience ceases to be a voice we listen to, for in a world of externals, we can't afford to listen. In its place, we learn obedience and conformity—doing what we're told and fitting in. No wonder crimes, including white-collar crimes, proliferate. The inner voices that would stop them have been silenced, and their intangible values dismissed. Educator Constance Kamii writes:

> We cannot expect children to accept ready-made values and truths all the way through school, and then suddenly make choices in adulthood. Likewise, we cannot expect them to be manipulated with reward and punishment in school, and to have the courage of a Martin Luther King in adulthood.[4]

For Socrates, it's unthinkable that justice should do this to us— should cut us off from our voice within. Not justice but *in*justice does such violence to us, which has to mean—and does mean for Socrates and Plato—that we're approaching justice the wrong way. In dialogue after dialogue, Socrates and Plato shift the focus in the opposite direction: from outer to inner concerns, from appearances to essences, from visible forms to invisible ideas and values. The dialogues aim to deepen our connection to what's within—to know ourselves—assuming that the

3. See Edward L. Deci and Richard M. Ryan, *Intrinsic Motivation and Self-Determination in Human Behavior* (New York: Plenum Press, 1985). This entire book—in full academic dress—reports on the extensive experimentation that has been done on this issue. The evidence is overwhelming that positive reinforcements (rewards) are only slightly less damaging than negative reinforcements (punishments) to people's inner motivation.

4. Constance Kamii, "Toward Autonomy: The Importance of Critical Thinking and Choice Making," *School Psychology Review* 20 (1991): 387.

inner reveals who we are and therefore stands as our true authority and guide.

Justice must serve this core relation we have to ourselves, if it's to function as something worthy and good, which Socrates and Plato assume it is. Justice can't be defined in terms of externals, in which case the "just deserts" model cannot capture what justice is all about. Indeed, it is a model of injustice, for in practicing it we do injustice to ourselves by denying what's most essentially us, our own inner experience.

Plato even ends *The Republic* with the near-death experience of a soldier and his account of the upper and lower worlds that souls travel to between lifetimes. He's clearly questioning the religious assumptions of his day about afterlife judgment and hence cosmic justice. Those who went to the upper world (rewarded) became arrogant and self-important and often made disastrous decisions in choosing their next lives, while those who traveled the lower worlds (punished) were humble and often made much wiser decisions. On strict reward-punishment terms, who was most blessed? Promises of rewards and punishments in the afterlife aren't as clear-cut as they seem.

Challenging that justice is about rewards, punishments, and each of us getting our due was philosophical bait for us—after all, isn't that what we think of first when we think of things being just or unjust?—but what threw us into the project was Socrates' astonishing suggestion of what justice may be beyond that, a radically different model.

It's a long story, and who knows what Socrates—or Plato—really intend, since they explore ideas through dialogue, a method which wanders up, down, and all around a subject with few clear-cut conclusions. Socrates refers to the utopia he describes in *The Republic* as a metaphor for the soul's self-government and not to be taken literally. Metaphors spark the imagination and lure us into considering possibilities beyond the status quo of what already exists. Socrates isn't a thinker to be easily pinned down.

As to Plato, he states in a letter that readers cannot know from the dialogues what he personally thinks. The dialogues, he said, were intended not to present doctrines but rather to raise questions for philosophical discussion. That they do. But tell us what to think? No, the dialogues don't do that; they merely get thought going, even if it's by proposing arguments that get us worked up into a philosophical lather, of which there are plenty in *The Republic*.

Given all this, our best guess is that Socrates places justice roughly in the vicinity of *each of us doing what's ours to do*, which is indeed how he describes justice in *The Republic* (433a–434c). Naturally, to do this, we have to know who we are, which is a core tenet of Socratic/Platonic thought. The more we're connected to our inner truth, the more we live true to our souls' purposes, and the more justice operates in our lives. We live the meanings we were born to live, meanings which, for those of a spiritual bent, are linked to the meanings we derive from the whole.

Implicit in this view is a deep sense of the sacredness of every being—that everything has a value that can't be compared with anything else and that's needed within the whole to be what it is and not something else. This core assumption is expressed consistently in indigenous philosophies from around the world. Rupert Ross, a Canadian crown prosecutor who has spent many years learning from Cree and Ojibway elders, writes how this view undergirds their view of the universe, using the forest as a teaching of this principle:

> I was reminded, for instance, of an Ojibway elder who told about how she understood some of the teachings of the forest. In the forest, she explained, there were so many different trees, bushes, and grasses, insects, birds and animals. You would not compare the worth of the white pine tree with the worth of the blue jay. You would not compare the worth of the juniper bush with the worth of the frog. They were all necessary for that place to continue in health. They were all sacred.[5]

Applied to human life, an Ojibway medicine man explained to Ross that this philosophy forms the Ojibway attitude toward children and so informs family structures. All children are born with gifts, which means families have the duty to support and help develop them for the good of

5. Rupert Ross, *Returning to the Teachings: Exploring Aboriginal Justice* (Toronto, Ontario, Canada: Penguin Books, 1996), 53.

everyone—an attitude that Socrates and Plato very much agreed with, as we'll see:

> Everyone was to be respected for their gifts, and everyone had a duty to help children find and develop their special gifts, whatever they were. All the gifts were sacred....The issue that engaged them, that came from their teachings, was how each of them could use their own unique gifts to the fullest so that the partnership would achieve its fullest potential, and the family would be as strong as it could be.[6]

Respecting each other's gifts and helping each other develop to our fullest potential, so our relationships and societies can be as strong as possible—this is the new/ancient model of justice in a nutshell. The trick is drawing out its implications: i.e., restructuring our minds, emotions, lives, self-concepts, relationships, families, businesses, institutions, and culture to reflect this way of understanding justice.

To start, let's think more about the core concept of justice as each of us doing what's ours to do. The model assumes, with indigenous philosophy, that we're each born with a certain character, set of qualities, and destiny—what psychologist James Hillman calls "the soul's code," a kind of consciousness-DNA that invisibly guides our psyche's growth and leads us to do what's ours. We have countless choices along the way for how we can pursue our destiny. "There's a divinity that shapes our ends," Hamlet says, "Rough-hew them how we will" (5.2.10). We're as free as any artist to create what we will with the soul elements we're given.

Yet there is one thing we must do, namely, honor our inner core, not brush it aside, not fall into the cultural mind-trap of believing that it's self-indulgent to seek inner well-being. Our essence is the root from which our lives grow. If we and our lives are to be healthy, we need our root to be alive, happy, and strong. Dismissing it won't do, no matter what the justification.

Accordingly, even though we may go against familial, financial, and

6. Ibid., 54.

cultural pressures, we need to let our souls guide our growth—to go where they lead—because this is what justice requires. Justice means each of us honoring our inner truth above externals and granting this same priority for everyone else, not encroaching on each other's inner mandate to be soul-guided. By listening to our inner DNA and letting it steer our life's course, we do what's ours, and that's the essence of justice.

This model stands against the notion that we're property for sale, ownable commodities, or that our souls can be used as bargaining chips. Bargaining our inner lives away to gain external approval or rewards cannot succeed. If there's any owning to be done, we own ourselves— our minds, loves, energies, passions, sexuality, bodies. To put it another way, our souls already own us. If we push this further, our souls are owned by God, the whole, the Creator, the reality that is our source, or whatever terms we use for what's beyond us but also within us—the origin of our consciousness-DNA.

Because of this prior "ownership," when we follow our souls' guidance, we find how we're related to the whole by doing what's most soul-fulfilling for us. We discover our place of meaning—the place where we can put to best use the abilities and interests that flow from our essence. In doing what's ours, we do what the whole needs from us. Rumi, the thirteenth-century Sufi poet, speaks directly to this call of justice in a passage which Coleman Barks and John Moyne, the translators, entitle "The One Thing You Must Do":

There is one thing in this world which you must never forget to do. If you forget everything else and not this, there's nothing to worry about, but if you remember everything else and forget this, then you will have done nothing in your life.

It's as if a king has sent you to some country to do a task, and you perform a hundred other services, but not the one he sent you to do. So human beings come to this world to do *particular work*. That work is the purpose, and each is specific to the person. If you don't do it, it's as though a priceless Indian sword were used to slice rotten meat. It's a golden bowl being used to cook turnips, when one filing from the bowl could buy a hundred suitable pots. It's like a knife of the finest tempering nailed to a wall to hang things on.

You say, "But look, I'm using the dagger. It's not lying idle." Do you hear how ludicrous that sounds? For a penny an iron nail could be bought to serve for that. You say, "But I spend my energies on lofty enterprises. I study jurisprudence and philosophy and logic and astronomy and medicine and all the rest." But consider why you do these things. They are all branches of yourself.

Remember the deep root of your being, the presence of your lord. Give your life to the one who already owns your breath and your moments. If you don't, you will be exactly like the man who takes a precious dagger and hammers it into his kitchen wall for a peg to hold his dipper gourd. You'll be wasting valuable keenness and foolishly ignoring your dignity and your purpose.[7]

This concept of justice as "using" ourselves according to our "valuable keenness," our "dignity" and "purpose" accords with a teaching of Emanuel Swedenborg (1688–1772), the scientist and spiritual visionary whose ideas on holism proved far ahead of his time. Through his inner journeys with angels, he developed a concept of "uses," namely, that everything in the universe is created for its own special use that serves the larger design of things. "Uses" is a holistic concept, because it says that we each have the whole embedded in us—indeed, that we are the whole expressed—and that therefore the whole manifests itself in our lives through our loves and what we're drawn to do. Our very being is how the whole guides us, which is why we need to accept who we are and allow ourselves to be guided by it, not to be distracted by external social pressures.

It's as if we're formed to do exactly what's most needed within the whole, even though we don't have access to the big picture and don't realize how we serve it by doing what's ours. "The universe is a lan-

7. John Moyne and Coleman Barks, trans, *Say I Am You: Poetry Interspersed with Stories of Rumi and Shams* (Athens, Ga.: MAYPOP, 1994), 21.

guage of uses, where each individual has his or her own particular con-tribution to make: this is one's mission."[8] By using our time, energies, and resources to do what's ours, we do justice to ourselves by fulfilling our mission, and we do justice to our communities and world by con-tributing what they most need that we have to offer. All this depends, of course, on our connectedness to who we are, on our being inwardly guided, and on our not being "owned" from without, therefore com-pelled to act against our souls' intentions.

This inner-directed model of justice grabbed us—and sparked a flood of questions. So we went back to *The Republic*. This is a radical treatise, one that calls for lifetimes of study. No wonder it was found among the Nag Hammadi scrolls in Egypt with the sacred texts of the Coptic Gnostics, including the Bible. Apparently the most revered ancient thinkers didn't sugarcoat their ideas and critiques, neither did they bow to political, moral, social, or religious forms of "correctness." These were no-nonsense thinkers, intent on making us think for our-selves outside convention, and this was evidently considered a sacred endeavor.

How to create justice: that's what *The Republic* is about. To work toward a more just life and society, we must address the factors that get in the way of this process. If a just society needs each of us to be who we are and to do what's ours to do—if we're born as we are because that's what the whole needs to prosper—and if we as individuals want to live from who we are as well, then what's the problem? What prevents us from living inner directed and fulfilling our life's callings?

Being essentially holistic, system thinkers, Socrates and Plato address the most formative system in human development: the family. What is it for? Is the family's function first a social duty to make new generations of people who will conform to social expectations, hence abandon the inward call for the sake of external acceptability? Or is the family's function first a sacred duty to nurture human beings in their souls' uniqueness, as the Ojibway elder described, so that new genera-tions can blossom as individuals, fulfill their potential, and make the

---

8. Anders Hallengren, *Gallery of Mirrors: Reflections of Swedenborgian Thought* (West Chester, Pa.: Swedenborg Foundation Publishers, 1998), 112.

contributions they were born to make, wherever that takes them? In short, is the family's role to suppress the inner or to call it forth?

The film *Dead Poets Society*, starring Robin Williams, posed the same questions for today: Are we free to respond to our souls' leadings, or must we fulfill our family's expectations of who we should be and what we should do with our lives? The film doesn't veil its answer, for when the young man succumbed to his father's pressure to abandon a life in the arts, he committed suicide. What is life, if the inner has no place in it?

For millennia, though, the first goal for families has prevailed, namely, to raise people who will put aside who they are in order to fulfill what the group (family, religion, nation, tribe) asks of them, whether it's to kill enemies or herd cows. Evolutionarily, all sorts of arguments can be made for this function of the family: the survival of the group is seen as more important than the survival of the individual, or keeping the family structure in place, though it disregards individuals, provides social stability.

To achieve the goal of obedience and conformity, the family unit in the West and certainly in ancient Athens was structured so that women and children (boys too) were given the status of property, owned and controlled by the male head of the family. Property does not have a say about how to develop its potential. Following a different drummer is not an option. Reducing people to the status of property is the ultimate statement that their inner experience doesn't count and that conforming to externals is all that matters.

Socrates and Plato clearly have a problem with this model. Families that function this way don't serve justice, nor are they just. Socrates and Plato don't like the price that the model exacts from individuals, but they especially don't like that societies lose the unique talents that individuals could contribute. So they rally one of the most radical assaults in history against the notion of human beings as property by challenging the traditional model of the family. If society needs each of us doing what's ours to do, then it won't work to subject everyone to the control of parents or spouses who impose their own notions about what family members should do with their lives. Family life must be rethought from the ground up, which is what Socrates and Plato proceed to do.

To remedy the injustice of young Einsteins or Mozarts being forced to bale hay or flip burgers in the family business all their lives, Socrates and Plato suggest that people should not know with whom they've had children nor who their biological children or parents are. Those who love children should be specially trained to take care of them, watchful of each child's special talents and equipped to develop them. People should not have children only because they're biologically capable of doing so, because they wish to increase their property holdings, because they feel obligated to carry on the group name, or even because they're carried away in passionate, romantic feelings. These reasons do not signify preparedness to nurture a unique and creative contributor to society.

Their point wasn't about intimacy or child-parent bonding. These issues, as important as they are, aren't what *The Republic* is about. Justice, that's the issue, and whether we ever have it when an externalizing model governs our most intimate and formative relations. To grow into doing what's uniquely ours to do, we need to access our inner resources and pursue our souls' callings, whether it's to become an actor, grow food, work with people, do abstract math, or become a wandering philosopher. The traditional family model doesn't invite this open exploration.

Whether Socrates and Plato intended the argument literally, metaphorically, or only as a thought experiment, we don't know. But they make their point. If we really want to change the world so that there's room for more justice in it, the family is the place to start. Everything else grows from there.

Today, we know this is true. We develop our most fundamental patterns of interacting with others in the family, and it's also where we form our most basic concepts about ourselves. Whatever we learn growing up in families—constructive or destructive, soul-affirming or soul-denying, just or unjust, free or not free, expansive or repressive, self-accepting or self-scolding, outer-image oriented or inwardly directed—we carry through life and into the world. We perpetuate the models we experienced early on.

Socrates and Plato knew the power of family systems and knew how destructive they could be to justice—to each of us doing what's ours to do. In the name of sacrificing ourselves for the group, we deprive society of what's ours to give.

Confucius argued similarly in *The Great Learning*, the central text of Confucian philosophy, namely, that we can experience virtue and goodness in the world only when we have healthy families, and we can have healthy families only when we blossom as individuals—when our minds, thoughts, hearts, and persons are nurtured to be healthy and happy, when we properly "cultivate" ourselves:

The ancients who wished to illustrate illustrious virtue throughout the kingdom, first ordered well their own states. Wishing to order well their states, they first regulated their families. Wishing to regulate their families, they first cultivated their persons. Wishing to cultivate their persons, they first rectified their hearts. Wishing to rectify their hearts, they first sought to be sincere in their thoughts. Wishing to be sincere in their thoughts, they first extended to the utmost their knowledge. Such extension of knowledge lay in the investigation of things.

Things being investigated, knowledge became complete. Their knowledge being complete, their thoughts were sincere. Their thoughts being sincere, their hearts were then rectified. Their hearts being rectified, their persons were cultivated. Their persons being cultivated, their families were regulated. Their families being regulated, their states were rightly governed. Their states being rightly governed, the whole kingdom was made tranquil and happy.

From the Son of Heaven down to the mass of the people, all must consider the cultivation of the person the root of *everything besides.*[9]

Granted, the lengths to which Socrates and Plato would go to break the externalizing model seem shocking. And yet so much is at stake. Freedom, self-determination, and justice aren't all that's sacrificed on a control model of families. Meaning and intimacy suffer as well. How can there be real intimacy when we don't feel free to express who we are?

9. James Legge, *The Four Books* (New York: Paragon Book Reprint Corporation, 1966), 310–313

Who is left in us or in others to be intimate with if our inner truth and reality aren't welcome?

Whatever the best remedy may be—and our vote is always with a philosophy shift and inward spiritual evolution—Plato and Socrates were right that justice must be lifted up before we can replace bondage with bonding and begin to explore genuine intimacy with those we love.

Such is one of countless thought-experiments posed in *The Republic*. We'd read them before; but, until we started digesting the core idea that justice is each of us being who we are and doing what's ours to do, we didn't see the logic. Once we did, though, we started applying the inner-oriented model of justice to our lives. Time and again, issues came up—not only intellectually but also socially, emotionally, and personally—that proved the power of this understanding: that we're each called to do what's ours, and that following this call is the core of justice. We were amazed at how its meaning clarified thorny issues and gave us peace on tough life choices. This soul-honoring model of justice has carried us through some of the biggest transitions we've faced.

Indeed, that's what we've loved most about this model of justice, namely, the strategy of life suggested—that justice means each of us being guided by our essence and that, if we each aim for it by being true to who we are as best we can, we'll bring greater justice into our lives together.

There's so much we don't know: How can we find our way? Which way is best? Justice says, "Trust your souls. Connect with who you are on the deepest levels of meaning, purpose, and unfolding process, and then follow where your own being leads! Do what's yours to do, as best you see it!" It takes huge trust, and even greater trust in the soul-guidance of others, but not without ground and reason—the philosophy that undergirds it.

Trusting our souls and inner guidance lifts from our shoulders the weights of the old model. Comparisons, expectations, competitions, outward successes or failures, judgments, "if onlys" and "what ifs," even the best of intentions: they start falling away. They're not relevant to our souls' agenda. As we stick doggedly to the course that our souls set for us, justice emerges, bringing with it peace, harmony, meaning, and real happiness.

Some scholars interpret Socrates' vision of justice as if he were saying we should all conform to the social roles dictated to us by society—that society should take on the controlling, externalizing functions that families have. But this interpretation of *The Republic* doesn't wash. The model would be the same, just some other social unit performing the externalizing role. If it were right, *The Republic* would contribute little or nothing to what already existed in Greek society, neither could it stand the test of ages as a sacred and mind-challenging text, nor would it be consistent with a philosopher famous for being the healer of the soul, one who taught that the unexamined life is not worth living and that "Know thyself" is a divine command.

Indeed, Socrates chose to drink hemlock rather than abandon his soul's calling to do philosophy in the streets of Athens. Uncomfortable as his presence was to the status quo, he argued that Athens needed him as a philosopher. That was his to do. He functioned as their gadfly, stinging the sleeping horse that was Athens into some philosophical and spiritual awareness. By contrast, had Socrates defined justice as conforming to social roles, he would not have chosen to drink the hemlock, nor would he have ever been brought to trial. What he taught would have threatened no one. The sleeping horse of Athens would have long since drifted into a full-throttle snore, and he with it.

Why is the call to live from our souls, from the divine spark that called us into being, so compelling? Because our lives are at stake, our happiness and meaning, as well as our relationships, families, businesses, culture, and now our planet. An externally lived life, even in the name of justice, lacks the meaning of life lived from our essence. Millions of us are exploring what it means to live differently, more from the inside out and less from the outside in. We're seeking to connect more deeply with who we are and to live from our souls' guidance. Hamlet says to Ophelia, "God hath given you one face, and you make yourselves another" (3.1.145–146). We want to know our original, God-given face beyond the masks we've created.

Whether we do this through recovery, twelve-step groups, self-help programs, therapy, a spiritual path, meditation, yoga, Eastern philosophy, astrology, esotericism, dream study, the classics, literature, political, social, and environmental activism, family life, a meaningful career, or religious devotion—which is to say, through our own blend of many methods—we're not only changing our own lives but simultaneously revolutionizing justice. As we come home to who we are, we're actually making the world more just.

Given this understanding, justice ceases to be a static condition that does or does not hold, in which case it makes no sense to say, "There is no justice." Justice isn't apart from us. It's what we create by being true to who we are. The Socratic revolution moved philosophy from outer considerations to inner ones. Applied to justice, Plato's *Republic* suggests a revolutionary model—one that in 2400 years we're just beginning in Western culture to wrap our minds, hearts, lives, and even institutions around. That's way too exciting to pass our notice.

THREE

Restorative Justice in Action

WHERE DO WE START if we want to think through justice
from a completely different set of assumptions? What are
the practical implications? How would an inwardly oriented, soul-honoring model of justice deal with all the different hurts that occur? What
would such a different philosophy of justice look like in practice?
Frankly, not moving in criminal justice circles, we didn't know.

But help came beyond our wildest hopes. Pat Carnes, a pioneer in
recovery and sex-addiction therapy, told us about the work that Ojibway
elders in Canada are doing to shift the model of justice in their communities. His colleague, Geral Blanchard, had recently visited the Hollow Water First Nation on Lake Winnipeg and observed their healing
approach firsthand.[1] Building on their indigenous teachings, the community's elders have created healing and sentencing circles for members who would otherwise be sent to prison.

These circles made the link we sought because they integrate a spiritual philosophy, including a respect for the dignity, divinity, indeed the
"use" of each individual, with a need to change the behavior of some
badly wounded people in their communities. They put a philosophy of
justice not unlike Plato's into practice in ways Plato didn't describe or
likely imagine.

Specifically, the healing and sentencing circles have the primary aim

---

1. Geral Blanchard, "Aboriginal Canadian Innovations in the Treatment of Sexual
Violence," *The Carnes Update* (Summer 1997): 4–6. This newsletter is available from
The Meadows Institute, 1655 N. Tegner Street, Wickenburg, AZ 85390, telephone:
800/621–4062.

to support healing and transformation. To this end, they bring together not only the victims and offenders but also the extended communities of each along with the elders and law enforcement people. Everyone is involved. The principals tell their stories, as do their families and friends. Expressing feelings is essential to the healing dynamics, from remorse and apology on the offender's side to pain and possibly forgiveness on the victim's.

Through this revolutionary justice process—new to European-Americans but ancient to indigenous peoples—everyone is touched and transformed in some way. The elders don't view offenders as the sick ones and everyone else as healthy. Their perspective is holistic, that is, whole-system oriented. If one person in a community is in pain, the whole community shares in the process that culminated in hurt or sickness, which means they view everyone as being in need of healing and essential to the healing process.

Or, to put it differently, when one person acts out of balance, this is a symptom of imbalance in the whole system. Since everyone is part of the same system, everyone has been affected by whatever is causing the pain. As a result, everyone must be involved in the healing process, and everyone will be blessed by the healing. That's why in these circles everyone goes on the healing path together.

Nor do they believe in punishment. It's not part of their cultural philosophy. In a position paper on incarceration, the Hollow Water Community expresses their Holistic Circle Healing Program's policy:

> Our tradition, our culture, speaks clearly about the concepts of judgement and punishment. They belong to the Creator. They are not ours. They are, therefore, not to be used in the way that we relate to each other. People who offend against another (victimizers) are to be viewed and related to as people who are out of balance—with themselves, their family, their community, and their Creator. A return to balance can best be accomplished through a process of accountability that includes support from the community through teaching and healing. The use of judgements and punishment actually works against the healing

process. An already unbalanced person is moved further out of balance.[2]

In his book *Returning to the Teachings*—an inspiring account of what he learned from these elders—Rupert Ross describes more fully the profound healing work that these communities are doing, based on original Native teachings.[3] The Euro-American model of justice does not work for them and never has. One Cree elder in Alberta reflected, "We know you have a *legal* system; we're just not sure it's a *justice* system."[4] All the Euro-American system does is transport multigenerationally traumatized people off to prison—a "solution" that functions as the current version of cultural genocide in Native communities. No young people are left to carry on the traditions. When they return from prison, they're more traumatized than when they went in. Unchanged and unhealed, they're likely to repeat their offenses.

This situation spurred the elders to act. The Ojibway would have no future if they did not devise an alternative. Those whom the official model labels as "offenders," the elders see as people in such pain that they pass their pain on to others through crime. Pain is not relieved—nor the real problem solved—by inflicting more pain. Since acts of violence don't come out of nowhere, what everyone needs—victim, victimizer, and community—is healing.

Healing is a mystery, a gift, but some conditions are more conducive to it than others. Prison is not conducive; neither are courtrooms filled with accusations, judgments, revenge, and punishments. Instead, the Hollow Water First Nation found that a holistic approach designed with healing as its primary aim is highly conducive:

We are attempting to promote a process that we believe is more consistent with how justice matters would have been handled

2. The Church Council on Justice and Corrections, *Satisfying Justice*, op. cit., xxiii.

3. Rupert Ross, *Returning to the Teachings: Exploring Aboriginal Justice* (Toronto: Penguin Books Canada, 1996). This book cannot as of this writing be obtained within the United States but may be purchased from The Albert Britnell Bookstore in Toronto, tel.: 416/362–0022 or 800/387–1417.

4. Ibid., 253.

traditionally in our community. Rather than focusing on a specific incident as the legal system does at present, we believe a more holistic focus is required in order to restore balance to all parties of the victimization. The victimizer must be addressed in all his or her dimensions—physical, mental, emotional, spiritual—and within the context of all his or her past, present, and future relationships with family, community, and Creator. The legal system's adversarial approach does not allow this to happen.[5]

Learning about this program cinched it for us. What Socrates and Plato envisioned as a utopian ideal of justice could in fact be practiced. But it takes healing to get there. To follow our souls' guidance, we must first heal from the traumas and anti-soul programming that gets in the way. Realizing this, we can commit ourselves and our communities to supporting the healing process, and as we do, we find true justice emerging. That's what the elders at Hollow Water are doing—not as a new program but as a return to Native American wisdom and practice.

In other words, what Socrates and Plato tried to express to their rabidly patriarchal, dominator, externally oriented society was an echo, a glimpse of justice lived in ways that many different indigenous peoples have put to the test for millennia. Plato referred to a Golden Age in the distant past when justice didn't need to be taught or enforced, where justice was a natural way of life. Was he perhaps referring to the Neolithic period (before 4000 BCE) when indigenous Europeans lived in more egalitarian "partnership societies," as Riane Eisler's research suggests?[6]

Interestingly enough, from his other-dimensional discussions with angels, Emanuel Swedenborg described a similar memory of wisdom communities in our ancient history. During a time when Christianity was not known for its tolerance, even burning believers for simply translating the Bible into the vernacular, Swedenborg maintained great

5. Ibid., xxiv.

6. See Riane Eisler, *The Chalice and The Blade* (San Francisco: HarperSanFrancisco, 1987).

admiration for traditions that preserved the "Ancient Word." He referred to the "Most Ancient Church" followed by an "Ancient" one, both of which long predated the "Israelitish Word" (*Apocalypse Revealed* §11 [1].[7] By "Church," Swedenborg meant not an institution like the Christian one, of which he was often critical, but a community governed by wisdom, where people lived in mutual respect, peace, and harmony. Somewhere in our ancient bones, we humans know what justice is and how to live it.

In *Restorative Justice: Healing the Effects of Crime*, Jim Consedine, a New Zealand prison chaplain since 1979, explores indigenous models of justice from around the world—Maori, Australian Aboriginal, Samoan, as well as Celtic and Hebraic (biblical) philosophies.[8] His treatment of biblical justice is an eye-opener; for he, like Mennonite Howard Zehr, presents a radically different understanding of biblical justice from the judge-and-punish, hit-back image. The prevailing retributive paradigm, it seems, has made use of the Bible for its own purposes by making revenge (in the form of judicial punishment) synonymous with divine justice.

The actual orientation of ancient Hebrews toward matters of justice seems to have been something else entirely. Their emphasis wasn't on punishment but on making things right between people and within the community. This, Zehr and Consedine claim, was the real spirit behind the Mosaic law of "an eye for an eye." The point wasn't to punish according to some abstract standard of retribution but to right wrongs on a practical level by limiting revenge and instead seeking simple compensation and amends, so that broken relations could be restored and the community made whole again.

Not that indigenous practices can transfer wholesale into modern

7. See Hallengren's chapter "The Secret of Magna Tartaria" in *Gallery of Mirrors*, 17–41, in which he discusses Swedenborg's views on the wisdom of the ancients as well as subsequent attempts by scholars to figure out what he was referring to in time and culture.

8. Jim Consedine, *Restorative Justice: Healing the Effects of Crime* (Lyttelton, New Zealand: Ploughshares Publications, 1995). This book can be ordered directly from New Zealand: Ploughshares Publications, P.O. Box 173, Lyttelton, New Zealand.

life. As Jim Consedine's book illustrates, indigenous peoples have an astonishing diversity of practices, most of which are not likely to become part of Western culture. One that comes to mind is the Australian Aboriginal rite of penis-holding. An accused man offers his penis to a brother or male friend to hold, who, if he accepts the offer, undertakes to plead for the accused.[9]

The outward form of this rite isn't likely to catch on in courtrooms as we shift to restorative justice (though it might boost the television ratings if it happened on one of the law shows), and yet the meaning of it has much to offer. Someone accused is now the vulnerable one, and what's at stake for that person is most personal, namely, his life and future. If we're accused, we need friends to plead for us, people who know all about us and understand us and who realize that they hold our best interests in their hands. We need such trusted bonds with the community, so that we can pay our debts and go on to create a good life. Jim Consedine writes, "The whole emphasis in this type of penalty payment is not to punish the debtor but to recognise that law has been broken and ritual is needed to restore the proper balance within the tribe."[10]

When we turn to indigenous traditions for insights on justice, we're not looking to adopt their customs literally, for the obvious reason that they don't fit us now. Rather, we're looking for their perspectives—the intentions behind the ritual forms. What we're really looking for is their time-tested wisdom about restoring damaged relationships.

Indeed, as indigenous peoples talk to each other and compare perspectives, they find beneath their diverse symbols and rituals striking similarities in orientation. Living in smaller communities, they didn't have the luxury of disposing of people as permanent undesirables. They had to make relationships work, so their communities wouldn't disintegrate.

It is not surprising, then, that these various new/old paradigms offer a kinder, gentler justice—a real justice—one that works for us through healing rather than against us through blame and punishment. Restorative justice embraces human concerns because it's about restoring

9. Ibid., 116.

10. Ibid., 116.

ruptured relationships and making things right, whatever this means on a case-to-case basis.

In these restorative models, justice takes life not from external arrangements (who gets what in carrots or sticks) but from the emerging integrity of our inner being and our ability to connect soul to soul. If we're broken within, we can't expect justice without. It won't happen. But we can heal, and healing broken relationships works better when we do it together. Isolating a person and labeling him or her as the problem only increases the harm done. Healing, restoring, making things right: this, and not punishment, is the job of justice.

As we researched the subject, one thing led to another; and before we knew it, the picture emerged that, around the world and often independent of one another, private citizens, communities, law-enforcement groups, and even state judicial systems are reclaiming justice as a hope-restoring, healing, transforming process. Often led by indigenous communities as well as by some religious groups—the Mennonites in the United States have been developing restorative justice models and practices since the 1970s—justice means transforming painful, broken relationships into mutually supportive, genuinely healing communities.

Stories of Restorative Justice at Work

Stories of this quiet revolution in justice have been finding their way into the media for some time. And yet it's been slow to catch on. We're all so heavily conditioned to view justice in terms of rewards and punishments—and when harms occur, to think exclusively of punishments. We react automatically, based on childhood programming. We were punished when we did something wrong, so that's what should happen. Punishment will fix things. It will restore justice. We have trouble imagining that justice could create health, harmony, and happiness, if we simply used a model oriented this way.

Yet think about it: what does punishment actually do for either victims or offenders? Even if we feel justified in not caring about offenders, we should care about helping the victims of crime. And yet the punishment model does nothing for them. Very often it puts them through investigative, legal, courtroom, and bureaucratic nightmares, as if the original injustice wasn't traumatic and disruptive enough. Sometimes the courts award victims money, but more than money is needed to restore a sense of well-being in society.

Howard Zehr explains in *Changing Lenses* that victims' needs are by definition peripheral in the current system, since the state is the one officially injured.[11] State-oriented criminal justice is not organized around helping victims put their lives back together. The entire focus is on determining the guilt or innocence of the accused and, if guilty, exacting punishment. Beyond that, victims are on their own.

The offenders' needs for healing aren't a priority either, yet this policy is dangerously shortsighted, given packed prisons and early parole. Neither does punishment hold offenders accountable for the harm they've done. Yes, offenders do time in jail—a payment to the state—but the human victim receives no closure or resolution. Prison sentences are an easy payment for offenders compared with looking into the faces of the people they've hurt and taking steps to find resolution.

With neither victim nor offender healed, how is the community made more safe? Having "paid their debt to society," offenders leave prison angry, frustrated, hardened, less prepared in job qualifications and normal-life coping skills, more skilled at crime, and now connected with a network of prison and ex-prison associates.

These failures of our current criminal justice system cry out for the restorative justice movement (see Resources, p. 287). For the sanity, peace, and happiness of everyone involved, people have been demanding a completely different approach to crime, conflict, and hurt. With healing as the common goal—making things right—restorative justice brings together all those touched by crime or conflict and appeals to the humanity in everyone to find a way. Usually, it's by sharing stories, expressing feelings, and hearing what has not been heard on all sides.

---

11. Zehr, *Changing Lenses*. This is another core book in the field of restorative justice that has been hugely helpful to us—one that can be easily ordered through bookstores. It's clearly written and gives a real feeling for the paradigm shift from retributive to restorative justice. Zehr has several point-for-point comparisons of the two models that are both clarifying and compelling.

Offenders are given the opportunity to hear the human consequences of crime, to express remorse to their victims, and to take part
in making things right, all of which can have a powerful, transforming
effect on offenders. Victims are given the opportunity to express their
pain, fear, confusion, and anger about what has happened. They also
have the opportunity to hear the offender's story, how he or she came to
be the person he or she is today, as well as to hear whatever the offender
is able to express to them. People from the community who participate
have the opportunity to function *as* a community, to lend support, to
express concerns, to gain a deeper understanding of and compassion for
others, as well as to use the experience for their own soul-searching,
deepening, and healing.

Restorative justice practices are emerging as a powerful force for
healing in our society. They inspire tremendous hope for who we can be
together and for the positive transformation that people, no matter how
violated or damaged, can experience when they come together honestly
and openly in the sincere quest for healing. All our descriptions of the
process, though, can't capture the emotional impact of the actual
accounts.

During our research, we've encountered many stories about how
restorative justice "turns suffering into meaning," to borrow Pat Carnes'
phrase. There's no single formula. Each person's path is unique. Healing can't be forced or legislated even with the best of intentions. But
with time and a model of justice that supports healing, it does happen.
And when it does, the experience proves powerfully convincing that this
is what justice is all about.

One of the best places to read about the global revolution under
way in justice is a thoughtful and wide-ranging book entitled *Satisfying Justice*, put out by The Church Council on Justice and Corrections
in Ottawa, Ontario. It describes one hundred different programs
around the world that experiment with restorative justice, exploring
methods that support victim, offender, and community healing. The
book also reflects on the strengths and weaknesses of these different
programs. For example, the compilers are skeptical about programs
that change techniques without adequately shifting the paradigm of
justice behind them.

Satisfying Justice begins with one woman's story—told by Wendy Keats of MOVE, a New Brunswick initiative in restorative justice—that highlights many of these issues:

Elizabeth had been extremely traumatized by the armed robbery during her shift at the convenience store. The crime scene had been absolute chaos. The masked robbers had screamed death threats as they held her captive with a knife to her throat. She had wet herself from sheer terror.

Even months after the robbers had been caught, life did not return to normal. Word had got out about her fear-induced loss of bladder control, and customers and co-workers teased her mercilessly afterwards. Not only did she have to cope with fear and shame, but past traumas in her life returned to haunt her. She became ill with bulimia and lost 85 pounds. Insomnia kept her awake night after night.

Friends and family quickly became impatient with her. "Look, you didn't get hurt. Let it go. What's your problem?" (This impatient response to a victim's torment is typical.)

Elizabeth herself couldn't understand the unrelenting torture. Why did she suffer nightmares every time she closed her eyes for a few moments? Why couldn't she resume her life? As her health deteriorated, her marriage broke down and her relationship with her children changed dramatically.

Meanwhile, Charles, the 21-year-old offender, was serving five years for the offence in a federal institution. He had been raised in a violent environment by a family deeply involved with drug and alcohol abuse. His string of surrogate fathers were mostly ex-offenders and addicts themselves. He and his sisters were victims of continuous abuse and poverty.

He had committed minor offences as a juvenile, but this was his first serious crime. To him, the offence was the result of an extremely bad acid trip. Completely out of his mind on booze and drugs, Charles had no idea of the trauma caused by his actions.

Charles first learned of Elizabeth's situation when he became aware of her insistence that the court allow her to submit a victim impact statement. She had not been invited by the courts to submit a statement as she was not identified as the victim. The convenience store was.

As Elizabeth fought for her right to somehow be included in the process, her anger and frustration grew. She was terrified that Charles and his accomplice would come back to get her as they threatened they would. She was isolated from her family and friends by this time. She was frightened, emotionally haggard, and physically sick.

Finally after two years and many counseling sessions, Elizabeth realized that she had to find a way to "let it go." She realized that, in order to do that, she had to try to find the answers to the questions that haunted her.

So when Charles' parole hearing came up, she traveled by bus for four hours to the institution . . . alone and suffering from pneumonia. During the hearing, Charles turned around and tried to say something to her, but victims and offenders are not allowed to speak to each other during these hearings, and he was cut off.

Back on the bus, she kept wondering, "What did he want to say to me?"

At this point, she contacted the National Parole Board with a request for a face-to-face meeting and they referred her case to MOVE. I was the assigned mediator.

When I first met Elizabeth, I asked her why she wanted to meet her offender. "I cannot live like this anymore," she said. "I have to get the answers to my questions. I have to find out whether he is coming back to get me or my family. I have to tell him how I feel. I have to look him in the face and tell him how he has changed my life."

All valid reasons for mediation. And so I went to see the offender.

Charles was amazed by Elizabeth's fear. "Doesn't she know I wouldna' never hurt her? Don't they give them convenience store clerks some training that tells them to just hand over the money and nobody will get hurt?" he asked incredulously.

"Doesn't she know that every robber says, 'don't call the cops or I'll come back an' git ya?' That's just the way it's done. Gee, I'm really sorry about this. . . . I had no idea."

Without hesitation he agreed to meet with Elizabeth to try to do whatever he could to make up for what he had previously thought of as just a bad night . . . too drunk . . . too stoned . . . and one for which he felt he was the only one paying a heavy price. By this time, Charles had been in prison for two years and it was no picnic. He slept with a knife under his pillow because there were so many stabbings going on around him. Like Elizabeth, he lived in daily fear.

The mediation was arranged to take place in a room within the prison itself. Neither of them slept the night before . . . each racked with doubts and fears. By the time the two of them came together, face to face across a 30-inch wide table, they were both peaked with emotion.

However, the controlled process of mediation soon took its effect and the story telling stage began. Elizabeth said everything she had been thinking for the past two years. Charles listened intently, and when it was his turn, he answered most of her questions as his own story unfolded. As the dialogue continued, they started to chuckle about a detail. This broke the tension and they really started to talk: face-to-face and heart-to-heart. They had shared a violent experience, albeit from entirely different perspectives. A relationship had been formed that night that, until now, had been left unresolved.

Elizabeth got the answers to all of the questions that had haunted her that day. She learned that Charles had never intended to come back and harm her, and that he was genuinely sorry for what he had done. They struck an agreement about how they would greet each other on the street when he is released from prison and returns to their home town. As they finished, they stood up and shook hands. "You know," Elizabeth said, "we will never be friends, you and I—we come from different worlds—but I want you to know that I wish you the best of luck and when I think of you I will hope that you are doing okay. I forgive you."

Leaving the prison, I asked her how she felt. "It's over. It's closed. It's done."

Five months later, she tells me that she has not had even a single nightmare since. "I don't feel like the same person anymore. There is no more fear. It's just gone."

I have learned from Charles' case manager that he is doing well. Staff feel it was a maturing experience for him and that there is a much better chance of him responding to rehabilitative treatment and taking life more seriously. No guarantees. He's twenty-three years old. My own guess is that he will never forget this experience, and that it will have a profound effect on future decisions.

After mediation, Elizabeth requested that a letter be sent to the National Parole Board. She no longer wants to be used as a reason to keep Charles incarcerated. "If they want to keep him in prison, that's their business, but I don't want it done because of me. For me, this matter is over. I am healed."[12]

Restorative justice is a growing revolution because it works so powerfully to heal what's broken by crime. Much of this revolution in our model of justice has been pioneered by individuals like Elizabeth, people who honored their souls' urging to heal and wouldn't be put off by a model that ignores human needs or dismisses victim pain. Her unyielding feeling of trauma had a purpose, a reason for persisting. By listening to it and taking steps to deal with those reasons, she not only healed herself but changed Charles as well, which in turn makes their shared community more secure. Perhaps that's why traumas that others might consider relatively insignificant can nonetheless have devastating effects on people's lives. The traumas, big or small, raise larger-than-personal issues and therefore call for a process of healing that more people than just the victim need.

12. *Satisfying Justice*, op. cit., vii–ix. Reprinted by permission of The Church Council on Justice and Corrections, Ottawa, Ontario, Canada.

In Elizabeth's case, no one died or was maimed. Can restorative justice work its healing power, we wondered, in more tragic cases? In an article in *Yes!* magazine entitled "Restorative Justice," Tag Evers tells the story of Thomas Ann Hines, whose son was murdered:

Burying her son and walking away from his grave were the hardest things Thomas Ann Hines had ever done. Meeting her son's killer 13 years later was the second hardest.

In 1985, Paul Hines, Thomas Ann's only child, was a student at University of Texas in Austin when he was murdered three months before his graduation. He was 21 years old. A 17-year-old stranger had approached Paul in a video arcade and asked him for a ride.

Once inside Paul's Camaro, the young man demanded the keys to the car. When Paul refused, the would-be thief shot him once in the chest and fled. Paul was found dead later that evening, slumped over in his Camaro, the car still running.

Thomas Ann was devastated. She wanted the death penalty, but due to the offender's age, he was given a 40-year sentence instead.

"I was filled with rage, anger, fear, and pain," says Thomas Ann, who lives just north of Dallas, Texas. "Every six months, without fail, I went to the parole board and asked, 'Is he dead yet? Does he have AIDS? Has someone killed him?' I was so angry at the system. My son was executed without warning. Yet this person could sit in prison and watch television or play basketball, things my son enjoyed."

She vented her grief through letter-writing. Mother's Day, her son's birthday, her own birthday, and the anniversary of Paul's death all became opportunities to express her anger and loss. The letters fattened the offender's file, adding testimony upon testimony against the occasion of his possible parole.

"Everyone says 'seek closure,' as if you're supposed to fix it," says Hines. "But it never goes away. You close the coffin, and it never goes away."

Yet 13 years later, this past June 9th, at the Alfred D. Hughes

Correctional Institute in Gatesville, Texas, Thomas Ann sat across from "Charles," her son's murderer, now a 30-year-old man. "I wanted him to look in the eyes of the mother of the boy he had killed," says Hines. "I wanted him to know there is love in the world."

Hines met with Charles under the auspices of the Victim Offender Mediation/Dialogue program operated by the Texas Department of Victims' Services. She had decided to participate in the program in 1995. It took Hines three years of mental and emotional preparation, both on her own and in consultation with people from the Mediation/Dialogue program, before she felt ready to meet Charles. The result, for both parties, was profound.

"The intensity and depth of emotion ran the whole gamut—from hopelessness and sheer despair to hope and a sense of faith," says Dave Doerfler, who mediated the session. "Charles was locked in his pain, saying there was nothing he could do to bring back Paul's life. But Thomas Ann was relentless—she broke through—and insisted while Charles couldn't do anything about her son's life, he could do something about his own."

At the close of their emotional six-hour session, Thomas Ann and Charles reached an agreement whereby Charles would indeed do something about his life. He agreed to work on his GED and pursue vocational training. Additionally, with Thomas Ann's support, Charles listed personal and spiritual goals that might strengthen him as he prepared for his eventual release from prison.

Up to that point, Charles had amassed 148 disciplinary violations, losing up to 10 years of possible "good time." But he now had something he did not have before: hope and the knowledge that someone loved him.

"You can't take away the sense of hope," says Doerfler, who manages the Mediation/Dialogue program, which currently has a waiting list of 250 victims and survivors who wish to meet their offenders. "It's not just one thing, but a combination that makes the difference in these dialogues. They provide a real release for the victim from the bondage and obsession of the past. And the offender gains a sense of emotional and personal accountability, a sense of empathy that is often lacking in the repeat offender.

"Additionally, a ripple effect is created that starts with the personal and extends to an examination of the social, political, and economic realities that undergird our violent society," continues Doerfler. "In other words, these dialogues are about peacebuilding in the most fundamental ways." . . .

It's not an easy process for offenders to go through. When Charles walked into the room with Hines, she saw "the pain in his eyes." After explaining how difficult it was to finally meet the man who killed her son, she said, "But I will not be unkind to you in any way."

Charles began crying, a flow of tears that continued for nearly the entire session. Victims often have questions for which they need answers. "Why did you pick me?" is a common line of inquiry. Hines, as a victim survivor, wanted to know how her son died.

"Charles," she said, "you were the last person to see my son alive. Tell me what happened that night." At that point, Hines relates, "It wasn't about me anymore, it was about Charles."

Charles recounted the details of the fateful evening as they both cried and took turns wiping away each other's tears. "I thought you'd holler and scream at me," said Charles. "I thought you'd want me dead."

"Yes, I did. I once wanted you dead, " said Hines. "But you never had a chance, Charles." In her preparation for the dialogue, Hines learned how Charles had been put out on the streets at the age of 13, how he had taken up a life of crime and drug-dealing to survive. "My little boy went to bed every night," said Hines, "tucked in by a mother who adored him. You never had that, Charles.". . .

There were two major turning points in Hines' long, painful journey leading up to her meeting with Charles. The first, she relates, occurred four years after Paul's murder, when she began to reach out to other parents of murdered children.

"When you're talking about restorative justice," she says, "it began for me when I started reaching out to others and helping them through their pain, because I didn't have anyone to help me when I was there."

The second turning point took place in 1994, when Raven Kazen, director of the Texas Department of Victims Services, asked Hines to participate in a victims' panel at a maximum security prison in Huntsville.

"Oh my gosh, I went with the intention of giving them a piece of my mind," says Hines. Instead, when she took her place on the panel, before an audience of 200 prisoners, all she could see was "a sea of broken pieces of humanity." It overwhelmed her, she claims: "I looked at them, and all of a sudden, I became a mother again."

After her presentation, one inmate stood up and asked her why she bothered to come to the prison. "The question hit me right smack between the eyes," recalls Hines. "I looked at him and said: 'If my son was sitting in this room, I'd want someone to reach out a hand and lift him up.'"

Hines says the experience helped her take her anger and transform it into something positive, both within her and in the lives of prisoners. She has become somewhat of a prisoner's advocate and speaks several times a week at prisons all over the state of Texas. Each time she goes with a mother's love.

"The criminal justice system operates on the principle that if someone is down, you kick 'em," says Hines. "Until we start looking at the roots of crime instead of the results, it's not going to change." . . .

"At the close of our session, I said to Charles: 'I had a choice—I could spend the rest of my life hating you. But I don't hate you. I just want you to move forward with your life.'

"As we parted, Charles reached out and wrapped his arms around me. I've had lots of hugs in my life, but besides Paul, I can't think of a person in the world I'd rather have hug me."[13]

13. Tag Evers, "Restorative Justice," *Yes! A Journal of Positive Futures* (Fall 1998): 35–37. Reprinted by permission of the author. This journal can be obtained from

Obviously, this woman is extraordinary, and what she does is extraordinary. Every healing is. But it's also true that she started from a very ordinary human response of emotional pain, anguish, and obsession for revenge. What makes her story amazing is that she followed a path of healing and wouldn't abandon it until healing became her reality. As it did, it became the reality of Charles and all the other prisoners she touches. It also becomes part of our reality and yours in reading about the choices she has made and the path she has pursued.

What is not usual—extraordinary—about Thomas Ann Hines is that over a span of thirteen years, faced with one of the worst things that could ever happen to a person, she made the paradigm shift from retributive to restorative justice, and no one benefited more than she.

Using Justice to Liberate Ourselves

The shift that Thomas Ann Hines made, as great as it seems, is yet greater, because of the power of her inner change. Shifting our model of justice involves more than changing how we deal with a specific compartment of social experience—that part of life affected by crimes, offenders, trauma, lawyers, courts, and other government institutions. As we've seen, ideas about justice affect us every day and in every facet of life. That's because, at its root, the deepest impact of our model of justice is within.

When we have trouble letting go of a desire for revenge and punishment, chances are we've internalized a judge-and-punish model and are applying it to ourselves, even though it's causing us unhappiness. Rooted in this worldview, we project it onto others and can't imagine an alternative. We live in a retributive world that affects how we experience both ourselves and everyone else.

For example, we may go through life blaming ourselves or feeling blamed, as if someone is keeping score on us, always afraid something will be our fault. Or we may suffer guilt for past mistakes, not granting ourselves the freedom to learn and grow beyond them, which means it's hard for us not to hold grudges against others for wrongs they've done.

Positive Futures Network, P.O. Box 10818, Bainbridge Island, WA 98110, tel: 206/842–0216.

Or we may judge ourselves by externals or feel anxious around author-ities for fear they'll do the same and not kindly. Then again, we may feel we're not getting what we deserve in life, which makes us all the more determined to see that others get their due. Or we may tolerate unsatisfying jobs and relationships because we fear we deserve no bet-ter or that social order requires us to suffer in silence, so it annoys us when other people make radical changes to improve the quality of their lives. We may imagine that we live under a strict, stern standard that we aren't allowed to waver from—no leeway, excuses, exceptions, or com-passion—so this is invariably what we extend to others. Or, finally, we may feel we have to be perfect all the time and never grant ourselves the normal human space to make mistakes, so we expect the same from oth-ers and feel betrayed and violated when they don't measure up to our expectations of perfection—the same expectations we suffer from.

If we live under all this, we probably feel fairly unhappy with our-selves, nervous about whatever we do, and fearful that if anyone really knew us, they'd judge us as being no good and think we deserve pun-ishment. So this is precisely what we assume to be true for others. We're suspicious, perhaps misanthropic, and ready to accuse and punish peo-ple the moment it appears to us that they've stepped out of line. That way, miserable as it makes us, we uphold justice.

All these are issues of justice, except that they come from shadow justice, a justice that negates who we are and attacks what we do. Shift-ing to a soul-affirming, wholeness-restoring model of justice requires that we release both ourselves and others from the accusing inner world that shadow justice creates. The more we release ourselves from it, the easier it is for us to release others.

The releasing can also start the other way. We may find a sponta-neous compassion welling up in us when we witness the suffering that false justice inflicts on others. We see their worth beyond the narrow ways that retributive justice measures them, and this new sensitivity demonstrates for us the compassion we need for ourselves—and that a soulful model of justice requires. Our compassion for others makes us begin the work of releasing ourselves from the heavy curse that ret-ributive justice puts on everyone.

This is the core issue that Thomas Ann Hines tackled, whether she intended to or not. In forgiving Charles—even loving him, having compassion for him, and working for his highest good—she entered a new world of hope and healing that included her. She didn't want to live in a world of hate, so she had to let it go within herself. She embraced herself as a mother, someone who nurtures growth and healing, rather than as an avenger of retributive justice.

When Thomas Ann Hines made the paradigm shift from revenge and retribution to restorative justice, she shifted to a model of justice that's liberating not only to Charles but to herself too, as well as to all the prisoners she helps, and indeed to all of us. When we shift from an oppressive model of justice to one that "restores our souls," we're all freed, and our whole world changes. That's the power of true justice.

❧ FOUR

A Timeless Method
for Evolving Our Philosophy

THE ACTUAL EXPERIENCE of restorative justice is powerfully transforming. There's nothing like it. It gets us out of our heads and into our hearts—into the realities of people who have been through real experiences and have real needs for healing as well as real potentials for doing so. It also demonstrates the real powers we all have to help each other, not from a "have-all-the-answers" position, but from the simple, honest expression of our feelings and experiences. Expressing our deepest truths to ourselves and others is healing, and listening to ourselves and others express them is healing too.

Philosophy doesn't replace this real experience, but it can either support this process or sabotage it, depending on the models we use. When the crisis has passed—after the dramatic experiences have happened—we want to ground the transformation that has occurred in a philosophy that reflects what we've experienced. It doesn't feel right to go back to our "mindsets as usual," the habits of thinking about justice in blaming, judging, or win-lose ways, even though much of our cultural conditioning inclines us this way. We want our philosophy to come up to speed with our experience, which means we want it to evolve with us.

That's because our philosophy affects everything about us, from how we feel about ourselves to how we handle relationships to how we interact with the culture. Philosophy provides the channels through which our life's energies flow. It's as if our energies get funneled through a cookie press, and our philosophies are the different shaped gadgets we put on the end to form the dough as it comes out.

The trouble is, these different elements—our philosophies, models of justice, social systems, and personal lives—aren't always in sync. We may want our cookies to come out one way, but we're using a gadget that's making the dough come out differently. For example, even though we're drawn to peacemaking, the essence of restorative justice, we may still find ourselves stumbling over ingrained mental and emotional patterns that don't bring peace. Behaviors that are controlling, judgmental, or self-justifying obviously aren't the right philosophy gadgets to use, and yet it's easy for us to have picked up such patterns from families, schools, religions, workplaces, and other cultural sources. Unless we clean our philosophical houses, we may not realize that old habits are getting in the way of new learning.

Or, to consider another philosophy gadget, peacemaking requires radical tolerance. We all aspire to tolerance, having been on the receiving end of intolerance one time or another, and yet somewhere in our lives—school is definitely one place, religion another—we may have developed a visceral response that says we have to settle on one right view, answer, or approach and then persuade everyone to agree to it. If so, we face a discrepancy—a discontinuity between our philosophy and where we want to go with justice—that makes peace unlikely.

Such discontinuities are fruitful, because they generate discourse between our philosophies, our views of justice, our cultural traditions and institutions, our models of relationships, and all the other elements that make up who we are. Because we're evolving, these elements do tend to get out of sync. It's only natural, since some aspects change faster than others. Certainly, individuals change faster than institutions. Within ourselves, our intellectual concepts tend to shift faster than our emotional structures or social habits. Yet the very friction among these elements triggers growth.

Indeed, that's the aim: to evolve our philosophies, our models of justice, and our ways of life. We want to continually investigate how these elements add up, and we can use discontinuities as an impetus for self-reflection and growth. Granted, in practice, we're often unsure about what needs to change, since these elements run together. We talk about them as distinct to try to gain some clarity, but we experience them as one process, which ultimately they are. The fact that they are so interlinked keeps them moving together.

Native American teachings express what we're evolving toward, namely, justice as a total way of being, expressed in every attitude and action. It's how we treat everyone, animals and nature included, because it stems from an overall way of understanding life. Justice follows from who we are in our wholeness, that is, who we are when we live a philosophy that honors the sacredness of life and carries a "holistic respect for everything" to every action. The 1993 *Report of Grand Council Treaty Number 3* states,

> Respect for each other and a universal appreciation for the power of the creator kept everyone walking down a path that encompassed honesty, truths, respect for everything in their immediate life or ecosystem, whether it was your fellow man or beast or plant life. It was a holistic respect for everything that the Anishinaabeg could see, smell, hear, taste and feel.[1]

The idea is that justice is not a separate category of society, something bureaucratic that kicks in only after harms have been done. Rather, justice is an all-encompassing way of life not only for individuals but also for societies, such that justice pervades every detail of social and cultural experience. How could it be otherwise? Everything we do together needs to be balanced—designed to support mutual good. Justice has to do with creating this quality in every facet of human experience.

Rupert Ross, researcher that he is, wanted to record Native views on justice, so he and his staff plied elders with questions about how they define justice and the specifics of their techniques in dealing with offenders. Their best skills of interrogation got them nowhere, however, for the elders would instead launch into discussions about legends and child-rearing, breast-feeding and nature—anything but what would qualify in Western terms as a good, concise definition. "Why, I asked, did those reports spend so much time trying to describe how the whole society functioned, when all we asked about was the justice system?" After awhile, Ross got the point:

1. Rupert Ross, *Returning to the Teachings*, op. cit., 254–55.

I'm not sure why it took me so long, but it is now clear that the elders have been giving their researchers—and the rest of us— one single, coherent and powerful message: justice involves far more than what you do after things have gone wrong. Instead, it involves creating the social conditions that minimize such wrongdoing. In short, a "justice system" in their eyes does indeed encompass much more than a "legal system," as the Cree elder suggested in his own way. It involves instead all the social mechanisms that teach people from the moment of their birth how to live "a good life." In fact, "good life" is often an expression that has the same meaning as "the law."[2]

This whole-philosophy, whole-society, whole-life view of justice seems to be how Socrates and Plato reason in *The Republic*. When asked for a definition of justice, Socrates replies with an entire vision of society—a quest for utopia—based on key principles, ideas, and values. What matters for these philosophers is that we are clear on the intangibles, because everything else grows from them. They form the unseen web that holds our relationships in balance.

Philosophy's job is to attend to the web—that is, to clarify the first principles on which we build the rest of life. Our core assumptions about who we are and what we're doing here establish the framework. They give us an idea of what we're looking for in happiness and quality of life. The "good life" is what our first principles say it is.

Applying this approach to justice isn't easy, though, because it is so big, involving everything we do. It takes self-reflection as well as mindfulness about our patterns and the right time to shift. We have to recover from the programming we've internalized—self-judgments and accusations, the cold, unfeeling, distanced cruelty that the official model requires. If justice is not fundamentally about rewards and punishments, for example, what will it take to leave this model behind—or, if we decide it has some limited use, to put it in its proper place?

Perhaps that's why Socrates didn't say, "Let's do this." The Athenians weren't ready. Instead, he invited his listeners to try a thought experiment:

2. Ibid., 256.

"Let's imagine this." That's the first step. Entertaining the vision, we can incorporate it into our lives as we're ready, slowly changing both ourselves and our social structures. As we grow, we're able to imagine and incorporate more. The *Grand Council Treaty Number 3* refers to this process: "Justice to our people means allegiance to the integrity of our spiritual principles and values. Simple in meaning, but difficult to practice; to be pursued rather than attained."[3]

Pursuing justice along these lines is exactly what we'd like to do for the rest of this book. We'd like to explore the total philosophy of life, the "spiritual principles and values," that lie behind restorative justice. What core principles can give us our bearings in thinking about justice in a larger way? How do we evolve our philosophies and with them our notions of justice?

We've learned that big subjects such as this—justice—reveal their treasures when we have some ordered framework to guide our investigations, rather like an idea-map for a treasure hunt. During our research, it took time for a framework appropriate to justice to appear, though in hindsight it seems obvious. Here's what emerged.

The Four Virtues of Platonic Philosophy

Justice that honors our souls has to build on values that go beyond externals. Big-picture justice must be grounded in values that speak to meaning and that help us connect with who we are deeply, beyond our immediate social or economic roles.

In *The Republic*, Socrates and Plato consistently appeal to four "virtues," four basic values that shape consciousness and guide us in life: wisdom, courage, moderation, and justice. These ideas work together to cultivate justice in human experience. It's as if these virtues are the seeds we need to grow a hefty crop of justice. The virtues channel our energies in constructive, justice-producing ways. They're tried and true: we can rely on them.

Wisdom focuses us on spiritual principles and values. It inquires about our overall philosophy—the web of ideas—that we use as the basis

3. Ibid., 257.

for thinking about justice. Wisdom makes us ask the basic questions: what's the purpose of justice? Is it to punish or to restore, to win a case or to create harmony and happiness? Is it about controlling people, assuming their inner guidance is a threat? Or is it about affirming the innate worth of every being and creating opportunities for that worth to be expressed? If justice is about each of us being who we are and doing what's ours to do, then we need to think about who we are: what's our nature? Wisdom urges us to explore these issues to get the big-picture perspective—the wisdom that informs everything else.

Courage gives us the guts to go where wisdom leads, even if it entails no small change for ourselves, our relationships, our social structures, cultures, and philosophies. Integrity is a closely related quality. We need both courage and integrity to tackle what's not working in our lives and to alter our course. Integrity makes us look at why things aren't working—personal reasons, yes, but also institutional, social structure, cultural context, and philosophy reasons—while courage strengthens our resolve to embark on personal and whole-system change as it's needed.

Moderation—the ancient Greek ideal of the Golden Mean or the Buddhist Middle Way—adapts change to where we are and to what's achievable. This third virtue accepts change but also accepts that we shouldn't kill ourselves, hurt others, or become fanatics doing it. Meaningful change happens step by step, not all at once. It has cycles and rhythms, and we can't push things out of their natural order.

During the step-by-step healing process—coming into who we are—we need compassion for ourselves and others, given what change demands. We also need patience, tenderness, and trust. Paradigm shifts are no small job. It took Thomas Ann Hines thirteen years with a horrendous event spurring her. How long does it take an entire culture with all its beliefs and institutions, especially when we've grown accustomed to many forms of injustices—wage slavery, for example, or work schedules that leave little time for real life? For this reason, we'd like to add *love* and *compassion* to Plato's moderation. We need these qualities to change, heal, make things right, and keep growing.

Justice emerges through the process; the virtues generate it as surely as crops grow from good seed and soil. Even if we make mistakes, they're fixable because the virtues channel our energies in ways that connect us with who we are. We gain access to our inner resources, and these show us how to put things right as best we can. Wisdom, courage, and compassionate moderation put us on the path of doing what's ours to do, and hence they make justice a lived experience.

Through these intangible virtues, we experience justice as something dynamic and evolving, something we work on every day. We frame our lives as experiments in justice, and as we do, we learn more of what justice means and how it works. We see what a model of justice that honors soul and meaning can do not only for healing our brokenness but also for creating happiness. Justice operates both as an ideal and as the process of getting there.

Plato's four virtues express values that are archetypal in human consciousness. We say this because they share themes with many fourfold teachings from spiritual traditions around the world. For example, they pattern the "gifts of the four directions" in Native American philosophy.[4] The four directions signify the fundamental elements of a creative process, which on a deeper level expresses reality's self-dynamics. We humans don't create the seasons or make them happen; neither are we responsible for keeping night and day going. There's a dynamic beyond us that includes us, symbolized by the medicine wheel with its four directions. By adhering to these values, we harmonize with the larger reality. In the case of the four virtues, the greater reality we're harmonizing with is the greater reality of who we are.

4. Many wonderful books are now available presenting Native American teachings, and the four directions are considered fundamental to all the Native teachings we've studied. Jamie Sams's book *Dancing the Dream: The Seven Sacred Paths of Human Transformation* (San Francisco: HarperCollins, 1999) offers an excellent expression of the four directions as a spiritual path in chapters 3–6, pages 43–162. The little book we will be often quoting in our own has been produced collaboratively by Judie Bopp, Michael Bopp, Lee Brown, and Phil Lane Jr., entitled *The Sacred Tree* (Lethbridge, Alberta, Canada: Four Worlds International Institute for Human and Community Development, 1984). This book, which can be special ordered through bookstores, includes a forty-page discussion and two-page summary of "The Gifts of the Four Directions," (pages 32–73).

Three Levels or Perspectives

Fourfold processes, such as those described by Plato's virtues or the four directions of the medicine wheel, operate on many levels. They can guide us in taking care of our bodies, our psyches, our relationships, or our communities. They can also speak to how we run businesses, settle disputes, or raise children. As a result, we can consider these values from different points of view. For instance,

(1) **The larger reality.** We can consider how these processes shed light on our relation to the larger reality of which we're a part, the larger reality of all that is. What is the essential nature of things, and how can we work in harmony with this nature? For Buddhists, wisdom means accepting the impermanence of things, which means not expecting things to remain the same, not trying to impose change but not resisting it either. For other traditions, wisdom means seeing a meaningful order unfolding through experiences, even if we don't recognize it at the time. The virtues reveal our connectedness to a wider reality, and this changes how we think. We see our lives nested within a bigger picture.

(2) **Our reality.** Since we're part of reality, we also experience the virtues as helping us find ourselves—who we really are. Wisdom, for example, brings the big picture home to us, shifting our views of our nature. Whatever reality is, we are too, because we're not outside reality. Reality's nature is in our bones. If reality is impermanent, then we're beings of change as well. Or, if life has some meaningful order, then that's true for our lives as well, and it won't do to abandon this meaning or ignore it. By focusing us on what's essential about us, the four values help us find who we are and live from our essence. They protect us from losing ourselves in externals.

(3) **Grounded in action.** We can also think of the virtues as operating in whatever we do. As we bring these qualities to our relationships and endeavors, the four values guide us in everyday affairs. They speak to how we form intimate relationships as well as how we manage careers and professions. Come to think of it, we have to use

wisdom, courage, moderation, and justice every time we drive out on the road.

Indigenous teachings offer a simple image for these three different perspectives.[5] When we stand on the earth, we stand connected to all of them at once:

Looking up. We look up to the whole universe that's the context of our existence. We look up to all that is and feel how we're related to everything—how we exist from our connectedness. Without this whole context in which we're embedded, we don't exist.

Looking within. We also look within to our inner life, our soul center, which serves as our touchstone. What we see of the world is filtered by our minds and interpreted by our psyches. We experience life from the vantage point of our self, a human. This humanness means being engaged in inner processes: care, understanding, love, joy, compassion, creativity, or pure awareness. Because we're autonomous beings, we have some say in what goes on with us—which processes we engage with. Certainly healing, inner growth, and transformation are processes we all find valuable.

Looking down. And we look down to what we stand on, to the earth that grounds us. Being on the earth gives us opportunities to focus our energies. We have endless choices in how we participate with creation. Through our choices, we aim to focus (1) our relatedness with all that is and (2) our unique human perspective in ways that (3) put our energies and talents to good use. On the third level, our experience of the totality becomes concrete and specific. We connect with earth experience in ways that are ours to do.

Psychologists sometimes discuss the human self as operating on these three levels. Social psychologists Edward L. Deci and Richard M. Ryan in *Intrinsic Motivation and Self-Determination in Human Behavior*— a book written in technical language for psychologists—cite considerable research on what either supports or damages intrinsic motivation. They depict every human as needing three factors in order to feel "intrinsically motivated," that is, motivated from who we really are, dis-

5. See Jamie Sams, *Dancing the Dream*, chapters 7–9, pages 163–254.

tinct from being motivated by internalized programming.[6] We need to feel *related* to our world, so that we can have some positive effect on it. We need a sense of *self-determination and autonomy*, so that we're not controlled from without but can make our own choices about our own lives freely. And, finally, we all need a sense of *competence*, that we can do something well and feel good about it, that what we do is meaningful and worthwhile.

Combining these insights, we can describe these three different perspectives as:

(1) *looking up to our relatedness*, which explores who we are as whole-connected beings;

(2) *looking within to our autonomy*, which explores who we are as dynamic processes where healing and transformation go on; and

(3) *looking down to our competence*, which explores who we are as a focus of activity—as doing what's ours to do.

Root Principles for Evolving Our Philosophy of Justice

The four virtues can be viewed from any of these three levels. For the purposes of this book, we will consider them only from the first level, namely, of looking up to our connectedness. As we go along, we're asking: what vision of reality emerges from a wider, "looking up" perspective? And how might a more holistic philosophy of reality's nature inspire us to think differently about justice?

These are important questions, but how do we explore them? What wider vision of reality does wisdom, courage, moderation, and justice give us as we "look up"? Once again, we went looking for help in sacred teachings.

The Sacred Tree, a book written by Native Americans for Native Americans to help them reclaim their spiritual heritage, presents "first principles" considered common to all Native American philosophies,

6. Deci and Ryan, *Intrinsic Motivation and Self-Determination in Human Behavior*, see Chapter 2, "Conceptualizations of Intrinsic Motivation and Self-Determination," 11–40.

no matter how varied the different traditions are.[7] Each First Nation has its own teachings, customs, and practices, and they're not the same. Apparently, though, among the core perspectives that they share are these root principles—principles which ground their differing philosophies.[8] The book presents twelve root principles, but we will consider only the first four:

(1) wholeness and the correlative truth of universal connectedness;

(2) change, which is universal and includes both development and disintegration;

(3) cycles of change, which hold meaning and are not random or accidental; and

(4) the seen and the unseen, both of which are valid and which together give us a balanced perspective on life.

In writing this book, we're using a specific method of philosophical and spiritual reasoning, namely, thinking in categories and blending them. We're blending (1) the virtue with (2) the level with (3) the root principle. Exploring how these categories converge yields insights. Together they tell a spiritual story about justice. Yet what we've written by no means exhausts the possibilities. Were we to do it again, surely other insights would emerge, and were you to do this, insights would come to you beyond what we've expressed. We're simply getting the philosophical ball rolling.

So, in each chapter, we'll discuss the blending philosophically first, and then we'll explore what the philosophical insights might suggest for

---

7. Bopp et al., *The Sacred Tree*, 26–30.

8. We prefer their term of "first principles," because it expresses so clearly that these core concepts provide the ground from which everything grows, the first among all the rest. First principles is an honored term in the West as well, the metaphysical premises on which we build our lives. Yet as we went along in writing, the language became awkward—first "first principle," fourth "first principle," etc. So we've adopted the term "root principles." We also considered "core" or "primal" principles. In other words, these aren't just any principles. These principles lie at the heart of our total way of being.

a different approach to justice. For example, in the next chapter, we first discuss what wholeness means as a philosophy of life—how it shifts our worldview about who we are—and then we explore how the idea of wholeness challenges us to think about justice differently.

The matrix on the following page shows how we need to "look up" to evolve our philosophy of justice. It does this by showing the different categories we're blending and how they come together.[9] It represents the idea-map we're seeking to help us evolve.

---

9. Reasoning in categories and blending them are ancient methods. In the West, they go back to at least Socrates and Plato, who taught, for example, that the good is the good only if it also partakes of truth and beauty. Justice is justice only if it incorporates wisdom, courage, and moderation. This way of reasoning occurs frequently in Plato's dialogues. Denise learned this method of reasoning years ago from Max Kappeler, a Swiss economist who became a lifelong independent researcher of Christian Science. The method assumes a coherency and interrelatedness within the unseen world of ideas and maps this relatedness to provide a guiding context for how we negotiate our lives in the seen.

"LOOKING UP" TO EVOLVE OUR PHILOSOPHY OF JUSTICE

	Wisdom: seeking the big picture, the aim and purpose of justice.	*Courage, integrity:* following through with personal and social change.	*Moderation, love and compassion:* adapting change to where we are.	*Justice:* a way of life that we create from who we are and that evolves with us.
The question for this book: How can we evolve our philosophy of justice?				
Looking up: Exploring how we're connected to all that is and how this sheds light on our nature.	*(1) Wholeness:* all things are interrelated, connected, which means every one has a value, no one can be left out, and every experience tells us something about the whole system. (chapter 5)	*(2) Change:* all of creation is in a state of constant change, which means change is our nature, and justice must help us change both ourselves and societies. (chapter 6)	*(3) Change occurs in cycles,* though it is hard to see the meaning of them clearly. This means we need justice to adapt to our cycles and help us move from where we are to the next step. (chapter 7)	*(4) The seen and the unseen* are two aspects of one reality and must be honored and kept in balance. Justice, itself unseen, protects the seen. (chapter 8)

All of this comes together in the spiritual law:
What blesses one blesses all.
(chapter 9)

PART II

What We Need —
The Root Principles of Justice

ᚥ FIVE

Wholeness

Wholeness. All things are interrelated. Everything in the
universe is a part of a single whole. Everything is connected
in some way to everything else. It is therefore possible to
understand something only if we can understand how it is
connected to everything else.   —*The Sacred Tree*

THE ROOT PRINCIPLES suggest where to start in expanding
our assumptions about who we are and hence the kind of
justice that is appropriate to us. The first root principle "looks up" to
wholeness—to how everything is interrelated in an unbroken whole.
Nothing exists in isolation or as an isolated entity. It's the fundamental truth of universal connectedness: everything comes from something
else, which in turn comes from something else—the Buddha's teaching
of dependent arising—all of which moves within the whole. "Everything is connected in some way to everything else," the first root principle states. Wisdom in human life means acknowledging our
connectedness in all its implications—no small trick.

To start closest to home, this principle changes how we approach
human nature. If the bottom-line truth about us is our connectedness
within the whole, then it won't be wise to define our nature as a separate thing—abstract and unrelated to the systems around us. It's a
wrongheaded approach. When we come to investigating our nature,
instead of debating whether we're all bad or all good, we need to investigate the systems on which we depend: "It is therefore possible to
understand something only if we can understand how it is connected to
everything else." That's true for everything in the universe, including us.

The first principle's method for thinking about human nature,

83

therefore, takes us beyond judgments, good or bad. We reason from the premise that we're connected and that our connectedness makes us what we are. The principle speaks to our basic character not from studying this or that human behavior but from considering the nature of the reality of which we're all part. We participate in the systems around us; more than that, we're formed from these systems and reflect them. We exist as whole-participating beings, and without this connectedness, we wouldn't exist.

In other words, if we're exploring who we are, wisdom "looks up" to our inescapable connectedness with the whole and to the infinitely diverse systems that the whole includes as the place to start. Whatever else we are—and untold possibilities flow from this—we're connected beings. This is our core nature, and if justice is to serve and help us, it has to be adapted to us, which means it has to take this root principle as its starting point. This chapter is about trying to figure out what this means—how the core truth of our connectedness within the whole invites us to think about ourselves and justice differently.

And it is a different way of thinking from what we're raised with. In Western society, we don't experience ourselves as connected but as separate and often isolated. We feel as if we're on our own, struggling to make our way in a world where everyone else is struggling to get what we want too, and we can't all have it. It's competition, the old "struggle-for-survival" model that strikes fear in all of us. So when we first consider that justice might mean each of us being who we are and doing what's ours to do, we think, "No way. That would be a nightmare—more struggle only worse, with the lid off."

Indeed, it's anarchy that scares us. We'll take up this issue again at the close of this book, but it's good to name the challenge up front: if we each connect with our souls and live from our essence, won't society fall into utter chaos? We've seen rioting mobs on television. We've seen people act irresponsibly, abandoning children or behaving unconscionably at work. We've also seen terrorists and bombers. Isn't this what happens when we each do what's ours to do? It's all well and good for the few who have the nature of saints to heed their souls' callings, but doesn't the great mass need to be kept in line and told what to do, with social expectations and everyday economic constraints—that is, the need to hold a job and make some money—providing the necessary restraining force? In other words, how can Socrates and Plato be even remotely serious about proposing an inward-oriented model of justice, given human nature as it is?

Whether or not we're moved by this fear depends on our philosophy. What do we assume about human nature? Who are we really? What's our paradigm's "wisdom" as we "look up" to the larger picture of being human in society, on the planet, and even in the cosmos?

The Monster Paradigm

The general Western assumptions about what it is to be human, drawn from both religion and science, scare us out of our wits, making us frantic to control people before the veneer of civility peels off and we're left at the mercy of the emotional chaos beneath. We think control will save us. We think it will create order and help us keep it.

But control is no panacea. If anything, it's the chaos maker. The unresolved question of who controls whom makes the "solution" of control problematic.

First, who controls the controllers? What guarantees that they'll be servants of the larger good? Whatever human nature is, they've got it too. If human nature is nasty, power-over positions will only inflate the nastiness.

Second, when those in control positions—whether in marriages, families, schools, businesses, religions, professions, or governments—use their position to extend their advantage over others, people become unhappy, frustrated, and cynical. We suffer chronic discontent, fed up with bottom-of-the-rung status and inwardly exhausted from external control. Not allowed to live our own lives, we lose our will to live at all. Under these conditions, no relationship works well, either at home or at work.

Third, given that bottom-of-the-rung status isn't much fun, who doesn't want to be on top, the one controlling others? Who wants to be at the mercy of someone else's "human nature"? The no-holds-barred contest for control that power hierarchies inspire stirs up no small amount of chaos of its own, proving the "cure" more dangerous than the original condition.

Which brings us to the core question: what original condition does the dominant European philosophy diagnose our species with? What is our real nature? It's not pretty. Presumably beneath the appearance of well-meaning, caring people lie seething, angry, greedy, selfish, aggressive, insatiable, ignorant, lazy, yet competitive and ready-to-fight beasts.

Psychology, for example, often assumes that we're psychological messes at our core. Part of this is due to our psychological makeup, the other part to how society suppresses our nature. It's a nagging question for psychology: are we just too much of a mess inside to trust our inner processes or to be guided by them?

Christianity has often painted us as bad or worse: we're born sinners, cursed and driven from the Garden, and deserving no less. Original sin justifies parental, teacher, clergy, and self-abuse: the bad must be humiliated, shamed, punished, exorcized, and if need be, beaten out of us, just as criminals, those in whom sin has prevailed, must be punished and driven from society.

Business management tends to view employees with an equally stern and disapproving eye—"You have to supervise workers and ride them constantly to get a decent day's work from them"—whereupon workers suggest that management wrap their golf-loving, golden-parachuted psyches around the concept of projection.

Government officials apparently view citizens with similar contempt ("the masses are asses"), and their conduct—granting government agencies powers over citizens that would make Hitler jealous—seems consistent with that philosophy. Alfie Kohn, who writes extensively on human behavior and social theory, summarizes the view:

> We raise our children, manage our companies, and design our governments on the assumption that people are naturally and primarily selfish and will act otherwise only if they are coerced to do so and carefully monitored. We assume that genuine generosity is only a mirage on an endless desert of self-interest.[1]

---

1. Alfie Kohn, *The Brighter Side of Human Nature: Altruism and Empathy in Everyday Life* (New York: Basic Books/HarperCollins, 1990), 4.

If this is who we are and nothing more, then the idea of connecting with this essence and following our souls' callings doesn't look promising. Instead, domination, intimidation by authorities, enforced discipline: such measures seem necessary for our species to live in some semblance of social order. Persuade people from birth to conform to the rules of society by giving them one simple message: "Who you are is dangerous to our well-being and yours too! Become who we tell you to be, for only then will you be accepted and happy." Monsters we may always be, the philosophy tells us, but we can be cowed into good behavior if we're sufficiently intimidated or bribed. That's why we have the model of justice we do.

The problem with this self-portrait is not that it's entirely false. Thanks to television, even small children witness the human capacity to be selfish and cruel beyond our worst imaginings. Monstrous behavior exists, and it would appear that we all have a capacity for it. What's wrong with the grim portrait, though, is its one-sidedness—its reductionism. It reduces human nature to what we can become under fear, stress, trauma, and abuse—how we act when our psyches have been seriously messed with since birth. Yes, we have the potential to behave selfishly, aggressively, and cruelly, but why structure our societies to develop this potential to the nth degree through systems that artificially heighten fear, insecurity, and stress? Why fill each other with messages of failure and rejection? Why focus exclusively on the destructive end of our spectrum of potentials?

Failing to distinguish between what's installed and what's innate, the monster model takes a photo of us when we're most desperate and traumatized, and then presents this dismal image as the sum total of our nature. Such characterizations are as accurate as if we were to capture a baby animal, torment him as he grows, and then draw conclusions about the nature of his species from how the adult animal reacts, trauma being all he has known.

Dr. Sandra Bloom of "The Sanctuary" at Friends Hospital in Quakertown, Pennsylvania, deals with traumatized people everyday, yet this has led her not to draw conclusions about human nature in general but to confront the trauma-organized, trauma-inflicting character of our social systems. When we are traumatized, she observes, we are not ourselves.

In her book *Creating Sanctuary*, she explains how drastically we change:

It is when we are severely stressed, when the expected routine of daily life is disturbed by traumatic events, that our bodies respond in primitive ways and we find ourselves in the midst of a storm of emotional and physical reactions that we cannot understand or control. In many ways, we are not the same people when we are terrified as when we are calm. Our bodies change in remarkable ways, as do our perceptual abilities, our emotional states, our thought processes, our attention, and our memory. When under this kind of stress, it is as if we become another person, no longer able to respond to others as we would under less threatening circumstances.[2]

Granted, if external control is the agenda, then institutionalizing trauma—artificially creating it through yelling, threatening, punishing behaviors or through institutional versions of the same—can make external control easier. One wouldn't think so, but it's true. Why else would parents spank children? The assumption is that a traumatized child is more controllable. Why else do we have prisons and death penalties? Trauma or the fear of it supposedly makes us more controllable. We more readily fall in line, because we're too scared to do anything else.

Our increased controllability comes from the toll trauma takes on our inward resources, debilitating them. Bloom explains that trauma is a time when our internal controls go haywire, and we no longer have the capacity to think clearly:

How impaired our thinking becomes depends on the magnitude of the danger and the possibility of loss. When frightened, our thinking becomes overly simplistic and we are unable to deal with a variety of categories of thought. We do not recognize all the alternatives open to us and instead tend to focus on the

2. Sandra Bloom, *Creating Sanctuary: Toward an Evolution of Sane Societies* (New York: Routledge, 1997), 15.

quickest way to escape. When severely stressed, we are unable to think clearly, to consider the long-range consequences of our behavior, to weigh all of the possible options before making a decision, to take the time to obtain all the necessary information that goes into making good decisions. As a consequence, our decisions are inflexible, oversimplified, and often very poorly constructed. . . . The problem, of course, is that modern life provides us with many situations that induce acute stress that are not, in fact, life-threatening situations, but our bodies and minds still respond as if they were.[3]

Too stressed to wrap our minds around complexities, we become more susceptible to accepting how others package and present things—more prone to adopting simplistic, polarized, reductionist responses and having them stick, given the intensity of emotion that attends trauma. Afterward, we believe that the narrowed ways of thinking got us through, and we're loathe to give them up, even though they're perpetuating a trauma-centered mindset and experience.

This mental impairment under stress opens the door for external controls to move in. When we're in trauma, we enter a trance-like state. Our focus narrows to deal with the immediate stressors, diminishing our ability to access our full personal resources. We don't, as Bloom says, seem to recognize options that we would otherwise see. We become highly suggestible, since our thinking processes are impaired but our neediness is heightened.

And because we're looking for a way out of the immediate fear, pain, and anxiety, we're more likely to accept directives that we would otherwise reject. After all, we're in crisis; we'll do anything to alleviate our condition. Under stress, we're more receptive to outside control than when we're secure, confident, fully in touch with the full range of our abilities, and free to explore multiple options of our choosing.

If control is the ticket for maintaining social order, instituting traumatizing behaviors, belief systems, and social mechanisms would appear to make the job easier. Under stress, we're less of a force to be reckoned

3. Ibid., 23–24.

with, because there's less of us present to be controlled. Blasted out, we're just not all there.

Short term, that is. Measured in immediate, outer effects, the control method has its day. Long term, however, it's another story. The toll that control-by-trauma takes on human psyches surfaces, revealing trails of trauma everywhere—more than what control can make go away. Control exacts a fearful price that, sometime down the road, we pay.

Whether by dark intent or by hapless entrapment in self-perpetuating, multigenerational patterns, trauma permeates society. We don't have to scratch the surface very hard to find it. On page after page, Bloom presents statistics documenting the high levels of trauma that surround us from childhood on—trauma levels that then manifest in trauma-related behaviors. These behaviors range from being emotionally shut down or unavailable to being volatile, irritable, angry, or violent—an emotional tinderbox. Trauma can manifest in mood swings and depression, or it can come out in a hardened facade of cynicism or apathy. The very fact that trauma patterns are so common—all we have to do is turn on the television or pick up a newspaper to find them reported—tempts us to draw conclusions about human nature as a whole.

Indeed, virtually all the moral-monster qualities attributed to human nature by Western philosophy—qualities that justify tight controls and ready punishments—are characteristics of humans who have suffered abuse, grief, and trauma but have not yet healed from them. We become frozen in trauma patterns and don't know how to break them.

The growing literature on trauma and addiction clearly describes the relation between trauma and destructive behavior.[4] Those who manifest destructive behavior, whether toward themselves or others, have suffered some trauma, some loss of soul and inner integrity. Traumatized and traumatizing reactions become a way of life, which then are acted out on others.

The practical question is, how do we as a society respond? So far, institutions that deal with traumatized people are designed not to help

4. Dr. Bloom's book has an extensive bibliography on trauma research, while Dr. Patrick Carnes' book, *The Betrayal Bond*, gives an excellent bibliography on how trauma relates to processes of addiction.

them heal but simply to contain out-of-control behavior, usually by inflicting greater trauma through external controls and punishments. Institutions become locked in patterns of using force to restrain traumatized individuals, which not only further traumatizes the individuals but also extends trauma to others.

Given institutions whose de facto message is that we're guilty of a rotten nature until we prove ourselves good (and no good is ever enough to be convincing) or that force, punishment, and control are appropriate methods for treating citizens, it's no wonder that Western thinkers found a raging, semi-psychotic beast under every emotional stone: the Euro-American "solution" of control intensifies and escalates the cycle. It multiplies—and through child-rearing methods creates—the very trauma effects it intends to contain.

Oblivious to these circular dynamics, though, virtually all our social institutions—families, schools, legal systems, businesses, prisons—use the control "solution." Our social systems are long on methods for controlling the monster but short on methods for cultivating anything else. How surprised should we be when the monster complies by emerging? French philosopher Gabriel Marcel captured the dynamics: "Man depends, to a very great extent, on the idea he has of himself, and . . . this idea cannot be degraded without at the same time degrading man."[5]

Moreover, the assumption that our core nature is aggressive, selfish, and traumatizing makes us think that, when we act any other way, we're being fake, not true to who we are. The effort to cultivate other qualities seems futile, an exercise in self-deception. If we're aggressive, greedy, and selfish by nature, then war and domination for selfish interests are the natural order for our species. This is assumed to be our reality. Why hope for anything better, since that only sets us up for disappointment? Why attempt other models of behaving? Why seek nonviolent, cooperative, mutually beneficial, even altruistic methods and solutions? We assume they'd fail, given who we think humans are. The philosophy becomes self-fulfilling: we become what we assume ourselves to be.

5. Gabriel Marcel, *Man Against Mass Society*, trans. G. S. Fraser (1951; reprint South Bend, Ind.: Gateway, 1978), quoted in Kohn, *The Brighter Side of Human Nature*, 181.

In *The Brighter Side of Human Nature*, a compelling book for anyone pondering this subject, Alfie Kohn dismantles the reductionist assumption, concluding as follows:

> Finally, and most insidiously, there is the phenomenon of the self-fulfilling prophecy. . . . The simple assumption that we cannot help being aggressive helps us to continue being aggressive. No circle is more vicious than the one set up by the fallacious assumption that we are unable to control an essentially violent nature. Aside from the respect in which it proves itself true, then, this belief is not only inaccurate for all the reasons reviewed here, but also deadly. While the various other psychological and social factors that contribute to aggressive behavior cannot simply be wished away, assumptions about the nature of our species can be—and, given the stakes, must be—reconsidered.[6]

Unchallenged, the moral-monster assumption gets written in cultural stone: our species is a mess inside. If we follow what's within, we'll have an outer mess too. The only hope for social order is to cut us off from our inner mess-in-the-making as early as possible, replacing our inner motivation with external incentives. That way—cut off from our presumed mess inside—we're rendered controllable. The more we conform to external rules and regulations, enforced through rewards and punishments, the more we'll have social order.

The success of this "monster-containment" formula depends, of course, on our assent and consequent cooperation—our compliance in rejecting ourselves and agreeing that it's better for us not to be who we are. We have to agree that the monster lies at our core and that our own essential nature is dangerous to us. Then we have to agree not to miss our inner motivation, not even to notice that it's gone. We also have to not mind being controlled by people and not mind spending our lives chasing after the externals they control. In other words, we cooperate by playing along, not claiming our freedom to be ourselves.

---

6. Alfie Kohn, *The Brighter Side of Human Nature*: Nature, 58–59.

Restorative justice assumes a different philosophy of human nature, mainly because the monster model doesn't describe much about us that's restorable. Granted, we don't know all that we are, but we do know we're more than what a reductionist model paints.

If the monster isn't all there is to us—indeed, if the monster comes out precisely when we've been traumatized out of our skulls by people, philosophies, and institutions who treat us as if we're nothing but monsters—then what more are we?

In *The Brighter Side of Human Nature*, Kohn offers evidence against the monster paradigm. One example that stands out is Kohn's discussion of human behavior during warfare. If we're innately selfish, aggressive, violent, and ready to kill, then what accounts for the following anomalies? First, drafts must be instituted because too few people volunteer for the opportunity to kill with state sanction and pay. Second, military training requires (a) that both the draftee and the enemy be dehumanized, the first by training, the second by propaganda, (b) that individual, critical thought be replaced with mindless obedience, and (c) that "an abhorrence for taking a life [be replaced] with either indifference or positive enthusiasm."[7] Kohn asks: "Why the universal need for this deliberate and involved process if we are innately disposed to kill?"[8]

But even dehumanizing the soldier and the enemy has proven insufficient for turning humans into killers. In 1947, military analyst S. L. A. Marshall, who later served as a general in the Korean War, conducted interviews with hundreds of infantry companies in the central Pacific and European theaters of World War II—and was most alarmed at the results from a military point of view. Kohn quotes his findings, summarized in Marshall's book *Men Against Fire*:

> On average not more than 15 percent of the men had actually fired at the enemy positions or personnel with rifles, carbines, grenades, bazookas, [automatic rifles], or machine guns during the course of an entire engagement. . . . The best showing that

7. Ibid., 48–49.
8. Ibid., 49.

could be made by the most spirited and aggressive companies was that one man in four had made at least some use of his fire power. . . . The 25 percent estimate stands even for well-trained and campaign-seasoned troops. I mean that 75 percent will not fire or will not persist in firing against the enemy and his works. These men may face the danger but they will not fight.[9]

The combat soldiers were not driven by fear for their own survival. They feared killing more than dying—not the instincts of an innately selfish, violent creature. Marshall concludes: "It is therefore reasonable to believe that the average and normally healthy individual—the man who can endure the mental and physical stresses of combat—still has such an inner and usually unrealized resistance toward killing a fellow man, that he will not of his own volition take life if it is possible to turn away from that responsibility."[10]

The very fact that intense and consistent conditioning is necessary to overcome our innate resistance to killing suggests that aggression and violence are not our first choices. These aren't the potentials that, left to ourselves, we choose to develop. As Kohn goes on to document, from babies to adults, culture to culture, humans manifest a remarkable sensitivity to each other's welfare and a desire to help others beyond what self-interest would require. The moral-monster paradigm asks that we disregard as anomalous a great deal of human behavior.

On this point, Gandhi observed that the vast majority of human interaction goes on everyday without violence. Our lives are filled with peaceful, mutually beneficial exchanges, not to mention spontaneous acts of kindness and generosity. When an acquaintance of ours took on the responsibility for raising her brother's three children after he committed suicide, a friend of hers gave her the money to buy a house with no strings attached or expectation of repayment. The friend wasn't wealthy, but she had the money to give and wanted to help.

In China, the philosopher Mencius (c. 371–289 BCE) championed human nature as essentially compassionate and given to fellow-feeling.

9. S. L. A. Marshall, *Men Against Fire* (New York: William Morrow, 1947), 54, 50.

10. Ibid., 50.

"Humaneness," justice, propriety, and wisdom are innate virtues, he said. They exist in us ready to be developed. True, we may not develop them as much as we could, but that doesn't mean they don't live in us as potentials:

> Meng said: "All men are such that they cannot bear seeing others suffer. The kings of old had this kind of compassion and it governed their policy. One could easily rule the whole world with attitudes like that: it would be like turning it round in the palm of the hand.
>
> "I say that men are like that because anyone seeing a child fall into a well would have a feeling of horror and distress. They don't feel this out of sympathy for the parents, or to gain a reputation among friends and neighbours, or for fear of being considered unfeeling. Not to feel the distress would be against human nature."[11]

It seems that our nature cannot be painted with one brush or degraded so readily. Examples of spontaneous altruism, generosity of spirit, and reverence for life will not, however, sort out the question of human nature. For every example of kindness, adherents of the monster paradigm can produce equal examples of cruelty and selfishness. We need to expand our ways of reasoning beyond either/or, "all-bad or all-good" categories.

Why? Again, because who we think we are determines what kind of justice we think we need. Justice flows from us. We create it in human society based on our self-concepts—on our notions of what it is to be human. As a result, no issue is more central to the kind of justice we either have or could have.

Certainly the retributive model tells us a lot about how we as a culture have thought about ourselves. Retributive justice is a collectivized, institutionalized model of self-hate and self-rejection. It says that if we're not perfect, if we're in pain and act badly, or if we make mistakes, the

11. Ninian Smart and Richard D. Hecht, eds., *Sacred Texts of the World: A Universal Anthology* (New York: Crossroad, 1982), 316.

right response is to blame, shame, and punish us. No compassion, no help, no understanding or healing is offered.

If, however, we have potentials all along a spectrum of behaviors, then retributive justice cannot be the answer. Self-hate, compounding hurt with more hurt, won't move us to where we want to be. Yes, monster behavior needs to be restrained, whether it's a person, a corporation, or a government that's doing it. But we're more than these behaviors, stemming as they do from trauma, and our models of justice need to honor this "more" and give us room to develop it. The job of justice is to cultivate us all along the spectrum—to support our growth away from traumatizing, self-hating, self-abusive patterns and toward our creative, compassionate, self-accepting, and self-evolving potentials.

Exploring Our Whole-Connectedness

How do we move in this direction? How do we shift our concepts of who we are and with them, our models of justice? According to the first root principle, we start by considering our reality, our connectedness within the whole. We need to consider the larger context of our existence, for this context—our inescapable rootedness in reality—ultimately shapes our nature. If we go with it, things work; if we ignore it or try to go against it, they don't. Reality wins out.

When it comes to considering reality, the first root principle—wholeness and connectedness—functions as a core premise, a true first among first principles, for all spiritual teachings with a mystic bent. Nor is this up-in-the-clouds thinking. Native Americans and other indigenous peoples—the wholeness thinkers with the longest track record of practicing it—put the earth and nature at the center of their philosophies, underscoring the presence of wholeness right where we live. Their approach is completely practical and down to earth: the food on our plates and the air we breathe come from our connectedness to the whole. Nothing can exist apart from this, and if we ignore our primal connectedness with the earth, we jeopardize our own survival. Wholeness isn't therefore an abstract concept; it's the foundation of our existence.

What counts as dangerously abstract thinking is the notion that we can ignore our connectedness and focus only on what's immediate and short-term. In extreme forms, this way of thinking leads to criminal behavior. Those who hurt others for personal gain don't think about the effect their actions have on others. But being blind to our interconnections causes harm in many other ways as well—ways we've come to accept as normal.

For example, it's dangerously abstract to think that we can suppress alternatives to the combustion engine for decades, jeopardizing the health of people and the planet, simply to extend profits from burning oil and gas. The thinking is abstract because it ignores the consequences of this choice to the universe of connectedness—the pollution, the damage to the ozone layer, the permanent loss of the resource of oil. And it ignores who we are in our wholeness, namely, as beings whose meaning comes from more than the single relationship to money.

Thinking from wholeness as our first root principle is practical. It's practical for forming big-picture concepts of who we are, and it's practical for framing wise, long-term plans of what to do. Honoring our nature as whole-connected beings works; ignoring it doesn't.

Asian philosophies offer compelling images of wholeness and what it's like to live in harmony with it. Teachings on wholeness and connectedness from Hindu, Buddhist, Taoist, Zen, and Shinto traditions are becoming better known in the West, but Confucian thinkers also have much to say about wholeness, and their ideas relate directly to who we are and what's ours to do, hence to justice.

For example, on the highest levels of its meaning, *li* expresses the ultimate order of things as they flow from the Tao, the whole that is beyond words or concepts. We express our true nature when we live in harmony with reality's order, as best we understand it. We can't possibly know the whole as such, but because we're part of the whole and made of it, it forms us and lives in us. The whole order, *li*, that's embedded in us serves as our guide for how to live in harmony with the universe of connectedness. *Li* functions like an inner gyroscope that spins in us in sync with the whole. Following *li*, we move with the whole rather than at odds with it.

Indeed, if we try to force our inner gyroscope to spin some other way, it won't work; it'll topple. Hsün-tzu (third century BCE) wrote of *li*:

"When the world follows it, there is good government; when it departs from it, there is anarchy [chaos]. One who follows it is safe; one who deviates from it is in danger. One who follows it endures; one who deviates from it perishes."[12]

Why does he make such claims for *li?* Because following it means allowing everything to express its whole-imbued nature. There's a basic goodness to things that comes not from the things in themselves but from their innate participation in reality. Following our innate nature, we naturally move with reality. Chu Hsi (1130–1200 CE) wrote of our whole-nature:

> Fundamentally there is only one Great Ultimate, yet each of the myriad things has been endowed with it and each in itself possesses the Great Ultimate in its entirety. This is similar to the fact that there is only one moon in the sky but when its light is scattered upon rivers and lakes, it can be seen everywhere. It cannot be said that the moon has been split.[13]

When we follow our whole-born nature, Hsün-tzu suggests, everything works together effortlessly, but when we depart from it, nothing works. When we ask ourselves not to be ourselves—to act from some nature that isn't us or from narrow slices that don't reflect our whole being—we create chaos and suffering, trauma. Hsün-tzu's response to the monster model's fear of social chaos sets the logic straight. Because our original nature is formed, imbued, and guided by the whole, chaos happens not when we follow our nature but when we lose touch with it—when we believe we're separate from the whole and isolated, cut off from who we are. Ignoring our whole-connectedness—not being who we are—leads to chaos in our relationships.

Wang Pi (third century CE), who embraced both Taoist and Confucian teachings, wrote in his commentary on the *I Ching* that everything makes sense and works together when we understand "the many" as coming from, reflecting, and moving within "the one," the whole.

12. Ibid., 310.

13. Ibid., 309.

Following the "ruling principle" of our existence, our whole-connected-ness, is the antidote to chaos and confusion:

> Now, the many cannot be regulated by the many. They are reg-ulated by the smallest in number (the one). Activity cannot be controlled by activity. They are controlled by that which is firmly rooted in the one. The reason why the many can exist is that their ruling principle returns always to the one and all activ-ities can function because they have all come from the same source. . . . Therefore, though complex, they are not chaotic, and though many, they are not confused.[14]

The System Dynamics of Our Existence

Because the principle of wholeness differs radically from our ordi-nary categories, it challenges us to rethink who we are from the ground up. We're called to rethink not only our nature but, even more, the dynamics of our existence, namely, that we're not separate beings, how-ever much we appear to be. Because we experience our bodies as distinct from each other and our minds as walled inside our brains, we're used to framing our lives in terms of personal separateness—an issue we'll pursue further in the next chapter.

Yet in spite of appearances, we know that many things that seem unrelated are highly related. They participate in shared systems, even though we can't see the connections. We feel a pulse in our wrists that, if we didn't know physiology, would seem completely unrelated to some-thing going on in our chests. Or the tides seem unrelated to the moon, and yet they're connected by fields of gravity.

So, too, our personal ways of being emerge from our relatedness to the systems within and around us. Most basically, we all participate in systems of nature, both through our bodies and through the natural world. We all need air, water, food, and sunlight. In human worlds, we participate in families, schools, religions, businesses, economies, and societies, all of which leave their mark. They encourage some habits of

14. Ibid., 296.

mind, emotion, and expression, while discouraging others. According to indigenous and other spiritually oriented cultures, both the natural and human worlds participate in overlapping systems of energy and consciousness fields, unseen worlds of spirits, guides, and the Creator.

By expanding the context for understanding ourselves, we develop a more open, accepting, and nonjudgmental self-awareness. Why? Because we see more clearly how we came to be as we are, and we discover expanding frameworks for exploring our potentials for who we might become—other dimensions of ourselves that we could develop. We embrace ourselves as part of the universe and as reflections of it. This is the first root principle's method: "It is possible to understand something only if we can understand how it is connected to everything else."

Einstein's insight that the field forms the object is another way of expressing this principle of wholeness. It says our being comes from the whole systems of which we're a part—that fields create and form us.

Yet because we're of the fields, they're not outside us. We're not pawns of the systems around us but participants in them, which means we have a role in shaping both their course and ours too. We sense what's going on in systems, precisely because we're so utterly connected to them. In a real sense, they are we and we, they. We think and experience what we do in response to them. Whether we choose to perpetuate patterns or to change them, we react, and our choices affect the entire field.

From our ordinary perspective, we believe that what goes on with us is ours alone, because that's how it seems. From the perspective of wholeness and connectedness, however, we're system beings, evolving in intimate relation with all the systems around us extending out to the whole: families, communities, societies, culture, consciousness, and meaning. Who we are is all bound up with these dynamics every moment, and it's misleading to draw lines that separate what's us and what's not us. From a connectedness view, the processes of life don't have the hard and fast boundaries that we put on them. Buddhist Joanna Macy writes:

> I used to think that I ended with my skin, that everything within the skin was me and everything outside the skin was not. But

now you've read these words, and the concepts they represent are reaching your cortex, so "the process" that is me now extends as far as you. . . . What I am, as systems theorists have helped me see, is a "flow-through." I am a flow-through of matter, energy, and information, which is transformed in turn by my own experiences and intentions.[15]

We're beings in processes of connectedness, engaged with all sorts of systems that operate in and around us. Accordingly, whatever we do flows out to the universe through all sorts of links, ties, and trails of connections.

Granted, our ordinary perspective is too immediate—too accustomed to the skin-bound view of ourselves—to see how larger systems affect us or how we affect them. On one hand, we think we're either a bad person or a good person, but whichever, it's all our doing—our fault or our virtue. On the other hand and for the same reason, we don't see the roles we play in collective change and transformation. We feel small, insignificant, unimportant, as if what we think and do doesn't matter—the grain-of-sand view of human life.

Wholeness and connectedness say both perspectives are too narrow. It's impossible for us not to be engaged in two-way processes with systems on many levels, because that's how we're constructed. Systems affect us, and we affect them. We can't escape these dynamics of connectedness, because that's our reality; we can only be unaware of them.

Claiming our connected nature starts with recognizing our connectedness: observing how we participate in family systems, educational systems, social systems, economic systems, work systems, religious systems, media systems, political systems, as well as systems of meaning, philosophy, consciousness change, and personal and spiritual growth. We're both products of all these different systems and changers of them.

Failing to notice this two-way dynamic, some critics interpret holistic perspectives through one-way, top-down, dominator categories, as if the whole were a monolithic entity imposing itself on its parts against

15. Joanna Macy, *World as Lover, World as Self* (Berkeley, Calif.: Parallax Press, 1991), 12.

their will or well-being. It's a short step from this conceptual image to a political version in which people like Hitler, Stalin, or Mao Tse-tung step in for the one system and run things as if they were *it*—as if they could know what's best for humanity or society.

But the criticism doesn't hold water. The dominator view isn't reality's way of operating but a human distortion of it. Reality's whole can't tyrannize its parts, because the parts are the whole in action. They're not separate from the whole, and neither the whole nor its parts have a separate agenda for the other. That's like saying the body tyrannizes the lungs or heart by making them breathe or beat. Systems don't work on dominator dynamics. If they did, they'd break down. According to chaos theorists, reality is made up of self-organizing systems that are open and constantly changing. They have their own rhythms of moving through order to apparent chaos to new forms of order. Order emerges, but it's not imposed from without.

As to the political version, "the one," "the ruling principle" is not a human being; neither is any human mind so great as to be able to fathom what's best for everyone. Wholeness is a call to humility before the infinite connections that sustain us. It's a call, as indigenous peoples say, to walk gently on the earth, honoring the connections we know and being even more respectful of those that lie beyond our knowledge. It's not a call to arrogance, presumption, or domination.

Socrates and Plato tried to beat the "power-over" model at its own game precisely by shifting the consciousness. If we must have hierarchies in society, they reasoned, instead of putting the most brutish, greed-for-power-and-wealth mentalities at the top, why not put at the top the most carefully trained-in-virtue souls—people (men *and* women, they specified) who have given up all private ownership and therefore whose complete concern is focused on the common good?

Actually, Hindu scholars say that this was the original ideal of the Hindu caste system. But it hasn't worked in the West or in India in the ways that Plato, Socrates, or Hindu seers hoped, because the dominator consciousness keeps creeping in, invited there by a model of hierarchy. Over time, the ruling head and torso sit too heavily on the rest of the body.

Indeed, the relationship among the parts—the balance among them and how they work together—marks the difference between dominator wholeness and real wholeness. In real wholeness, if our toes hurt, it's hard to think about anything else, especially if we're trying to walk. All parts participate in the experience of the whole, which means all parts are affected by the joy and pain of every other part. It's a never-ending source of amazement how the tiniest thing—a milli-ounce nerve in a tooth or splinter under a nail—can send a one- or two-hundred-pound body into total agony.

Exploiting one part for the benefit of another cannot, therefore, be a strategy in systems without weakening and ultimately destroying the whole. If our minds drive our bodies, forcing us to do things that make our stomachs turn, our bodies eventually give out. Bodies don't tolerate minds in tyrant mode. They rebel in ways that we can't ignore.

When our bodies finally break down, we don't heal them by beating up on the ailing parts. If our stomachs hurt, we don't cut them out, lock them in a closet, and then bring them out later sufficiently chastised and expect them to work. We find out why they hurt and make changes, so our stomachs can heal.

The same system thinking applies to how we work with the systems around us. One sector prospering at cost to another is not a successful strategy; neither is further hurting a part that already hurts. In the short term, dominator methods can seem successful, but in the long term, they fail. They're ignorant of how things got to be how they are because of the workings of systems: their health or illness, harmony or discord, functionality or dysfunctionality, balance or imbalance. System imbalances must be righted, or system ills go uncorrected. Imbalances make problems multiply, until systems fail, and we with them.

Another reason dominator methods don't work is that they don't value what each part means to the whole—that the whole couldn't be what it is without each of its aspects. What we call parts are the whole in expression, which means they're not dispensable. The whole permeates the parts—all of them—and each part participates in the whole and contributes to it. Each is needed for the whole to be what it is.

This understanding underlies the spiritual conviction in the sacredness of life and in the Hindu tradition of *ahimsa* or nonviolence to all creatures. Ecology arrives at a similar understanding, namely, that all facets of the earth's systems are necessary for the whole to thrive. The loss of a species threatens more than that species alone, because each species contributes to the balanced working of the ecosystems as a whole. We may not recognize the role or appreciate its importance, but we're learning. Bugs aren't our favorite creatures, but if we kill them all, we won't have birds either.

The systems of the body offer another example. Every organ has a value to the body, even organs whose roles science couldn't at first identify. But the participation of our organs in the whole that is a conscious human being goes far beyond biological functioning. In his book *The Heart's Code*, Paul Pearsall presents anecdotal evidence from organ-transplant recipients that our organs participate in our emotional, intellectual, intuitive, relational, and physical lives.[16]

We've pictured our brains as all-knowing command centers dictating orders to an unconscious body, but this view turns out to be false. Our organs register not only memories but also language and food preferences. In fact, they appear to embody a knowledge of who we are on many levels. A proper, lace-clad, marzipan-loving aunt threw off her lace and started wearing jeans and drinking beer after she received a kidney from a young man killed in a car crash. Transplanted hearts carry the feelings, memories, and ethics of their donors into their recipients' lives. Our organs are evidently even attuned to our soul's meaning in life, for they can rebel with sickness if we lose sight of it.

Because the whole permeates the parts, no part is expendable or insignificant. Whatever our nature may be and wherever our journeys may take us, we are each sacred and precious to the whole, for we are the whole made manifest. Such is the core assumption about who we are from a mystic perspective, drawn from the first root principle, wholeness.

True, confronting patterns of selfishness, cruelty, violence, and destruction is evidently part of the larger story of evolution that we're engaged in telling with our lives; yet the principles of wholeness and connectedness say there's no wisdom in attaching these patterns to our nature in some final way. Storytellers and their stories are not the same,

16. Paul Pearsall, *The Heart's Code: Tapping the Wisdom and Power of Our Heart Energy* (New York: Broadway Books, 1998).

and we miss the possibilities for us as storytellers to tell other tales if we reduce ourselves to one plot line.

In other words, if we're working out issues that arise within certain systems, what sense does it make to slap labels on us, as if who we are under these conditions is who we are absolutely? Were we to interact with different systems, we'd have different meanings to explore. We'd behave differently. It makes more sense to map systems, our roles in them, and how they promote certain behaviors while discouraging others. Then we have the information we need to evaluate the dynamics with an eye to changing them—shifting to new systems.

Mindful of our connectedness and how it works two ways—it to us and we to it—we understand ourselves better. We see how we've come to be who we are now, and we see our potential to be more. We also see how we can be creative with the two-way flow we have with our connectedness. We can use it to develop real wisdom about human nature in general and our personal natures in particular. And then we can use this wisdom, Plato's first virtue, to change systems.

Humanity as One Body

Western thinkers who have taught wholeness—and we have a long tradition from Pythagoras, Plato, and Plotinus through Swedenborg and Leibniz to the Transcendentalist and New Thought movements in America to physicists like Einstein and David Bohm—have attempted to do precisely this, namely, to take a holistic, connectedness approach to everything. They've attempted to step back and look at the wider systems that shape us, from socioeconomic and political levels to metaphysical, consciousness, cosmic, and "meaning-of-life" levels. In many cases, they've used the body as an image of wholeness and how it works.

On a socioeconomic level, for example, revolutionary thinker Thomas Paine wrote *The Rights of Man* to oppose Britain's colonial policies. He used the image of blood in the body—that it must flow freely for the whole body to stay healthy:

> Every kind of destruction or embarrassment serves to lessen the quantity, and it matters but little in what part of the commercial

world the reduction begins. Like blood, it cannot be taken from any of the parts, without being taken from the whole mass in circulation, and all partake of the loss. When the ability in any nation to buy is destroyed, it equally involves the seller. Could the government of England destroy the commerce of all other nations, she would most effectually ruin her own.[17]

Paine was drawing on a long tradition of wholeness thinkers who conceive of humanity as a unified body, functioning as one in spite of the perception of ourselves as separate entities—separate nations, businesses, religions, races, cultures, families, or persons. We move as one system, and the appearance of separateness, compelling as it is, is illusory. It's as illusory as if we were to focus a video camera on one of our hands and then believe, since we saw nothing else, that the hand was separate and had a life apart from a body. Since we wouldn't see a body, we'd assume it didn't exist.

A holistic perspective explores what it means if we're no more separate from humanity than our hands are from our bodies. Just as our hands serve as sensors for our bodies and tools for carrying out its different purposes, so are we sensors and tools for humanity's whole being. We are how humanity experiences itself from a certain point of view, as if we're each the eyes and ears of humanity's one body, providing information about the larger dynamics. The philosopher Leibniz described us as windows on the whole. With our unique set of sensors, we offer feedback to the one body that's made up of all of us. Whatever is going on with us says something about what's going on within humanity, starting with our most immediate and close relationships and moving out.

Granted, separateness can be a convenient illusion, insofar as it gives us the practical job of looking after the piece we've been assigned and seeing what we can do with it. But the illusion isn't convenient if we forget that what we do with our "piece of the continent" affects "the main," the entirety. John Donne's famous "Meditation XVII" is a straightforward meditation on our whole-connected being, using the body as a central image:

17. Thomas Paine, *The Rights of Man*, Part II, Chapter V, *Basic Writings of Thomas Paine* (New York: Wiley Book Company, 1942), 211.

When [the church] baptizes a child, that action concerns me; for that child is thereby connected to that body which is my head too, and ingrafted into that body whereof I am a member. And when she buries a man, that action concerns me: all mankind is of one author, and is one volume. . . .

No man is an island, entire of itself; every man is a piece of the continent, a part of the main. If a clod be washed away by the sea, Europe is the less, as well as if a promontory were, as well as if a manor of thy friend's or of thine own were: any man's death diminishes me, because I am involved in mankind, and therefore never send to know for whom the bell tolls; it tolls for thee.[18]

To our surprise, given the use made of his ideas by gung-ho capitalists—proponents of the "greed-is-good" philosophy—eighteenth-century economist Adam Smith shared this holistic understanding and thought it should inform our actions, particularly in business life. Coming to economics from moral philosophy, Smith admired the holistic views of the Stoics. In a book he spent his life revising entitled *The Theory of Moral Sentiments*, he wrote:

Man, according to the Stoics, ought to regard himself, not as something separate and detached, but as a citizen of the world, a member of the vast commonwealth of nature. . . . Whatever concerns himself, ought to affect him no more than whatever concerns any other equally important part of this immense system. We should view ourselves, not in the light in which our own selfish passions are apt to place us, but in the light in which any other citizen of the world would view us.[19]

The fact that we regard Adam Smith today as the champion of

18. John Booty, ed., *John Donne: Selections from Divine Poems, Sermons, Devotions, and Prayers* (Mahwah, N. J.: Paulist Press, 1990), 271–272.

19. Adam Smith, *The Theory of Moral Sentiments*, III.3.11, eds. D. D. Raphael and A. L. Macfie (Oxford: Oxford University Press, 1976), 140–141. See also David Korten, *The Post Corporate World: Life after Capitalism* (San Francisco: Berrett-Kohler and West Hartford, Conn.: Kumarian Press, 1999), 152–154.

selfishness in business indicates the power of paradigms to twist people's ideas, making them fit the paradigm's agenda. Adam Smith wrote *The Wealth of Nations*, first published in 1759, to limit the exploitative actions of rapacious merchants in England. That his name should now be invoked to defend unchecked greed is a gross injustice to him. But he is by no means alone in having his work misconstrued down through history, for this is precisely what has happened to some of the most powerful wholeness teachings in the West: the esoteric traditions.

Astrology, for example, by its very structure conceives of individuals as one with the whole, inseparable from it, and always moving within it. Astrology is a symbolic meditation in meaningful whole-connectedness, not as something static or fixed but as a dynamic unfolding of meaning. Pioneering astrologer Dane Rudhyar, who, along with psychologist Carl Jung, integrated astrology with humanist psychology and Eastern mysticism, believed that the universe calls us into being. Who we are is precisely what the whole needs us to be at this point in time, space, and consciousness. Because we come from the whole, we can rely on our whole-formed being to guide us. Doing what's ours to do and doing what the whole needs are one process: our lives—our lives, that is, when we're living from our essence.

Our natal charts offer keys and clues to this essence—to the coincidence of who we are with what the whole needs. And our transits, the ongoing movement of the planets, show how our essence unfolds through the rhythms and dynamics of our experiences, coordinating our development with the larger evolution. Well used, astrology is a powerful tool for affirming the sacredness and meaningfulness of each life and its journey. Being who we are and doing what's ours to do is our purpose here, and astrology is a symbol system designed to help us pursue this purpose mindfully and creatively.

Emanuel Swedenborg, another Western visionary who has been relegated to the intellectual sidelines for his unconventionality, also reasoned in whole systems. His holistic sense of reality can best be described using the metaphor of holography—that each part bears the image of the whole and patterns it. In the heavenly realms he traveled, he perceived angels moving as one body on any given level, each themselves drawing life from their connectedness to the whole. The power of the whole is behind their every action—hence their quality as angels—because they act from their seamless connectedness with the whole realm of which they're part.

Here on earth, Swedenborg said, we experience this same unseen coordination of our efforts through "the unity of uses." Each human and indeed every form of nature have "uses" unique to that person or life form. We each have a special value and make a special contribution to the whole, which we do through all that we are—our thoughts, feelings, relationships, actions, even our very existence, grounding a certain quality of consciousness. The unique puzzle piece that we are completes the mosaic. This is Swedenborg's doctrine of uses, which we mentioned previously.

Whether we take Swedenborg's visions metaphorically or literally (or both), his teaching is one of wholeness and connectedness. Wholeness and connectedness are both our reality and a guide for how to act wisely.

We don't have chaos, therefore, when zillions of life forms do their own thing, for the same reason that our bodies don't fall into chaos when our zillions of cells go about their individualized functions within the body. An organic unity integrates our cells into a functioning form, just as on a far wider scale an unseen unity harmonizes our many voices into a chorus. According to Swedenborg, the whole melds our many individual efforts into a larger good we neither contrive nor even have the perspective to see. The larger good isn't our creation; it's not something we're responsible for making happen. Rather, the whole-good is something we participate in creating the more we're true to ourselves and live the meanings we have from the whole.

In *Gallery of Mirrors*, Anders Hallengren quotes Swedenborg when he explains that, when we're each doing what's ours to do—that is, when we're doing our "duty" to ourselves, to the moment, and to the whole—

"the welfare of the general body of people or mankind is being cared for." There is a unity of all uses. "In the Lord's sight the whole human race is as one man. . . . It is the uses with them that do so."[20]

20. Hallengren, 112.

This unity of uses holds not only for individuals but also for group differences among us. Our differences serve to create a unity, a diversified whole—a body that's not all feet. "According to Swedenborg's visions, all religions and all cultures have some important part to play in the body of humanity. Each simply has different missions."[21]

In other words, because our nature stems from our connectedness to the whole, in being true to our nature, we do what the whole needs. Our essential nature guides us to be of greatest good both to ourselves and to the people and systems around us. We're back to Hsün-tzu's idea that, in following *li*, we are safe, we endure, and we achieve balance and harmony in all our relationships.

Interacting with Humanity's Body Day to Day

Again, a whole-system approach is not up in the clouds. It's entirely down to earth and applicable in the most tangible and mundane of affairs: business. Adam Smith's way of thinking about economies exemplifies this, for it bears striking similarities to Swedenborg's holistic approach.[22] Perhaps Smith was influenced by the interest of many of his fellow Scotsmen in Leibnizian, Swedenborgian ideas of holism, especially as they relate to scientific knowledge. Or perhaps the holistic approach just made sense to his practical mind.

In any case, Smith viewed society and its economy as a great organism, one body. He didn't favor one economic class over another in his theories but sought to understand how society hangs together as a whole. "No society can surely be flourishing and happy," he wrote, "of

21. Ibid., 112.

22. Adam Smith also shared with Swedenborg the experience of going into trances, although, unlike Swedenborg, Smith either retained no memory of what he experienced or kept it to himself. The trances, described as "absences of mind" or "falling into a reverie," would come on unexpectedly, and he could walk fifteen miles in this condition before coming to again. His neighbors in Edinburgh regularly saw him "walking down the cobbled streets with his eyes fixed on infinity and his lips moving in silent discourse. Every pace or two he would hesitate as if to change his direction or even reverse it." Robert L. Heilbroner, *The Worldly Philosophers: The Lives, Times and Ideas of the Great Economic Thinkers* (New York: Touchstone, Simon and Schuster, 1953, 1992), 45.

which by far the greater part of the numbers are poor and miserable."[23] Robert Heilbroner writes of Smith: "…it is not his aim to espouse the interests of any class. He is concerned with promoting the wealth of the entire nation. And wealth, to Adam Smith, consists of the goods that *all* the people of society consume; note *all*—this is a democratic, and hence radical, philosophy of wealth."[24]

What sounds most remarkably like Swedenborg's unity of uses is Adam Smith's famous "invisible hand" that guides economies toward some mutually beneficial balance. The yet-to-be-realized condition for this happening is that everyone acts freely, not just politically but economically too. If we don't like our job, we can find or create another that suits us better—and, in today's terms, get the appropriate training and funding to make the transition.

In other words, what Socrates called "doing what's ours to do" and Swedenborg called finding and fulfilling our "uses" may be compared on the practical, everyday level to what Adam Smith called pursuing our genuine self-interest. Self-interest is not selfishness. It's attending to our legitimate needs and making the most of our lives—our talents, ideas, abilities, and indeed our souls' callings. Everyone should be free to do this, because what we have is what the whole needs. Only in tyrannies (which may exist in families, corporations, and economies as well as in governments) are people denied this freedom—and the whole body of humanity is diminished as a result.

As we fulfill our own needs by engaging in some activity that fits us, Smith said, we contribute to the good of society. Because we're part of the whole, we perceive the needs of the whole from our personal perspective as our needs. That's how the whole comes to us and communicates with us, namely, through the language of our own lives, needs, feelings, dreams, and longings. In striving to meet our own needs by doing something that's of value to others, we contribute to the good of the whole. Smith writes:

23. Ibid., 61.
24. Ibid., 53.

Every individual labours to render the annual revenue of the society as great as he can. He generally, indeed, neither intends to promote the public interest, nor knows how much he is promoting; . . . he intends only his own security; and by directing that industry in such a manner as its produce may be of the greatest value, he intends only his own gain, and he is in this, as in many other cases, led by an invisible hand to promote an end which was no part of his intention.[25]

Smith goes on to say that it's probably just as well that we don't know exactly *how* we're promoting the good of society because, in all likelihood, when we think we know what's best for the whole, our vision turns out to be too narrow, and we end up making a mess of things. Notions of dominating others "for their own good," popularized, for instance, in the 1980s and 1990s as the "trickle-down theory," start creeping in.

We're better off trusting the unseen order as it guides our steps through the language of our own skills, needs, and inclinations. Heilbroner writes of Adam Smith:

He was a philosopher-psychologist-historian-sociologist who conceived a vision that included human motives and historic "stages" and economic mechanisms, all of which expressed the plan of the Great Architect of Nature (as Smith called [God]). From this viewpoint, *The Wealth of Nations* is more than a masterwork of political economy. It is part of a huge conception of the human adventure itself.[26]

Naturally, if enough people decide their job is to dominate the body of humanity—to take control of markets, for example, by either buying up the competition or driving them out of business, after which they can charge the skies for inferior, even dangerous products—we're in trouble: humanity's body gets sick. The controlling hand ceases to be the

25. Adam Smith, *An Inquiry into the Nature and Causes of the Wealth of Nations* (New York: The Modern Library, Random House, 1937, 1965), 423.

26. Heilbroner, *The Worldly Philosophers*, 73.

invisible one of the whole guiding each part according to its whole-born nature. Social and economic orders break down for similar reasons that bodies do: some parts grow like cancers, devouring the systems on which they depend. Like parasites or viruses, they flirt with destroying their host body, because their wisdom cannot equal the wisdom of the whole.

Greed isn't the only thing that throws humanity's body off balance, however. Boring, meaningless, or frustratingly unsatisfying jobs grow like cancers as well, as does internal programming that makes us lose faith in our personal value to the whole. Social and financial expectations consume us too, brushing aside our longings to do what's uniquely ours. All these "cancers" prevent us from doing justice to ourselves and hence to our societies by giving them what's most ours to give.

Not that it's easy for us to know what's ours. What are we here to do? Or in Smith's terms, what is genuinely in our best interests, and how can we best pursue them? We haven't been raised to think about these questions freely. Instead, we choose work lives according to what makes the most money, what seems prestigious or acceptable, or what parents and family urge us to pursue.

If we're to do what Socrates describes as necessary for justice and what Smith describes as necessary for a balanced, wealthy economy, we need freedom. On one hand, we need the inward freedom to go for it— to do what's ours. On the other hand, we need outer freedom—the means to go where the inner leads.

As yet, we don't have that kind of freedom. The social and economic systems aren't in place to support our quests to do what's ours, supplying the quality of help we need during transitions. Education, for instance, is becoming more expensive, although the good of both society and the national economy depend on quality education. Without outer support, we lack the practical wherewithal to fulfill our souls' callings. Our freedom is theoretical, not lived. From monetary aid to counseling to education and apprenticeships, wisdom suggests that we put our social money where our political mouth is. Otherwise, freedom remains rhetoric laid over a reality of economic slavery: a population that feels compelled to pass the days doing things just for money. It doesn't matter whether we're rich or poor, the more our energies revolve around making money, the greater our slavery to it, and the less our freedom to do what's ours.

As important as what we do with our lives is, it remains an open and unresolved issue for most of us. Perhaps uncertainties go with the territory since we're more than what we ourselves can know. Whole-connected beings don't fit into neat boxes, and the things they love doing don't always come with a paycheck or meet with social acceptance. Whole-connected beings don't remain static either, which means what's ours to do continually evolves. Then, of course, we don't know what humanity's one body needs, any more than our hands of themselves know what to do to be most useful to our minds, bodies, or emotions.

All these factors make the quest to do what's ours no small challenge. It calls for methods different from the ones we're accustomed to following, like doing what people tell us, choosing what makes the most money, or even masterminding our own lives, trying to figure everything out. Instead of obeying conventional wisdom, we're called by wholeness and connectedness to cultivate qualities of patience in the quest, a trust that we have a value to the whole beyond what we realize, and open humility about our life's course.

On a personal level, we surrender to processes that surpass our concepts. We seek the good we know, but we also stay open to a good that's beyond our knowing and that interjects the unexpected. Collectively, we push our social structures to support us along the way, allowing us flexibility and room for change and experimentation, giving us room to try things out as well as to make mistakes and false steps, which every creative process involves. Not only our good but also the good of the whole grow from our endeavors.

A New Agenda for Justice: Monitoring Our Connectedness

What does all this mean for justice? It lays a new philosophical foundation—a new philosophy of life from which our ideas about justice can evolve. Specifically, the first root principle offers a new understanding of our nature as humans: who we are, what we're doing here, and how we can all be on earth creatively, happily, and without strangling each other. In light of the principle of wholeness, we're participating in the unfolding story of humanity as one body, and no one of us is expendable in that telling. Each life has a meaning from the whole and an importance for the whole of humanity.

Far from assuming that we're moral monsters, therefore, a wholeness-based model of human nature says we're all needed, wherever we are in our development, because we each have differences to contribute and perspectives on the whole that are important. Who we are makes a difference to the whole, beyond what we can know in visible, quantifiable, or outward terms. No one of us has a perspective adequate enough to judge the value of another life.

That's easy to see if we're talking about the apparently successful people in society—the heroes—but how about the rest, those in social, economic, or personal pain?

People in pain have perspectives on systems that may be the most important to hear, for they indicate that something is out of balance. If we're on the *Titanic*, who has the most important perspective for the safety of the ship: the passengers inside who see no danger because they're busy playing cards or the ones out in the cold on the decks of the ship who spy an iceberg ahead? If we silence those in pain or dismiss them—or if we silence or dismiss our own pain—we ignore early warning messages telling us that the systems on which we depend are out of balance and headed for danger.

Indigenous traditions understand this and practice its implications. One person's pain—whether it be misfortune, physical illness, psychological distress, destructive behavior, or social dysfunction—triggers self-questioning for the entire community. Myron Eshowsky, who takes his shamanic practice into prisons to work with the inmates, writes:

> In tribal cultures, soul loss, power loss, and spirit intrusions and possessions are not considered individual problems *per se*. To quote Larry Peters, an anthropologist and psychotherapist,
>
> "Rather, they are seen as problems involving the whole social network, and the balance and relationship to the spiritual forces of the cosmos. That is, because 'illnesses' are considered transpersonal and sacred crises, they involve the intense participation of deity, family, and social network. Thus treatment is simultaneously psychosocial and spiritual."

In this world view, illness (here defined as including prisons) is symptomatic of an imbalance between society and the spiritual realm. This larger view is critical to being able to do shamanic work in prisons.[27]

People don't become the way they are out of the blue, nor do events happen from nowhere. There's a reason, a history, a story of connections. Some ways of connecting honor our place within the whole, while others make us feel judged, rejected, degraded, and isolated. To help someone in crisis, we need to investigate these connections and to take part in changing those that cause hurt. We may not be the ones suffering today, but tomorrow may be a different story. In any case, we want our shared systems to be as healthy and nurturing as possible for the good of all. In *The Spirit of Intimacy*, Sobonfu Somé of the Dagara people in Burkina Faso, West Africa, writes:

In Africa they say that if one person gets sick, everybody is sick. The village or the tribe is seen as a huge tree with thousands of branches. When a part of this living entity is diseased there is a need to reexamine the whole tree. This is why when somebody is sick in the village, everybody is worried; it reminds everybody that there is something present that is potentially dangerous for all.[28]

In the 1980s, the Maoris, New Zealand's indigenous people, hotly contested the English model of justice, which removed young "offenders" from their families, in other words, blamed and punished the young people alone, as if that would remedy things. This practice violated the core understanding that Maoris have always held about justice and the connected nature of people, actions, community, and society:

27. Myron Eshowsky, "Behind These Walls Where Spirit Dwells," *Shamanism* 12, no. 1 (Spring/Summer 1999): 9.

28. Sobonfu E. Somé, *The Spirit of Intimacy: Ancient African Teachings in the Ways of Relationships* (New York: William Morrow and Company, 1997), 106–107.

Historically, Maori justice processes were based on notions that responsibility was collective rather than individual and redress was due not just to the victim but also to the victim's family. Understanding why an individual has offended was also linked to this notion of collective responsibility. The reasons were felt to lie not in the individual but in a lack of balance in the offender's social and family environment. The causes of this imbalance, therefore, had to be addressed in a collective way and, in particular, the harmony between the offender and the victim's family had to be restored.[29]

Once again, the first root principle states the logic: because "everything is connected in some way to everything else," "it is therefore possible to understand something only if we can understand how it is connected to everything else." Tracing the stories of connectedness as they ripple out from one person or event to include "everything else," we move from specific events to learning about the social systems within humanity's one body. We take humanity's temperature.

Because humanity's body is our body too—the only collective body we have to depend on—we care about the results and want to do what it takes to make humanity's body healthy. If connectedness with existing social systems has caused havoc to some parts of humanity's body, connecting with those same systems cannot be entirely positive for any of us. We need to know this, for our sake as well as theirs.

This first root principle suggests, therefore, that we shift the agenda for justice. If we start from the premise of "looking up" to our shared wholeness, justice cannot be about plucking out the "bad apples" among us, and certainly not about giving them more bruises. "Bad apple" isn't a category for wholeness-justice. Singling out one person as "the problem" makes no sense, since no one exists in isolation. It's scapegoating, aimed at purging ills, not at addressing causes. If we come to be who we are through our connectedness, then if we're in pain and passing it on,

29. Edward Durie, "Custom Law," unpublished manuscript, 1995. Quoted in Allison Morris and Gabrielle Maxwell, "Restorative Justice in New Zealand: Family Group Conferences as a Case Study," *Western Criminology Review* 1, no. 1 (1998).

our connections cannot be entirely healthy, however they may appear.

Neither can justice be about silencing the symptoms alerting us to social systems in need of change. When our shared systems function in sick-making ways, we all feel it. Those who feel it most, for whatever reason, aren't society's enemies but its friends. They sound the alarm through the pain of their own lives, alerting us that we need to change our shared systems before we all get sick (or sicker). Far from nailing individuals for being society's alarm bells—whether as victims, offenders, or both in one—wholeness-justice involves listening to the alarm, taking steps to change whatever isn't working, and creating a balance that supports everyone.

In other words, wholeness-justice has the job of monitoring our total connectedness: how we're connecting with each other and the earth through our shared systems. We can consider this connectedness from two perspectives: whole to part, and part to whole.

Looking from the whole to the part, wholeness-justice demands that our shared social, economic, educational, family, and political systems abandon soul-damaging patterns and function as good servants to us, providing the safe ground from which we all grow. Justice works to make our shared systems healthy and supportive to us, because that's why we have them. The reason for systems to exist is not to exploit, tyrannize, or dominate us; and if they start functioning this way toward one person or group today, they can do the same to others tomorrow. Real justice sniffs out such patterns—individual experiences providing the primary alarm bells—and changes them.

Looking at the connection the other way, namely, from individuals (parts) back to the collective (whole), wholeness-justice supports each of us in fulfilling our destiny to contribute what's ours to the larger processes—to humanity's body.

Both ways, wholeness-justice seeks health and healing. That's the aim, the agenda, what justice is driving at and what it must be all about.

In wholeness-justice, it follows that helping one helps all. This isn't spacey talk. It's turning rapists and murderers into contributing members of society. Or it's turning money and power addicts—white-collar addicts in business and government—into people who redirect their gifts for grand organizing onto solving some of the grand problems we face. The individuals break out of their addiction/exploitation/crime cycles, so they're happier. And they start giving to society what we all need from them, whatever their unique skills and talents may be, so we're happier too. Before long, the systems, patterns, institutions, and paradigms that formed them begin to shift. Wholeness-justice works in all directions. It draws everyone into the process of imagining, creating, and evolving greater justice among us.

In other words, because of connectedness, whenever shifts occur, everyone feels them. The social atmosphere changes. Within ourselves, we feel freer to move into our own soul-connecting processes and to do our inner work. If murderers can learn to forgive themselves—as they must to become functional—surely we can do the same for ourselves. We breathe an atmosphere of greater tolerance and compassion when the aim of justice isn't to nail people for this or that mistake, big or small, but to help each of us find who we came here to be and to fulfill our value to society.

Therapist and author Leonard M. Shaw has been conducting a three-day "Love and Forgiveness" seminar at Monroe State Prison near Seattle since 1986, a facility which holds those convicted of violent crimes (murder, rape, sexual abuse). He writes of his work:

It has been suggested to me (by professionals and nonprofessionals both) that since these men have committed such violent crimes, perhaps they do not deserve healing and peace of mind. It is very clear by the third day of these seminars that:

- We are all in this together, and if we refuse healing to these men, we are refusing to heal ourselves.

- When we love these men, we are loving ourselves.

- We are all much more alike than we are different.[30]

Because, as Sandra Bloom observes, we live in a trauma-ridden society, who among us is not in need of healing? If humanity's body is full

---

30. Leonard M. Shaw, "Love and Forgiveness Behind Bars," *In Context* 38 (Spring 1994): 50.

of trauma, we are too. The blatant and subtle abuses that we experience in schools, families, religious groups, jobs, government agencies, and all the other stress-inducing systems of society take their toll on us. Instead of pointing fingers at which parts of humanity's body felt the trauma first and reacted to it by passing it on, wholeness-justice adopts the approach of the Hollow Water elders: as soon as possible invite as many people as possible to go on the healing path together.

Marcia Blackstock, director of Bay Area Women Against Rape (BAWAR), came to similar conclusions when she and two of her colleagues were invited by a group of inmates to speak at what was then (1988) the largest prison in the industrialized world, California Medical Facility-South, holding 8,500 inmates. It was a scary experience for the women, surrounded as they were by thousands of men convicted of rape and murder. But as they met with the group over time, each listened to the experiences of the other. Joanne Lucas Cvar, who reported on the meetings for *In Context* magazine, wrote:

As they continued to work together, the group found that a healing process was occurring and that it was working both ways. The stories helped offenders as well as victims to share strongly felt emotions they had never before had an opportunity to express. When the men began to understand the abuse victims had suffered, many of them realized for the first time that they themselves had been abused in one way or another, often as children, and they wanted to share their own stories.

"Through listening to each other, we learned what we had in common—our humanity," Marcia says. "Stereotypes had helped to create and empower the monster image. With that realization, we could begin to accept them, and they could begin to forgive themselves."[31]

The more we heal, the more we make a paradigm shift in how we see ourselves. That's the crucial first step, because the kind of creature we

31. Joanne Lucas Cvar, "Transformation: Victim Offender Reconciliation," *In Context* 38 (Spring 1994): 50.

understand ourselves to be determines what kind of social systems we create. More to the point, it determines our concepts of justice—whether to blame and punish single individuals or to support everyone in healing and transformation.

Conceiving of ourselves as connected to the whole—as whole-formed beings connected to all that is—provides, then, the first root principle on which to build a new awareness of justice. But this is just the beginning of "looking up" to how we're related. Learning about our connected being inspires change and all kinds of it—the second root principle.

SIX

Change

Change. All of creation is in a state of constant change. Nothing stays the same except the presence of cycle upon cycle of change. One season falls upon the other. Human beings are born, live their lives, die and enter the spirit world. All things change. There are two kinds of change. The coming together of things (development) and the coming apart of things (disintegration). Both of these kinds of change are necessary and are always connected to each other.   —*The Sacred Tree*

"Looking up" to how we're all related as one body changes us. We think about ourselves differently. The idea that we're needed within the whole just for who we are—that all our voices have a place in this chorus—expands our frame for thinking about our lives.

Expanding our perspective is precisely what philosophy does. That's why the study of philosophy can be our best friend and guide through change. It offers different views of reality and who we are in its context, and these views expand our options for responding to change. Suppose we encounter a masked figure dressed in black leather, a big knife, and chains coming toward us on a dark street. Depending on our concept, we can see our life pass before us, or we can join a friend on his way to a Halloween party, complete with plastic props.

Philosophy works like that. This ancient but elusive discipline explores our mindset possibilities and, by so doing, offers us a mighty power both to respond to change and to shape it. This power is practical, inexpensive, and democratic, in that we all have it; yet despite these advantages, philosophy is a power that we as a culture have yet to tap.

There are reasons for not tapping it. If we'd prefer things to remain as is, philosophy is persona non grata, and we'd best avoid it. As long as we keep looking through the same lens, we're going to see things the same way, as is everyone else who shares that lens.

The second root principle suggests, however, that this strategy works only so long, and then we run into a second aspect of reality's nature: change. Nothing is immune to it. We live in a dynamic universe, and therefore we're engaged, willingly or not, in paths of transformation that weave together personal and collective shifts.

Given the fluid nature of reality—one that's regularly "coming together" and then "coming apart," as the second root principle states—we can have no better companion than philosophy, which can make change comprehensible (somewhat) and even fun (now that's pushing it) with "Aha!" experiences. Philosophy's job is to make sense of changing reality, giving us maps so we don't get lost in the flux. In Buddhist traditions, philosophy gives us methods for connecting with change openly and mindfully, so that we receive change with less suffering. We accept it as part of life's process and remain open to a basic goodness going on, as Tibetan Buddhist Chögyam Trungpa calls it, beyond our immediate reactions to change as being either "bad" or "good." Tibetans are not people for whom suffering is unknown, so his affirmation of a "basic goodness" carries weight.

Whatever philosophies we use, the trick is to coax them out into the open, so we can see who from philosophy's pantheon is guiding us and whether they're the kind of philosophy-companions we need. Some philosophy-guides are more helpful than others, and it's nice to have a choice.

Whether we think much about philosophy or not, though, we all have one, and we respond to change accordingly. This unseen captain of our ship permeates our thoughts and perceptions, frames how we interpret life's flow, and steers our actions.

In fact, we usually have multiple philosophies rattling around in us, like guests who wandered in and never got invited to leave. Unless we have an in-house conference of all the philosophies we've collected, we may not know which philosophies we're housing.

For instance, at home we have a view of life that involves mutual love, care, respect, and support, while at work we assume it's a different game, rougher and with the mutuality factored out—the "trust-no-one" and "every-person-for-him-or-herself" philosophy. One of philosophy's main activities is taking stock of who's in our house, and whether the philosophies living in us are helping us or making change harder.

Where do our philosophies come from? Various sources. Many come from our interactions with social systems, which communicate philosophies through every word, rule, policy, command, reprimand, and memo. Social structures install in us a certain view of things—certain ways of responding to change. Religious institutions do this outright, as do families and schools. But businesses, government institutions, and the media send equally powerful messages about which philosophies we're to accept. We could go so far as to say that our social institutions operate primarily to inculcate a philosophy, for once that's established in us, the rest is easy. When changes arise, we respond by trying to preserve the existing system.

In other words, once we "buy" an institution's philosophy, we do as it directs and flow in the institution's channels, whether it's the institution of marriage, religion, business, or, as African American scholar Carter G. Woodson explained, slavery. We may not realize it, we may not be benefited by it, we may even be harmed by following an institution-inculcated philosophy; and yet we act as we're directed. We respond to the expectations the institutions broadcast about who we should be and what we should do with our lives. We do as we're told, and we feel guilty if we do anything else.

When this happens, we stop reflecting on philosophies and get locked inside one in particular. If we hold to a philosophy organized around keeping things as is, we're going to find change a nightmare. What could help us through change turns into an obstacle. We won't welcome change, and when it comes, we'll think something bad is happening.

Given the freethinking, rebellious creatures we are, how do we get so stuck in one philosophy? How do institutions—families, schools, workplaces, religions—persuade us to stop listening to the natural voices of change within? Easy: the philosophy goes inside—we internalize it.

Somewhere along the line, we accept a philosophy so totally that we forget that it's not our idea. It permeates not only our thoughts and ambitions but also our feelings and emotional responses. Our entire inner experience gets stamped by the worldview. Believing the philosophy to be ours, we see the world as the culture inculcates, and we feed and defend the view as our own creation.

Fortunately, social institutions aren't the only sources for our philosophies. We don't come into this world as the *tabula rasa* or blank slate that philosopher John Locke imagined. We're born with our own orientation, or so Socrates claimed, and not he alone. Asian philosophies assert the same. We've lived before in the multidimensional universe, and we carry within us the philosophies forged through earlier experiences. We may also bear in our souls a remembrance, as Socrates suggested, of who we are in our essence, who we are from the whole. A meaning wider than this or that social institution called us into being and continues to call us. Our origins beyond here live in us, and these inner voices speak up.

Even in basic ways, we see hints that social institutions don't give us everything that's in us philosophy-wise. For example, when a child or animal is treated badly, something in them recoils and cries out, "This isn't right. I'm not to be hurt this way!" A truth is born with us that says how we should or shouldn't be treated—that our essence deserves respect, love, and nurturing. Whatever philosophies our particular culture may teach, a deeper reality lives in us, and its truth persists.

Given all these sources, more philosophies live in us than those installed by society and culture. Otherwise social order wouldn't be such a challenge. As it is, the course of mind-programming never does run smooth. Any parent can tell us that. Yes, we need to accept some basic rules in order to function in a culture—things like manners, mutual respect, honesty, and knowledge about which side of the road to drive on. But we have our own sources of philosophy too, sources that transcend the current social order. We have our souls' agenda, as well as our destiny and purpose from the whole.

Being personal vessels for multiple philosophies makes life interesting. Multiple philosophy-captains have multiple ideas about where to point the ship. Social conventions say one thing, our inner compass another. The dominant culture may teach that we're nothing more than bodies and brain chemistry, that making money is life's purpose, that obeying social expectations and conventions is the moral and good life, or that beating others is the way to get ahead. Everything within us may rebel at such notions, and yet we find it hard to live our truth given the cultural context. That's the downside to housing multiple philosophies.

But there's an upside: the struggle to sort them out spurs growth. Each perspective has its own truth to tell, even if it doesn't have the whole story. Philosophies guide us through change, but change also makes us rethink our philosophies.

Whoever our inner guides and companions may be, philosophies are central to our experience. They're also central to every one of our social systems and, by extension, to what kind of world we live in. But most of all, they're central to our peace and happiness when both we and our social systems undergo change.

The pre-Socratic Greek philosopher Heraclitus, the Buddha, and the second root principle all agree that change is the true constant in life—a coming together and coming apart that go on up and down, within and without, small scale and large, individually and collectively, in both the human and natural worlds. When we're immersed in change, philosophy is our best tool for survival: a change-friendly philosophy keeps us going; a change-resistant one makes a difficult situation worse.

What Is It to Be Individual?

Previously, we explored philosophies of human nature, because how we conceive of ourselves determines the kind of justice we create. Our general concept of human nature sets us up to think about justice one way or another.

In this chapter, the general becomes specific. Change doesn't hit human nature in general. It hits people—each of us—in particular. We're the ones coming together and coming apart as our life's processes, and justice needs to be right there in the middle of it, helping us find our way.

To ground our concepts of both ourselves and justice, therefore, we need to think about what it is to be us specifically. Depending on how we frame our individual existence—what it is to be us—we form our ideas about change: what it's doing with us, and how we can work with it. We also form our ideas about how justice can help us.

Because change is bigger than any of us, it makes sense to develop a change-friendly philosophy—a way of understanding change that makes our experience of it positive. If reality's nature is to change, then it's our nature too. Change isn't foreign to us. If anything, it's not changing that's alien. To be alive is to change; to remain static is to die.

Accordingly, the more we conceive of ourselves as beings in process, moving with a connected universe that's always in flux, the less threatening change seems. We not only expect change but also assume that it's in our nature to flow along. Yes, change is challenging, given all its comings and goings, but it's not out to destroy us; neither is it a declaration of failure if our lives undergo restructuring. Change is as natural as life itself, and we exist in webs of connectedness that sustain us throughout. Even so, change is hard. It pushes us to our limits, calling us to exercise powers and to develop potentials we didn't know we had. But we don't need to see it as bad, something to be resisted or fought. It's reality, therefore, our reality too. It's not our fault that we can't say "No" to what is.

Based on this philosophy of who we are in relation to change, we need to ask justice to support us through our shifts—to ease our comings together and comings apart. If we go through a coming-apart phase and act hurtfully, whether through lack of awareness or skill or simply because change can be painful no matter what we do, we need justice to help us to see what's happening and to move with the shifts as gracefully as possible. Something in us or in a situation needs to come apart for us to grow. Perhaps relationships or certain models of them need to loosen and restructure. Perhaps a model of doing business needs to shift. Maybe a parent-child relationship needs to be restructured. Or maybe we need to heal and expand our self-concepts. As we'll see at the end of this chapter, we need to design justice both to help us as we go through these natural processes and to change our shared social systems so that they treat us with greater understanding and support in our upheavals.

Unfortunately, many of us—too many—haven't grown up with a model that frames change as natural. Instead, the model we've learned makes it hard for us to respond positively to change.

Specifically, we've grown up assuming that individuality means separateness, that we're so many isolated entities trying to hold our own against a hostile world, and that any order or connectedness is imposed from without, therefore superficial, not flowing from who we are. A "me-against-the-world" or "me-against-change" stance is born, and what could be natural to us—change—becomes frightening and excruciatingly painful. Why?

On a model of separateness, connecting isn't safe. It feels external, imposed, never quite fitting. And that's on good days. On bad days, connecting can be downright dangerous. When people view connections as a chance to get the most and give the least, to control and dominate, connecting can mean losing our shirts. When this model rules, connecting with people, families, groups, or workplaces in adversarial, win-lose ways costs us dearly.

But there are inner costs as well. Connecting from the "outside in" throws confining nets over our individuality. We're asked—and not always subtly—to give up who we are and abandon what's ours to do in order to become what others want us to be, which usually means not changing, staying inside the box.

A fellow writer working with prisoners observed that a major impediment to personal change in prisons comes from fellow prisoners: they rally to shame and extinguish individual steps toward recovery and healing—change. Families often behave similarly, as do workplaces and religious groups. Connected to people or social structures who put maintaining the status quo first, we find it hard to be true to ourselves, especially when we undergo shifts. We're told what our lives should be and how to live them, even if it means not moving with our reality. That hurts. When we're not able to follow our life's path, we lose our will to live. We become empty shells of who we could be, frozen, not entirely there.

To protect ourselves, we try to establish an identity and keep it fixed. We build walls around our personal separateness so no one can mess with us. This may mean getting the best education in the hopes of getting the best job, raising the brightest children, having the healthiest body, holding the most powerful position, making the most money, adopting the most informed political views or even the most evolved consciousness. However we go about it, self-protection means covering our hearts, steeling them, hiding our feelings. That's because our hearts are attuned to our needs for change, and if we're not allowed to move as we're moved, we can't afford to feel the pain of being stuck, trapped.

In all these ways, we seek defining marks that say we're special, we stand alone. To earn our place in a world that seems not to have much time, place, or need for us, we try to prove our uniqueness. At the same time, we use these forms as shields to keep the world, change, and other people at bay. Once we get our islands of personal security established, change is the last thing we want.

This sounds like the all-American call to be self-made individuals, and yet achieving it isn't about Mom or apple pie. Likely the quest involves win-lose contests. Darwin's "survival of the fittest" gives the endeavor an alienating, us-against-them, I-win-you-lose view of life. Seeking individuality in separateness is a lonely road, since every relationship falls prey to the one-upping, who's-in-control contest. Intimacy, trust, mutual support, caring, compassion, honesty, integrity, openness, understanding, generosity: these experiences of authentic connectedness aren't welcome. Given a model of separate individualities, we can't afford them; they make us too vulnerable.

The quest for individuality in separateness also involves judgments and comparisons: Did we succeed or fail? Who's doing the more distinguished work? Whose social position, body, finances, relationship, or psyche is more enviable? Comparing ourselves with others becomes a knee-jerk response, trained as we are from childhood to do it. We don't do it to be perverse, though. We do it—and compulsively so—because we believe our survival as separate beings depends on our looking good and coming out on top.

And yet it's a right yearning to experience our individuality as something sacred and worthy. There's profound truth behind the desire: we owe it to ourselves and the universe to live wholeheartedly from our essence. The first root principle affirms that we are the whole in expression, therefore that we each have a contribution to make. We're all needed not as clones of someone else or as prefab images stamped out of society's mold but as who we uniquely are. Our being here enriches the whole design, and our individuality is a treasure, something worthy of our life's endeavors toward individuation. When we're most fully who we are, we're most fully what the whole needs—more, we're most fully the whole in expression. That's worth seeking.

So what gives? What causes the pursuit of individuality to become warped and damaging to us and the public good?

Saying that money and power corrupt dodges the issue. Of course they do, the same way alcohol intoxicates. But blaming money or power for individuality gone awry is like blaming alcohol for the way drunks drive. The real issue is: Why are we addicts—self-destructively insatiable—around money and power? Why is our society money and power driven, shunting aside such values as wisdom, foresight, shared interests, compassion, or even basic planetary survival needs (breathable air and nonpoisonous water)? Why do we feel we must postpone lives of meaning and happiness in order to make money? We've already explored this territory in two of our books, *The Soul of Economies*[1] and *The Paradigm Conspiracy*,[2] as have many researchers and writers on addiction. Suffice it to say, greed for money and power is a manifestation of addiction, not a cause. We must look deeper to discover what throws us off.

Another response blames individuality per se, or rather, a particular definition of individuality. In their best-selling book *Habits of the Heart*, Robert Bellah and his co-authors bemoan an excess of individuality in America, believing that this causes a declining sense of community and values.[3]

It's true. Accepting a philosophy of individuality as selfish, competitive separateness, Western thought assumes an inevitable dichotomy between the individual and society—that what's good for one must come at the price of the other. Exercising personal freedom must endanger society, and securing public good must cost us our liberty. Political philosophies take this as given, and, operating on the belief in personal separateness, we

1. Denise Breton and Christopher Largent, *The Soul of Economies: Spiritual Evolution Goes to the Marketplace* (Wilmington, Del.: Idea House, 1991).

2. Denise Breton and Christopher Largent, *The Paradigm Conspiracy: Why Our Social Systems Violate Human Potential and How We Can Change Them* (Center City, Minn.: Hazelden, 1996).

3. Robert Neelly Bellah, William M. Sullivan, and Steven M. Tipton, *Habits of the Heart: Individualism and Commitment in American Life* (Berkeley, Calif.: University of California Press, 1985).

do indeed generate win-lose situations that reinforce the dichotomy.

If we define individuality through a self-against-the-world philosophy, then we'd agree with Bellah and his colleagues: individuality is a problem. Living out this notion of individuality means constantly flying in the face of reality's wholeness and connectedness. For this very reason, though, there's something wrong with defining individuality this way. We're not separate beings. Connectedness is how we're born, how we eat, and what fills our time, thoughts, and energies. The problem isn't us as individuals but how we define what this means—namely, that it means being separate.

How then do we arrive at the notion that being an individual means being selfish, competitive, and cut off? The cultural philosophy—the one expressed most often by academia and the media—says we're born with it. We're not convinced.

Yes, we're born with the potential to view ourselves this way, but our cultural institutions turn this potential into a flaming obsession. It's not our personal creation to think of ourselves as separate and under constant threat. That's stamped in us kindergarten through college, graduate school through work life. We've been trained to believe that asserting separateness, even if it means beating others or profiting from their loss, is what being a successful individual involves.

Consider just one social mechanism that instills this philosophy. We're thinking of our old favorite, rewards and punishments, especially when the game is rigged with limited rewards (only a few can get them) but unlimited punishments (plenty to go around, starting with all those who don't get the artificially restricted rewards). This social mechanism programs us to think of ourselves competitively and selfishly, driving us to win at all costs, framing situations in power-over terms (who has the power to control the flow of rewards and punishments?), and habituating us to conceive of our interests as separate from and at odds with the interests of everyone else.

Not we but the cultural mechanism creates the mindset and instills the habit. It teaches a particular philosophy of individuality day in, day out, using shame, humiliation, and unrelenting fear and stress to drive the message home. We end up living a view of individuality that's blind to the universe of connectedness and how it forms our being.

The result? Acting from a separateness notion of what it is to be individual, we're guaranteed to make a mess of things, because we don't think about the connected reality in which we act. Perceiving ourselves as separate, we don't perceive real consequences, because we don't experience the deep, reality links that create them.

For instance, offenders don't feel connected to those they harm, for when they meet their victims in a victim-offender mediation program, they're often struck with remorse and profoundly changed by seeing the faces and hearing the pain of those hurt by their actions. Moreover, they're often amazed at the support they receive from their victims for doing something positive with their lives—support they obviously had not experienced before.

These offenders are simply carrying to an extreme a notion of individuality that is culturally accepted, inculcated at every turn. Their inability to live mindful of their connectedness dramatizes for everyone the consequences of a philosophy of individuality as separateness—a philosophy we've all been raised to accept.

In a universe of connectedness, hurting anyone hurts us—the boomerang effect. That's true whether it's the actions of a child bully on the playground or an adult bully at home, at the office, or in government. Crime exists because we're not separate beings, and we're still learning what it means to be connected.

To Be Individual Is to Be Connected

As it turns out, being separate isn't a practical or true-to-life definition of individuality. The words *individual* and *indivisible* share the same root. Western thought has taken *individual* to mean the smallest, indivisible unit of society, the social atom as a discrete, isolated entity. But we can also take *individual* to mean "indivisible from the whole," not separated but still distinct, much as a facet of a crystal offers a distinct image of the whole crystal. Or consider the individual parts of our bodies: thanks to our DNA coding, each cell bears the information of the whole but does something special with it. The whole isn't an amorphous blob but a differentiated whole, and we're all the differentiations.

An everyday experience of our whole-connected nature is our individual role in family life, especially in light of family-systems research. Each family member mirrors the whole family dynamics from an individual perspective. Members develop roles that serve their own as well as family good. In healthier family systems, individual roles change as everyone grows. In more rigid families, family members get locked in roles and aren't allowed to change. Expansively or restrictively, though, the family system gives rise to the individuals, who in turn both reflect the system and do something unique with it. Each member participates in the whole in an individual way, without being separate from it.

Family systems offer a microcosmic image of what mystics understand to be our macrocosmic truth. Our being is thoroughly wedded and woven into the whole. We draw our individuality from this source and exist inseparable from it.

A whole-connected sense of individuality is a core tenet of Swedenborg's philosophy, as it is of every mystical tradition and now, apparently, of quantum physics as well. The appearance of differentiation into separateness hides a reality of mind-boggling unity, such that subatomic particles that are split from each other continue to mirror each other's motions as they move toward opposite ends of the universe, apparently connected on some deeper ground.

This doesn't mean we're all the same or that we lose our individuality. It means our individuality flows from a much richer source—far greater than separateness could offer. In *A Scientist Explores Spirit*, George F. Dole and Robert H. Kirven explain this concept of "distinguishable oneness":

> While the form and the substance of an object can usefully be distinguished from each other, they cannot be separated from each other in actuality. . . . This principle [Swedenborg] extended to all of reality, insisting that nothing exists in isolation, and particularly that the Divine is essentially one in the special sense that it is wholly present everywhere and always, in an infinite number of distinguishable forms.[4]

4. George F. Dole and Robert H. Kirven, *A Scientist Explores Spirit* (West Chester, Pa.: Swedenborg Foundation, 1997), 66. See Swedenborg, *Divine Love and Wisdom*, §§14, 77–81.

Nor does it mean that we become lost in the whole, a criticism sometimes aimed at the mystic view. Blind conformity or living from a group mind—the mindset operating in cults, religious organizations, political parties, corporations and businesses, families, or any other group where dissension and individual expression are unwelcome—is a problem for humanity; but the mystic notion of individuality isn't the cause of it. If anything, it's the remedy.

If our source is in a reality that transcends all social groups and systems, then we have an alternative to social conditioning. We can be guided from that higher source. True, many religions interject institutions, doctrines, and traditions between us and these higher sources, as have families, political factions, and social classes. Even so, our rootedness in the whole is stronger. The "distinguishable oneness" living in us gives us the perennial option not to be stamped out of some social mold.

Star Trek: Next Generation wrestled with the issue of individuality and its relation to a whole through the image of the Borg, a mostly mechanical species functioning entirely from a group mind or hive mentality. What's missing from the Borg? What makes our condition different? Both Borgs and we have minds, and their group-mind, being computer-like, is superior in its memory-bank and speed of calculations. But the Borg's whole is a mechanical, one-dimensional whole. Unlike Borgs, we have the ability to tap higher sources, and more than one human has chosen to die rather than surrender the freedom to go where these whole-born impulses lead.

Swedenborg, for instance, affirmed free will—our power to choose which philosophy sources to follow. In his view, the two—whole-connectedness and individuality—go together: we're the whole individualized, and we're free to choose what to do with our whole-bestowed individuality. If we're the whole expressed, then we have the freedom of the whole embedded in us, the freedom to learn and explore, as well as to make "mistakes" while we're at it.

Moreover, if the whole isn't static but constantly changing, as the second root principle suggests, then being part of the whole means being in process. Processes unfold with endless variety without falling outside the whole. They're like the branches of a tree: branches grow in different directions as they respond to the sun and wind and yet remain one with the tree.

The fear that whole-connectedness reduces us to Borg-like, deterministically programmed robots may, as we discussed in the last chapter, lie with our assumptions about the nature of reality. When we think of the whole, the image of a totalitarian state isn't far from our minds—an image that Western religions sometimes encourage with notions of an all-powerful, judging, punishing God. We think of the universe in dominator terms, and then we assume that the whole systems in our lives—families, schools, religions, workplaces—should operate in the same monolithic, dominator ways, as if that's Godlike.

But what if that's not at all the way reality works? What if reality is a dynamic, open, self-organizing process like a tree, an image often used by indigenous traditions to symbolize the whole? The trunk does not exert power-over control of the leaves or punish them if they blow the "wrong" way, whatever that might mean. No two leaves are alike, and yet they're all one with the tree. The trunk continually supports the leaves, no matter what their shape, how tattered they become, or which way they blow. Even if they fall to the ground, they go into the soil, nourish the roots, travel up the trunk, and perhaps come out as new leaves.

Natural processes don't operate on a power-over, control model. They have a balanced system dynamics that both includes all the parts in a working unity and allows a diversity of expression, since that's what systems need to grow.

Not Whether to Connect but How

If free, open, creative connectedness better expresses our reality, then we have to rethink what being an individual means. It can't be about separating ourselves from our connectedness but rather about embracing connectedness in whatever ways are ours to do. Connectedness is a fact. It doesn't go away, no matter how separate we appear to be. Neither does imagining ourselves to be separate make us separate. In reality, our choice isn't whether to connect but how—what to do with our connectedness.

Connectedness is like breathing. We must breathe; we have no choice. But, as yogins explain, we can breathe in many ways—shallowly, deeply, long breaths or short, quickly or slowly—and each way of breathing has a different effect on our minds and bodies.

If our choice isn't whether to connect but how, then the more we know about our connectedness, the more creative we can be with it. Increasing our awareness of our connectedness expands our options for connecting.

In *Returning to the Teachings*, Rupert Ross recounts a teaching that an Inuit woman learned from her grandfather about connectedness. He told her that before she ventured out on Hudson Bay,

> she had to learn how to look for and understand how "the five waves" were coming together on any particular day. I'm not sure I recall each of those five waves accurately, because at the time I was trying to figure out what waves on Hudson Bay had to do with a justice system, but I'll give it my best shot. The first waves were those of the winds that were building but not yet fully arrived, the waves that would grow strong as a new weather system came in. The second waves were the ones left over from the weather system that was now fading, for they would still continue to affect the water even after the winds had gone. The third were the waves caused by all the ocean currents that came winding around the points and over the shoals, for they would present their own forces against the waves from the winds. Fourth were the waves caused by what Westerners call the Gulf Stream, and fifth were the waves caused by the rotation of the earth. Until you looked out and saw how all those forces were coming together, then developed some idea of how they would interact as the day progressed, it was not safe to go out and mingle with them.[5]

In a connected universe, we're in Hudson Bay all the time. Sensitizing ourselves to the waves moving within and around us increases our

5. Ross, *Returning to the Teachings*, 73–74.

options for responding. The more we're aware of connectedness, the more we act mindfully and creatively with our worlds. We see what's around us and appreciate its value to us and everything else. We perceive potentials—both as dangers and as opportunities—that we wouldn't otherwise see.

Since we're a culture that sorts things out in past, present, and future, we could use these categories to start noticing our waves of connectedness.

(1) *Past waves.* What is our history of connectedness? How has connectedness shaped and influenced us? All sorts of systems—biological, family, cultural, social, religious, economic, political, planetary, interdimensional, and spiritual—have become part of us, until it's not clear where systems end and we begin.

Come to think of it, which "we" are we speaking of? Not a separate, self-made "we" but the "we" that emerges from the interactions of all these waves on countless levels: family waves; school waves; media and peer waves; future-prospects waves; cultural fears and expectations waves; financial waves; religious, political, racial, and ethnic waves; and soul, spirit, and whole-born waves—all of which continue to splash inside us. Some waves have hit us hard, while others have lifted us up. We each have developed our own styles of deciding which waves to dive under, swim through, or surf over. Who we are now has emerged from all our choices about connecting.

Yet even that isn't quite accurate, since our ways of choosing have been wave-shaped as well. What feels most like us comes from the deeper levels of consciousness. Our essence waves—the ones that splash in us from the whole—express what's most abidingly us. These waves inspire us to make choices from our souls. The more outward waves shape our time-space personalities in this or that stage of life, community, and culture. These waves move us to adapt to the worlds around us.

From the most inward and essential to the most outward and impressionable, we're a convergence of more systems than we can name, and who we are now is a living history book telling the story of all these connections. To know how to put our individuality to good use in our worlds, we need to investigate how we got here. Which waves contributed to making us who we are and to making our connected world what it is?

(2) *Present waves.* What is the present of connectedness? How are we experiencing the universe of connectedness here and now? Are we aware of our connected being, and on what levels? In writing our books, for example, we feel more connected than we can process, which is the challenge of writing: which connections do we focus on? For instance, as we write, we're connected to:

- a vast and continually unfolding story of ideas that involves thinkers across time and culture and that brings in everything we've ever thought, read, heard, or studied;

- social and political issues, events, crises, trends, suffering—the whole drama of shared cultural, media-reported (and not media-reported) collective experience;

- our publisher and its team, which in turn connects us with the publishing industry—another story of connections;

- our readers past, present, and future, including commentators and reviewers;

- our families, friends, and colleagues, who nourish and sustain as well as challenge us;

- communities of acquaintances, whose perspectives and stories weave into our lives;

- the finances of writing, which for us, as for the vast majority of writers, turns out to be a not-for-profit activity;

- our personal experiences and day-to-day concerns, especially the upheavals, transformations, and restructurings we've experienced;

- our bodies, feelings, and emotions, including our inner journeys;

- our homes and all that goes into creating and maintaining them;

- collective consciousness, in which we're all participating, which includes consensus concepts of what's real and useful or not;

- collective unconscious, in which we're also all participating, which

includes a deep wisdom about human life, meaning, purpose, transformation, and destiny;

- other-dimensional consciousness, which, like everyone else, we catch
glimpses of or sense in fleeting insights—insights which nudge us to
look beyond personal and cultural norms.

And that's the short list. For example, did we mention nature, the
seasons, and the animals we live with and encounter on our walks? Or
our dream lives, which often help us with the writing? Let's not forget
how we're connected to language, English in this case, which brings its
own set of limits and possibilities, its own filters. Or the Internet and the
connections that blossom from there. And so on. We look like two separate people staring at computer screens miles from each other, but
we're connected every moment to the whole ball of wax.

(3) *Future waves.* How is our connectedness unfolding into the
future? Given our past and present experiences of connectedness, what
are our opportunities for creating new patterns? Which connections do
we strengthen, and which do we let come apart to be restructured? If
we're connected to all that is, everything we do affects everything else.

Every time we decide to purchase something, for instance, from an
apple to a sweater to a car, computer, or house, we send ripples into a
future that we're creating with our choices.

These material-culture choices reflect far deeper ones: What values
do we live by? What priority do we give our inner lives and emotional
well-being? What time, energy, and qualities shall we bring to relationships? Shall we have children, and how shall we raise them? What meaning does our connectedness to larger worlds hold for us—to
communities, society, nature, and the earth? Which philosophies make
sense to us and serve as good guides? Whatever our choices, they generate ripples that travel way beyond our circle of awareness. We're in the
Bay, and we're both receiving waves and sending them as we go.

Living from our fluid and changing connectedness doesn't diminish
us, then, as if we lose our distinctness; quite the reverse, it enriches us
in ways we can't experience as detached beings. The more we realize
how through-and-through connected we are, the more we have to
express, and the more creative we can be with our lives. We draw on a

reserve far more vast than we as separate entities could ever possess.

It's as if we're all tapping into a cosmic Internet of consciousness, but we don't know it, or if we do, we don't realize all that can be done with this resource. As we discover what's online in consciousness, both for expressing ourselves and for learning from others, we consciously engage with this unlimited resource, each in our own ways.

Living in the thirteenth century, Rumi used the image of a wicker basket in the ocean to illustrate our superabundant individuality as whole-connected beings, in contrast to the emptiness of living an individuality that's separate from the ocean:

A wicker basket sank in the Ocean,
and saw itself full of seawater, and decided
it could live independently.

It left the Ocean
and not a drop stayed in it.
But the Ocean took it back.

For no reason, the Ocean took it back.
For God's sake, stay near the sea![6]

"Looking up" to our relatedness takes courage, Plato's second virtue. We don't start thinking of ourselves as separate beings for no reason. As we've seen, connecting can be costly. Chances are we've been hurt by connections. In a reward-punishment world, any connection can go bad. Whether it's with families, teachers, peers, spouses, bosses, friends, employees, clergy, neighbors, the Internet if we download a virus, or even other drivers in traffic: connecting makes us vulnerable. We have reasons for isolating ourselves behind defenses.

As a philosophical strategy, this solution would be worth debating were it possible. As it is, connectedness is our reality, which means choosing a path of separateness isn't a genuine option. Yes, being con-

6. Coleman Barks, *Delicious Laughter: Rambunctious Teaching Stories from the Math-nawi* (Athens, Ga.: MAYPOP Books, 1990), 132.

nected makes us vulnerable, and what happens in the world of connectedness affects us profoundly, for better or worse. But ignoring our connectedness doesn't make it less our reality; neither does rejecting our
connections transform them, so that they're less threatening. We can't
opt out of being connected.

Instead, isolating ourselves sends the potential for harm through the
roof, because it shuts down the sensors that monitor what's happening
in the shared field. Indeed, we adopt the very strategy that makes our
connectedness risky. We become genuinely unconscious of harm being
inflicted, no matter who or what is causing it, because we adopt the cultural norm of going through life with our connectedness sensors
switched off.

We're leery of connectedness, though, for yet another reason, which
the second root principle names. "Looking up" to our relatedness takes
courage, because reality's connectedness is moving in continual flux.
Change is everywhere, nonstop, and universal. As Heraclitus said, it's the
only true constant in the universe. Chaos theorists of today agree. Being
connected means connecting with change—processes of both coming
together and coming apart, and usually both at once.

Insofar as we believe that our individual survival depends on keeping things as is, change is terrifying. In desperation, we resort to a control response. Granted, some changes fall within our control and
responsibility, but many changes don't. The wider our connectedness,
the less control we have. We can't control, for instance, what other people think and feel or how they develop. We can't control their path in
life. This lack of control makes it all the more scary, then, when changes
in others affect us. We react by trying to stop change, or if that doesn't
work, to bend it to our advantage. Fear makes us try to extend our
spheres of control beyond what is legitimately ours.

That's when we need philosophy to intervene. If change is reality's
nature, then we must think very carefully about our role in change. We
have to sort out which changes spring from the ground of our connectedness and which come from a model of separateness imposing control
where it doesn't belong. The latter category of change doesn't work,
not in the long run anyway. To move with change well and wisely, we
need to discern the larger dynamics, which give us clues as to why

change is occurring. Change that's controlled from a philosophy of separateness isn't going to harmonize with the big picture. Trying to manipulate change from a narrow perspective is like trying to control a few words in the middle of a sentence without knowing the whole sentence, paragraph, subject, or any other context. We might be able to control the words, but they won't make sense.

According to the second root principle, our challenge isn't to control change but to understand it within the context of connectedness. Only then will we have some idea of how best to respond—how to move with change and use what control we have to strengthen our connectedness.

We can't respond wholeheartedly to change, though, as long as we view it as going on "out there." To move with change, we have to change too. We have to allow change to go deep inside us, which means we have to develop self-concepts that include change as natural and necessary to our being.

Being in Process as Open Systems

We're back to the ongoing question of who we are. By expressing the universal truth of change, the second root principle suggests that change characterizes us too. We're connected to a whole that isn't static, which means we're not static either. Change is the story of our lives, and how we've danced with change makes us individual. No one's story is exactly the same.

If our deepest nature is change, the fear response, which we all have, is not entirely natural. It's not informed by our actual nature. As difficult as it can be for us, we actually need change and stagnate without it. Medical researchers combined with chaos theorists have discovered that a heart that beats too regularly is more likely to fail than one whose beat includes irregularities. Variations in beating rhythms keep the heart flexible.[7]

Change is our element. Taoists use the image of water in a stream.

7. John Briggs and David F. Peat, *The Seven Life Lessons of Chaos: Spiritual Wisdom from the Science of Change* (New York: Harperperennial, 2000), 64–65.

It's hard to move around in a river's swift current as a solid body, but not hard if we're the water whose nature it is to flow along. If it's our nature to live in process, somewhere in our bones we know how to do it. Everyone does. Somehow we know change won't be the end of us, indeed that we'd die if we tried to block change by keeping existing forms fixed.

Change is frightening, then, only when we feel cut off from our inherent change powers. Conventional wisdom contributes to this fear when it tells us that change is demeaning to our identity. Successful people, marriages, families, religions, as well as decisions and policies don't change; they've got it right. If we're supposed to be perfect—if perfect performance gets the reward—then change suggests that we've fallen short and must be improved before we can win the prize. We experience change as a slap in the face, a sign of failure.

As long as we interpret change this way, we're bound not to like it. Seeking perfect forms, we feel as if we're "in here" trying to keep our islands of perfection intact, and change is "out there" chipping away at us—a view that makes change maximally stressful.

Mystic and spiritual traditions don't start from an us-against-change premise, because they figure we can't get outside reality. If there's perfection, it belongs to reality. Our job is to move as we're moved from the whole, which means to allow change to work its purpose with us. Instead of positing us as separate beings existing apart from everything else, spiritual traditions assume we and reality are of the same stuff and engaged in the same process. Reality's nature is our nature too.

The big question, then, is: What is reality's nature? That's what these root principles address. If, as the first root principle states, wholeness is reality's nature, then we have the quality of wholeness too, and our being is embedded within the whole. We can't be tossed out of the whole, nor can we toss out each other. Within ourselves, we can't successfully toss out aspects of who we are either, whether it's our sexuality, intuition, or intellect, our sensitivity, assertiveness, or spirituality, or our pain, grief, anger, and sadness. Neither can we toss out our capacities to grow or our soul's callings to do so. Our wholeness includes them all.

Second, given that reality is dynamic and constantly changing, the strategy of trying to find security in fixed forms can't make us happy. We're not that sort of creature, because reality hasn't that nature. We can't be put inside a box and be expected to thrive there. We're like cats: being put in a box is good enough reason to try to get out.

A more realistic philosophy acknowledges our change-nature and supports it. Again, Buddhist philosophy teaches how to embrace the impermanence of things. Instead of looking to preserve fixed states that seem ideal, we connect with where we are and trust the wisdom manifested in each moment. We neither try to change things nor try to stop them from changing. Instead, we embrace "what is" by remaining present with what we're experiencing. Where we are now is the whole made manifest.

Buddhist nun Pema Chödrön writes that "this very moment is the perfect teacher, and lucky for us, it's with us wherever we are."[8] We're engaged in a sacred process, and remaining open to what's going on for us right now is how we honor and receive it. Pema Chödrön's point is that this is true whether we like what's going on or not, whether we feel happy or sad, pleasure or pain, benevolence or anger. The change process includes all phases, and all have a function in our development. Trying to accept some and reject others puts us at odds with the process. Change continues, but our experience of it becomes more difficult.

Given these two root principles, the only thing we can really say of ourselves is that we're beings in process moving within a dynamic whole. Many systems have brought us to this point and affected our development. Now we have choices as to how we'll move from here—choices that involve learning how to respond from our connected, changing being.

Learning to respond from our connected, changing being actually means learning what it is to be human—a core theme in many spiritual traditions. Life's challenge, they say, is to become "a True Human Being" by accepting our original, reality-given nature. In Confucian philosophy, for example, "the emphasis is on learning to be human, a learning that's characterized by a ceaseless process of inner illumination and self-transformation."[9] Just because we get our nature from reality

8. Pema Chödrön, *When Things Fall Apart: Heart Advice for Difficult Times* (Boston: Shambhala, 1997), 12.

9. Tu Wei-Ming, *Confucian Thought: Selfhood as Creative Transformation* (Albany, N.Y.: State University of New York Press, 1985), 19.

doesn't guarantee that we'll understand it or live from it. We can be walking in a beautiful garden but only see the dirt in front of our feet, especially if our cultural upbringing has taught us to look no farther.

The best way to learn what it is to be human, Confucians say, is to start with investigating ourselves—"self-cultivation" and "self-knowledge"—exploring who we are not as isolated entities but as a "broadening . . . of the self to embody an ever-expanding circle of human relatedness."[10]

Tu Wei-Ming, whom we're quoting here, is a Confucian scholar and long-time friend of Robert Bellah. In *Confucian Thought: Selfhood as Creative Transformation*, Professor Tu wrestles with the question of what it is to be individual from a Confucian perspective. He argues that we're fundamentally "open systems": "Asian traditions . . . perceive the self as a dynamic, holistic, open system, just the opposite notion of the privatized ego."[11] That's because Asian traditions conceive of reality as an ever-expanding "continuity of being": "the cosmos envisioned by Chinese thinkers is a 'spontaneously self-generating life process.'"[12] If reality is a dynamic, holistic, open process, then so are we. We're made of the same stuff and mirror the same dynamics. It's not that we have to stop being closed egos; we never really were in the first place. We just have to stop trying to impose that model on ourselves, because it does not fit. It's not true to our reality.

As open systems, we're subject to change beyond our control. We have to allow this and learn how to live with it. The control response, however understandable, is not the answer. Control requires closed systems, so that all the variables can be either eliminated or managed. But control exacts a price. Nothing new is allowed to enter, which means there's no opening for growth. Closed systems are entropic. Without sources of regeneration, they tend toward stasis, death. Treating families as closed systems, for instance, makes them stagnate. The relationships lose their quality of aliveness. People suffocate in roles that don't change. That's when family structures turn into psychological prisons,

10. Ibid., 57.

11. Ibid., 8.

12. Ibid., 9.

however well-intentioned or outwardly ideal. The sources of renewal have been cut off.

If we're open systems, which is how we stay alive and regenerate, then we have to relax the control response. Yes, we have some appropriate control over our lives, because we have choices. But making choices to keep things open and moving is different from choosing a closed model that shuts down change. Being open means allowing our connected being to guide us—to allow into our lives people, turns of events, and possibilities that we never envisioned—even if the consequences bring profound shifts, which of course they do.

Granted, open connectedness is a trip—sometimes a roller-coaster ride, other times a gentle float down a river. We can't control what comes to us, but we have a say in how we respond. We can support the processes going on within and around us, if need be to transform them, but never to exploit, damage, diminish, or drain them. For Confucian philosophy, doing this—participating in our connected, changing reality—in the ways that are ours to do reveals our destiny as individual human beings. It's what being an individual is all about:

> [C]ritical self-awareness, informed by one's openness to an ever-expanding circle of human-relatedness, is the authentic access to one's proper destiny. The reality of the human is such that an eagerness to learn in order to give full realization to one's heart, to know one's own nature, and to appreciate the meaning of humanity is the surest way to apprehend Heaven. Since our nature is conferred by Heaven, it is our human responsibility to participate in the cosmic transformation so that we can form a trinity with Heaven and Earth. Our proper destiny, personally and communally, is not circumspection; . . . our proper destiny is an invitation, a charge to take care of ourselves and all the beings in the world that is our abode.[13]

The more we know ourselves as connected, evolving beings—true open systems—the more we're able to nurture our spheres of related-

13. Ibid., 63.

ness. The open connectedness in us resonates with the open connect-edness in others, and a real, open exchange goes on, enriching both. Neither of us tries to make the other behave in ways that are contrary to our essential natures.

In wider social realms, accepting ourselves as connected and chang-ing makes us good stewards of our social systems. To function well, social systems must serve us, which means they have to reckon with who we are. If they ask us to be something we're not or to behave in ways that don't fit us, then we and our systems get out of sync, and sooner or later they move into the "coming apart" phase of change, as communism did in the late 1980s.

Specifically, if we're connected beings but social systems ask us to ignore this in favor of competitive separateness, or if we're beings of change but social systems ask us to remain fixed and static, something has to give. It's not a good fit. We won't be happy, and our unhappiness will become increasingly evident to the point of crises.

Since we know ourselves best, keeping systems healthy is our job. Only we know whether they're working for us or not. To this end, we have to resist being pushed, shamed, or intimidated into accepting struc-tures that one way or another violate who we are. Acquiescence serves neither our good nor the good of systems. To work well, our shared sys-tems—from very personal ones like marriages and families to big col-lective ones like corporations and governments—need to connect with our authentic reality. When the gap between our reality and the ways we're able to function in a particular system gets too large, the system tends toward collapse. The credibility gap is actually a survival gap—survival on both sides.

The remedy is self-knowledge. The more we're connected to our real nature, the more we can discern when systems are serving us, when they need adjusting, and when it's time for a complete overhaul, all the way down to a philosophy shift. Our honest self-knowledge makes us the stewards and watchdogs of our social systems, without which they can-not do their job well.

Professor Tu writes, "Those who are absolutely sincere in the sense that they, through ceaseless learning to be human, have become wit-nesses of humanity as such, 'can order and adjust the great relations of mankind, establish the great foundations of humanity, and know the transforming and nourishing operations of Heaven and Earth.'"[14]

Justice Nurtures Us through Change

All this lays the ground for making a profound shift in how we understand and practice justice. On an immediate personal level, a sense of who we are as connected and changing gives us a different approach to life. Instead of feeling driven by separateness or a desire to be perfect and fixed in outer forms, we live open to our intrinsic relatedness to people and processes, to the past, present, and future, to communities and nature, as well as to our own souls, our whole-moved being. We don't experience ourselves as cut off or isolated from any of these processes, because they're part of our existence. Neither do we feel bound to stay as we are. Instead, we feel free to move in webs of meaningful change that support us and others too.

This sense of who we are gives us a built-in knowledge of what crime is and why it's not a good choice. We live justice not from laws or other externally imposed "shoulds" and "shouldn'ts" but naturally from the inside out. When we feel how we're connected, we know that hurting others hurts us too. Our own connected being tells us from within what's just or not, what's harmful, and why harming is wrong. We'd no more inflict harm on the connected universe than drink DDT or dieldrin for breakfast.

Granted, outer laws can help us think through the complexities of connectedness. There's a place for them. We can easily bumble into doing harm unintentionally, since we're not omniscient, which knowing all possible connections requires. Laws serve as the warning voice on behalf of life's web: "Don't tread on me!" At their best, laws pass on a legacy of wisdom about what it means to live mindful of connectedness and how to evolve a fair balance of relationships. We don't have to reinvent the wheel as to what's likely to do harm, what's fair, and what supports healthy relationships.

14. Ibid., 63–64. Tu Wei-Ming is here quoting the Confucian classic *The Doctrine of the Mean*, translated by Wing-tsit Chan.

Laws also offer some protection from those parts of us which may not feel connected—which still smart from cultural programming or traumatic experiences—and may spur us to do harm without wanting to, "acting out" vestiges of old me-against-you conditioning.

Laws can help us, they have their role, but the seat of justice in society—the source of peace, harmony, and social order—lies with what mystics understand as true individuality: living attuned to our connected being, honoring and being creative with it, and then moving with our connectedness as it changes without letting fears of separateness throw us off track.

Ultimately, our connected reality, linked as it is to whole-born change, makes crime obsolete. The more we're mindful of who we are as connected beings, the less we're capable of harming our worlds of connectedness, even amid change. Whatever changes we experience have a common source that synchronizes our changes with what's going on with others. We move together in a dance rather than a fight or brawl.

The maypole dance symbolizes how this works. Each dancer holds a ribbon that's attached to the top of the maypole. When the dance starts, the ribbon keeps the dancers moving in harmony with each other. Even then, a good maypole dance can look chaotic to those who don't understand what's going on. As the dance progresses, though, a pattern emerges created by all the different colored ribbons woven on the pole.

In the grand scheme of things, mystics say, we're doing a cosmic maypole dance together, even though from our everyday perspective, life can seem like anything but. The potential for a brawl hangs over us, since the cultural norms that create patterns of separateness and alienation persist—the competition for rewards, the expectation of perfection, and the fear of being punished for mistakes, all of which leaves us feeling alone and isolated.

Shifting our models of justice can remedy this. Letting go of the punishment-reward concept removes a main cultural model that separates us. With it goes the expectation that we make no mistakes. Creativity involves "mistakes," as do learning and growth. "Coming together" and "coming apart"—the twin faces of change—means entering into a wilderness where we have no clear idea of what's right or best.

Worrying about whether we're making a mistake or not is no help, since our primary challenge is to engage with the process of change, wherever it leads. We need the inner freedom to explore what's unknown, and we don't need our courage blasted out of us with a fear of failure, missteps, and punishment.

Instead of asking justice to nail us when we go into the wilderness, we can ask justice to help us find our way. We need justice to put us back on our feet when we fall down, not flatten us even more. In other words, when we need help and don't know how to get it, we want a justice that's organized around providing what we need. Our philosophy of justice—and the institutions we create from it—should not only allow us to change but also support us in doing so.

When we make mistakes and harm our connectedness, we require a model of justice that shows us how to make things right again—that heals rifts and helps us learn how to connect positively. The entire field of restorative justice is responding to this call with a model of justice that gets in the trenches of human lives and feelings to do just that.

One highly successful example of this supportive role for justice finds expression in the drug court system, which has been growing over the past ten years. Drug courts are not about punishing people but about helping them heal from addictions—creating positive change. Judge Jeffrey Tauber, former president of the National Association of Drug Court Professionals, calls the process "therapeutic jurisprudence." Drug courts abandon the adversarial model to create a team of justice and law enforcement professionals working together to reclaim individuals from the grips of addictions. Their success rate is phenomenal: 85 percent—an astonishing figure given the tenacity of addictions. No other recovery program can match that success rate.

The assumption is not that people shouldn't make mistakes or experience relapses but that they will and that people need help then the most. The drug court model works with people through the agonizing process of breaking addictions, and it does this by creating a support community around the recovery, healing process. Yes, mandatory testing and the threat of jail serve as powerful incentives for people to stick with the program, but what many graduates say carried them through is the power of connecting with people totally dedicated to their healing and transformation, in spite of relapses. The care and support they experienced—the connectedness through thick and thin and the unwavering commitment to their change—made the difference.

Many of the professionals in the drug court system made the paradigm shift to therapeutic jurisprudence after they witnessed the bald disaster of the prevailing system. In most courts, the same sick, addicted, violent people cycle in and out of prisons with no sign of change except in negative, deteriorating directions. The punishment model fails to effect positive personal change for many reasons: (1) it fails to mend what's broken within; (2) it makes family and community connectedness break down further; and (3) it deals with our change powers as badly as possible, moving us in the worst imaginable directions, multiplying hurt rather than healing it.

Nurturing true individuality by rebuilding our connected being and tapping our potentials for change is the logical as well as practical alternative. Nadine Milford, for example, now the state chair for MADD in Albuquerque, New Mexico, got involved in the drug court system after her daughter and three granddaughters were killed by a drunk in a car crash. Through terrible tragedy, she experienced the dark side of connectedness, namely, that none of us is safe on the road when substance-addicted people drive. The dangers of connectedness moved her to dedicate her life to helping addicts heal—to making our connectedness positive. Like Thomas Ann Hines, her personal pain and grief led her to shift her model of justice from punishment to healing.

A nurturing model of justice works because it takes seriously who we are: we're connected, and we can change; indeed, we must change to be alive. Therapeutic justice looks at the "waves on Hudson Bay"—the changing connectedness that has contributed to who we are—and it uses these connections to build the good, to restore, and to heal. It acknowledges with Nadine Milford that we're in this together and that strengthening the web as a whole begins with nurturing individuals.

Given that we're connected beings with untapped change powers, our justice systems need to treat us as such, i.e., not in isolation, as if we're separate, or as if our problems are ours alone, and not as if we're permanently bad or flawed, unable to change. We're connected creatures, and change is our life's blood. Surely this nature of ours can be a powerful ally to creating a more just world, and surely our model of justice can do more to build on this nature and support it in creating real justice among us.

Using Connectedness to Change Shared Systems

So far, so good, but what about our social and cultural systems? That's the next logical question. If we're no longer accepting a model of justice that blames this or that person, we need to expand our categories for thinking about justice to address what throws our connected worlds out of balance—and us with them. Real justice must change the conditions that made us sick in the first place. Where did hurtful patterns start? To nurture us as individuals, therapeutic justice must create a nurturing nest, but to do that, it must confront the character of our shared systems. We and our systems are interwoven: they affect us, and we affect them, for better or worse.

This two-way flow gives us a power to change systems, since any shift we make registers on the collective. When we touch any strand of a web, the entire web moves. Our built-in connectedness to systems gives us a power to precipitate system shifts.

Unaware of these powers, though, we don't realize we have them, and they lie unused. We perceive ourselves as functionally helpless before the established might of existing institutions—that we're on the receiving end and have no leverage to shift their structure or course.

Gandhi and Martin Luther King Jr. broke through this perception by exercising the leverage that any connectedness offers, even though the leverage may seem minimal, in their cases, the leverage of the poor and socially rejected races. Both reformers pioneered not only cutting-edge social goals but also cutting-edge methods for getting there—methods that depended entirely on the powers we have by virtue of our connectedness. Our very connectedness to pain-making systems gives us the leverage we need for challenging and restructuring them. How?

To start, we have to make our experiences in systems known. If they harm us, we need to say so and skillfully enough to be heard. That's not easy when systems institute ways of silencing such messages. Even so, systems need feedback. In social systems, that means us: our experience within systems needs to be registered, so that our truth can contribute to the larger process of evaluating systems and changing them. Just as the tiniest nerves in our bodies can, if hurt, gain our attention, so too we have the power to make our experience of systems known, so that any pain we feel from them cannot be ignored or turned back on us through blame.

The trick lies in how to do this. We have to make system-engendered pain known without either paying a terrible price ourselves or destroying the good that's there in existing structures. It takes no small amount of vision, ingenuity, persistence, patience, skill, and above all courage to do this, since the method entails feeling the pain-making potential of systems to the fullest—bringing it to consciousness from the background of habit and conditioning.

Specifically, we have to speak our truth to those who don't want to hear it. Gandhi figured out ways to speak India's pain to the British rulers. He chose apparently innocuous actions, like burning identity passes or making salt, which didn't hurt the British but which focused the injustice of their rule. Like Gandhi, we have to find ways to speak our truth to people who identify with existing structures and don't welcome change.

Before we can do this, though, we have to speak our truth to ourselves, and that's hard to do as well. It's far easier not to face the pain we feel from being in systems. We'd rather blame ourselves, believing that something is wrong with us, that we're not good enough, or that we're not working hard enough, than say that systems are throwing us off balance. Part of the reason is loyalty: we become loyal to families, and then we transfer that loyalty to other groups. Loyalty is logical: we depend on our shared systems, and it's scary to think that they may not be all we want and need them to be. Another reason we resort to self-blame is that we can envision changing ourselves, but changing systems seems impossible. Blaming ourselves seems the more empowering route. Self-blame in general isn't empowering, but if it's a dodge to avoid a system problem, it's really not. When systems function out of sync with who we are, both we and systems need to change. We need to recover from ill-fitting patterns, and systems need to stop imposing models that don't fit us. Then we get somewhere.

When we finally name how we feel both to ourselves and others—how shared patterns are affecting us—we often meet with resistance: our concerns can be dismissed. Though our feedback is essential to the health, vitality, and integrity of systems, we're not usually thanked for giving it. Hearing the truth of system-generated pain is scary. It calls for change, and no one knows where that leads. Hard as it is to exercise these powers, though, we still possess them, because they're built into who we are. If we're connected to systems and we're changing, we have to change them too.

Justice traditionally has the job of intervening in situations that cause pain, and this role extends to correcting imbalances in our shared systems. By urging us to be true to who we are, healing justice gives us the courage to voice what we feel—to name system dysfunctions and craziness. We learn how to use our relation to systems as a conscious, active force for evolving them, and this makes us formidable reformers, whether we're called to reform our immediate family structures, local institutions, workplaces, corporations, or national governments. Size affects the degree of complexity and how long change may take, but it doesn't alter the principle. Change going on within us compels us to use our change-powers on our shared systems, so that they keep pace with our growth.

If we don't use our powers, our systems stagnate, and we suffocate inside them. Stuffing our pain so that systems can go on "as is" doesn't work. We stay unhappy, while systems roll on oblivious to their effects on us. Problems don't disappear as long as the structures generating them remain in place.

Many schools, for instance, remain committed to the reward-punishment, authoritarian model. Many marriages function on a model of ownership and control, with the loss of freedom, soul, and love that this model of connecting entails. Many businesses continue to set employees against each other in competition for merit raises or other "incentive program" carrots. Many corporations connect only to exploit. Many governments become obsessed with social order and grab more and more power to achieve it. Many professions—law, medicine, science, psychiatry—inflated by their expert status, abuse their authority for profit or power ends. And of course, many aspects of our justice systems fall short of their mandate to create a safe, peaceful, happy, and just world.

These systems aren't necessarily evil, but insofar as they function in these ways, they're not just. They don't do what Socrates and Plato said systems that embody justice should do, namely, support us in living our nature. Instead, their structures impose a philosophy that ignores our nature and shuts us down.

Sometimes, though, we're not even in sync with ourselves. When we join a group, the connection colors our perspective. Our inner life "entrains" with the group, which means we move in step with it, mirror and pattern it. We're drawn to groups precisely to use this entraining effect to help us develop, realizing that the group-mind will catalyze changes in us.

But unless personal change perfectly matches that of the group, we find ourselves in a fix. On one hand, we continue to grow in our own ways. We can't stop the process, since that's our nature. On the other hand, we internalize system biases, especially insofar as we identify our interests with the group's. If we sense something amiss that challenges group structures, the group-mind or system norm inclines us to dismiss our feelings. In work life, for instance, we speak differently as an employee than we do hanging out with friends. With friends, we speak our minds; at work, we're careful.

That's because we as individuals possess an inner freedom that makes it easier for us to see the truth and go with it. On our own, we can respond to calls for shifts far more quickly than can groups or institutions. As a result, our shared systems depend on us to keep them alive. They need our energy, vision, and change powers, even if everything about them resists a shift.

Nor is it a surprise that systems resist our efforts at change. We create institutions precisely to give us a certain measure of stability—to keep things "as is." It's not their job to pioneer change; it's not what we ask them to do, and it's not what institutions are good at doing. Initiating change is our job as individuals. Collective systems have the turning speed of the lumbering *Titanic*, whereas we as individuals can shift course at the first sign of danger. No wonder we and our social systems get out of sync when the channels for two-way communication break down.

How can we overcome the inevitable disjointedness between us and our systems? Two options come to mind.

(1) *Top-down Communication.* First and most common, established social institutions demand that we conform to them and put our objections aside. If we have concerns, we stuff them, so that shared systems stay on course, iceberg notwithstanding. If the official word is, "There is no iceberg," then there is none, and if we think we see something big and white and jagged off to starboard, that's our personal muddle-headedness. According to a one-way, top-down model, we simply must learn to accept that the way things are is the best way, and if we don't experience things that way, that's our problem.

This is when justice systems come to the rescue—in theory, at least. When we find ourselves asking, "What's one person against institutional might?," our justice systems go to bat for us, giving us a safe and fair forum for airing grievances against institutions. If we can make our case, the justice system has the power to compel society's systems to change, even the mightiest. In theory.

Unfortunately, our justice system isn't working this way, as Ralph Nader documents in *No Contest.*[15] When it comes to changing our shared systems, court processes all too often fail to do the job. On behalf of established systems with their substantial resources, lawyers find every loophole to direct blame and punishment at individuals, leaving the collective systems that generate crises unchallenged. Ills that suggest a need for altering systems are glossed over, while individuals take the heat.

But using justice to defend the top-down model is a disaster. Not only does it nail individuals who don't bear the full responsibility, but worse it lets the larger systems that are culpable off the hook. They must change to prevent future harms, but technicalities and legal maneuvers allow systems to remain as they are, no matter how dangerous they may be to the common welfare.

The *Challenger* space shuttle tragedy offers a good example. Individuals made bad decisions about safety and quality, but they made those decisions because of larger system pressures: concerns about not only

15. Ralph Nader and Wesley J. Smith, *No Contest: Corporate Lawyers and the Perversion of Justice in America* (New York: Random House, 1999).

budget but also schedules as well as public image. These priorities were set by people above the ones making the immediate decisions about the o-rings, which caused the disaster. Not the engineers but the political and economic dynamics of NASA and its relation to government, the public, and its contractors set the stage for lowered standards of safety and quality. Given the system, disaster was inevitable, if not the *Challenger* then on some other flight.

If we focus on individual culpability and not that of systems, then systems don't change, and more and more individuals pay the price. We preserve the top-down model, but we lose the justice of the system, i.e., its ability to meet the needs of the people in it. Published in 1516, Thomas More's *Utopia* stated this as clearly as ever. After recounting all the ways that social structures reduce people to poverty and keep them there—miserable, hopeless, and addicted—More writes:

> Until you put these things right, you're not entitled to boast of the justice meted out to thieves, for it's a justice more specious than real or socially desirable. You allow these people to be brought up in the worst possible way, and systematically corrupted from their earliest years. Finally, when they grow up and commit the crimes that they were obviously destined to commit, ever since they were children, you start punishing them. In other words, you create thieves, and then punish them for stealing![16]

Howard Zehr, who as a Mennonite draws inspiration from the Bible for an alternative paradigm of justice, argues that justice should be a progressive force in society, addressing the roots of crime by challenging social, economic, political, and legal structures. He does not see justice's role as one of defending the established top-down power structure.

Unfortunately, as in More's sixteenth-century England, defending the existing hierarchy is exactly what contemporary justice does. It throws its weight behind maintaining the established order with its one-

16. Thomas More, *Utopia*, trans. Paul Turner (London: Penguin Books, 1965), 49.

way method of communicating and with its scapegoating agenda to find single individuals to blame and punish. This orientation is inevitable as long as the state and its concern for order resides at the center of our justice systems. Individual well-being and strengthening the connectedness among us, especially if it means restructuring social systems, are not the priorities of "contemporary justice." Zehr writes:

> Biblical justice does not allow us to divorce questions of "crime" from questions of poverty and power. Justice is a whole. It cannot be fragmented. Corporations which commit fraud or which harm people through destruction of the environment are as responsible for their actions as are those individuals who commit murder. Moreover, the social context of crime must be considered. One cannot separate criminal acts or actors from the social situation which lies behind them. Unjust laws of whatever kind must be challenged.
>
> Contemporary justice . . . sees as its primary focus the maintenance of order. Because of this, and because it can separate questions of criminal justice from social justice, the order which it tends to maintain is the present order, the status quo. All too often, therefore, modern law is a conservative force. Biblical justice, on the other hand, is an active, progressive force seeking to transform the present order toward one which is more just. In doing so, it looks out especially for the poor and the weak.
>
> Contemporary justice puts the state and its coercive power at the center, as source, guardian, and enforcer of the law. Biblical justice puts people and relationships at the center, subjecting both law and government to God.
>
> Biblical justice, then, provides an alternative paradigm that critically challenges our own state-centered, retributive approach.[17]

(2) *A Two-Way Flow.* The second option for dealing with systems in

17. Zehr, *Changing Lenses: A New Focus for Crime and Justice,* 153–154.

need of change uses our connectedness to create a two-way flow of communication. We learn what it means to participate in our connectedness—to experience connectedness not as a yoke we passively accept but as a changing reality we actively create. Again, systems are connected to us as much as we to them. They need us; more, they need us healthy, happy, and functioning at our fullest, and this intrinsic connectedness gives us the power to change them. We simply have to develop the skills for exercising this power and using it wisely.

Fighting and confrontation, for example, though they assert a two-way interaction, have limited effectiveness, because they harden people into opposition. Based on a separateness philosophy—an "I'm-right/you're-wrong" approach—the options explored by this method are few. It starts off with only two options and reduces them to one. Given the complexities of life, that's too limited.

Gandhi and Martin Luther King Jr. made a paradigm shift beyond the opponent model by practicing nonviolent, noncooperation with injustice, inviting public dialogue on the values of society and its structures. They refused to be the other side—on the receiving end—of how top-down systems connected with them. In other words, they wouldn't tolerate connecting with their societies in the unjust ways that the established institutions demanded, and their refusal precipitated colossal system change. Their power lay not in a power to impose their order on society but rather in their power to refuse to be imposed upon—to reject any social, economic, or political order that violated their basic human nature.

Fortunately, more and more research is proving that one-way, top-down communication simply doesn't work, and one of the most powerful two-way methods emerging from this research is the art of dialogue. Dialogue shifts the model from a win-lose power struggle to a model in which all parties engage in learning. Dialogue puts us all on the same side, working together to gain a better understanding and to create mutual good.

To achieve these goals, we need to investigate all the perspectives involved: how others think and feel, what's going on with us, what we've experienced, how we perceive the situation, and how systems set us up to interact one way or another. We share our stories, fears, expectations, and hopes. We also investigate the underpinnings of our social structures—the philosophies involved. What messages are we getting from them?

Through dialogue, we seek to expand our view, assuming that, within the whole, there's a place, meaning, and value for everyone. By engaging everyone in learning, dialogue grounds change on a shared desire to understand our connectedness and to strengthen it.

Management consultant Peter Senge has applied a learning approach to business and corporate systems. In his book *The Fifth Discipline*, he explores ways to draw otherwise polarized factions together around the shared aim to understand real needs and seek real solutions. The way to do this is to understand how "structures of which we are unaware hold us prisoners."[18] Once we're aware of oppressive structures, we can start changing them.

But this is no small job. To do it, we need to pool our perspectives to find out what's going on system-wise, which Senge calls "the fifth discipline": team learning. The learning model calls us to transcend the philosophy of separateness for the practical purpose of solving problems and being creative. We come together to understand our connected experience and to see how our shared systems may be interfering with our abilities to change.

Given the challenges we face personally and as a culture, we need such open-minded, open-hearted joining. If we fry the earth or render it toxic and radioactive for light-years to come, who's right or wrong won't matter. If management refuses to listen to feedback from workers or consumers, the business will lose in quality and service. If students not only aren't learning but also aren't developing as whole and happy people, everyone in society will be worse for it. Deafness to individual voices calling for change will tell. When systems fail to serve us as we need them to, we're all in the same boat, suffering the consequences.

As a result, the larger job of justice has nothing to do with laying blame or pointing fingers. Neither does it have to do with justifying existing power structures. Its aim is to create systems that support the

18. Peter Senge, *The Fifth Discipline: The Art and Practice of the Learning Organization* (New York: Doubleday/Currency, 1990), 94.

best in all of us, and if this calls for changing existing structures, then that's what we have to do.

This constructive, learning-oriented aim for justice makes sense based on our experiences in personal relationships. If we want to live happily with someone, proving who's right or wrong won't help. Top-down, blame-oriented systems sabotage good relationships, whereas systems built on understanding, compassion, and mutual support create them. True justice helps us do the latter everywhere in our lives.

We don't have to wait until some mighty institution hits us with an injustice, though, to develop our skills at team learning and dialogue— i.e., to shift from a one-way to a two-way model of communicating. Personal relationships—marriages, families, friends, coworkers, and other everyday relationships—are the place to start. If we can't discuss our relatedness in our immediate spheres, we haven't much chance of doing it in the larger world. We won't have either the inner awareness or the outer skills to do it.

For instance, one partner won't know that some aspect of the relationship isn't working for the other until the other speaks up and says so. Hurt comes from not knowing this, so we contribute to our own hurt if we don't speak up. It sounds simple, and yet our experiences with one-way systems make us leery of establishing a free, two-way flow of communication. Our skills for dialogue aren't well developed, mainly because the culture's philosophy and institutions don't support them.

One book that, had it been written in 2 CE would have changed the course of history, not to mention married life, parenting, and childhood (although it never would have survived the book burnings), is *Difficult Conversations*, written by Douglas Stone, Bruce Patton, and Sheila Heen of the Harvard Negotiations Project.[19] Their insights, methods, and perspectives bring justice into our everyday exchanges by offering skills that move us beyond "me-against-you" to genuine "learning conversations."

What's the key? Two keys. First, self-awareness within: the success of dialogue depends on our knowing what we're bringing to conversations. Second, cooperative learning strategies without: dialogue progresses

19. Douglas Stone, Bruce Patton, and Sheila Heen, *Difficult Conversations: How to Discuss What Matters Most* (New York: Penguin Books, 1999).

with dogged commitment to learning about our connectedness on every level and to restoring broken connections—and this takes skill.

To consider the first key, self-awareness, we can't hold up our end of dialogue if we don't know where we are inside. We need to be clear about what we're experiencing in our emotions and around our identity issues, so that we know what's bothering us and what we need to express. Self-knowledge provides the foundation. Being aware of how we're experiencing people, relationships, and situations makes it easier for us to communicate clearly.

The more we're self-aware, the less likely we are to sabotage dialogues with pain, grief, anger, or other concerns that we haven't yet sorted out within ourselves. Self-awareness involves owning our feelings, accepting that we have them, and acknowledging that we have a right to have them, even if our reasons may be skewed by misperceptions that are later clarified. By knowing our feelings, they don't come tumbling out of us in confused or unhelpful ways, nor do they fill our minds so totally that we misperceive what others are communicating. The more we're self-aware, the more we can bring our feelings into dialogue authentically, openly, mindfully, and powerfully.

Self-awareness also enables us to stay focused on what matters most. We're not so easily sidetracked by triggering details. The more we identify what's bothering us deep down, the more we're genuine in our communication, speaking straight from who we are as best we know ourselves. We're aware of our own masks and defenses, and we've learned when we need them and when we don't. By inhabiting our own hearts and minds, we're able to speak from them.

In turn, dialogue deepens our self-awareness: the process makes us learn more about ourselves. Others mirror back to us what they hear us saying, and this enables us to see ourselves in new lights. Through learning conversations, we discover how our ways of expressing ourselves affects people. The experience promotes deeper self-awareness on all sides.

The second key—learning about our connectedness and developing skills for doing this—seeks mutual good by focusing on how we connect. With the second key, we accept connectedness as a fact and from this ground work to strengthen *how* we're connecting. Generally speaking, this means we don't budge from the learning model by slipping into blame or defending fixed positions. Instead, we become students and stewards of connectedness, as well as artists and architects of it. We learn skills for tending our connectedness as we would a garden. For example, before assuming we've understood what people are saying, we check by expressing what we heard and inquiring whether we've got it right—that is, whether what we heard is what someone else intended.

Or, instead of blaming a single person or event for a problem, we consider the system context and how we may have contributed to whatever went wrong. This isn't to shift blame to ourselves but rather to abandon the blame model altogether by seeking whole-system solutions that require everyone's participation. Whereas blame creates defensiveness, learning about systems and everyone's contributions to them puts us all on the same side, working to improve our ways of connecting.

Another skill that serves learning is listening openly and without preconceptions, also without preoccupation with what we want to say next. We open our hearts and minds to receiving what others want to express and understanding it as best we can. Again, this is a skill to be cultivated, since we often feel unheard and impatient to say our piece.

Two-way communicating requires many other skills, and stresses and difficulties present opportunities for learning them. Problems shed light on our ways of connecting, spurring us to become more mindful and creative about the process.

What's really happening through learning conversations is that we're learning how to change: change our self-concepts, change our views of others, change our relationships, and, ultimately, change our shared systems.

Indeed, practicing learning conversations in our everyday, personal affairs lays the ground for creating learning societies, namely, a cultural atmosphere in which we're actively committed to evolving our shared structures by listening to each other's experiences of connectedness. Learning societies don't find top-down, one-way models of communicating useful. Top-down communicating is like going to a movie and refusing to listen to any but one actor's lines; we wouldn't get the whole story. Learning societies depend on dialogue, for how else can we communicate to our institutions about our changing needs?

Our skills at dialogue make learning societies possible, whether they're small ones like marriages, families, and friendships, or bigger ones like churches or businesses, or really big ones like local school systems, international corporations, or national governments. Again, size doesn't change the principle. What matters is the quality and mode of connecting: one-way or two-way. Even the biggest systems depend on us to tell them what's going on, whether they're open to hearing us or not.

For instance, if we've had a traumatic, painful past, we do society no good by saying, "The past is the past. Let's put it behind us and get on with living the good life." Whatever pain we've endured didn't happen in a vacuum. Unless the structures that caused pain have changed, pain will recur. Webs of connectedness contributed to our experiences, and we need to look at these webs so that they don't cause further pain to us or new generations. If we quietly, resignedly accept how we're treated, systems won't change. Finding ways to talk back to systems—and to turn up the volume until the message is heard—was Gandhi's and King's genius.

It isn't easy, though. Systems are good at marginalizing people, disconnecting groups from systems, and then doing whatever they want to them—exploiting, oppressing, and killing them. This is what the U.S. government has done to the First Nations, which should have been our first alarm bell. Hitler did the same to the Jews, and the Chinese have been doing the same to the Tibetans. But miraculously, in spite of unimaginable pain and suffering, some groups survive. And now First Nation teachings about justice are slowly revolutionizing the very justice philosophy that did everything to destroy both their people and their teachings.

That's at least partly because the truth wins out, although it may take centuries to do so. A justice system that honors the truth of who we are is going to win out over a justice system that denies our truth and flies in the face of our real nature. In America, the justice system claimed it could protect the nature of the white race by denying the natures of the red, black, and yellow races. It didn't work. Aside from the blatant injustice of it, the nature that retributive justice denies is human nature. As a result, it oppresses everyone.

In speaking the truth of who we are, we cut to the heart of shadow justice's weakness and the weakness of every system based on it. Through the apparently innocuous method of dialogue, we call for a justice that fits us. We speak the truth from our core, and the process of telling our stories has a powerful, transforming effect. Not only do we feel heard and our pain acknowledged, but also our experiences catalyze others to share their truth. Our real nature comes into the justice process as a factor that won't be denied. We learn how systems actually function in people's lives, in contrast to the sanitized pictures those in charge often paint. In the process, we start rethinking social norms and values in light of who we really are. In 1955, Rosa Parks' refusal to surrender her seat to a white man and go sit in the back of the bus because she was black catalyzed awareness of racial discrimination and a refusal to tolerate it. Her actions spoke who she was, and the system had to change as a result.

As social systems change, human pain—however wrong it was that anyone suffered it—proves not for nothing. When we use pain to learn about our ways of connecting and to change them, we give pain meaning. Archbishop Desmond Tutu commented that the local hearings of the Amnesty Committee of the Truth and Reconciliation Commission in South Africa "were occasions when those who had hitherto been treated like rubbish could stand up and have their stories heard."[20] The result was a new, democratic South Africa with Nelson Mandela as its head.

By investigating our nature as individuals—connected beings engaged in change—we call for a model of justice that functions as our friend and helper, not as an accuser, as we undergo shifts. And as we develop the skills to communicate who we are with our systems—to voice our truth as we experience it—we give our shared systems the information and impetus they need to come up to speed with us. Our self-knowledge compels us to practice justice as a force for social transformation. To use Paul Ray and Sherry Anderson's term, doing justice to ourselves by embracing our root nature as connected and changing

20. Nigel Biggar, "Can We Reconcile Peace With Justice?," *The World of Forgiveness* 2, no. 4 (May 1999): 27. This publication is produced by the International Forgiveness Institute, P.O. Box 6153, Madison, WI 53716-0153.

beings, we exercise our power to be "cultural creatives": we create a new justice, and with that, we create new shared systems to serve us, patterned on who we are.[21] This is what being an individual is all about.

21. Paul H. Ray and Sherry Ruth Anderson, *The Cultural Creatives: How 50 Million People Are Changing the World* (New York: Harmony Books, 2000).

SEVEN

Cycles of Change

Changes occur in cycles or patterns. They are not random
or accidental. Sometimes it is difficult to see how a particular change is connected to everything else. This usually
means that our standpoint (the situation from which we are
viewing the change) is limiting our ability to see clearly.

—*The Sacred Tree*

C HANGE IS THE GREAT CONSTANT in the universe, but it's not
linear or uniform. Change means variation and diversity,
involving processes that sometimes appear one way, sometimes another.
Each stage has its own character, with pluses and minuses. In cycles of
change, processes take many forms. Acorns don't look like oak trees,
nor is it easy to imagine summer in the dead of winter. And while we're
at it, how does a sweet little boy turn into Darth Vader, or more common, a helpless infant into a functioning adult?

What makes change challenging is its unpredictability, as any parent can tell us; and yet, amid the confusion, we also sense an order operating, even if our categories aren't up to telling us what that order is.
Whether we're considering our own changing reality, that of people
and personal relationships, of communities, of business, economic, and
political life, of nature, or of consciousness in general, change continually surprises us. It never quite fits our concepts.

On good days, that's the fun of it: we're not likely to get bored in our
journeys to understand reality. On other days, "fun" isn't the word that
comes to mind. Just when we think we've got things figured out, change
bursts through. Happily surprised or disappointed, affirmed or challenged, we change with the changes going on within and around us, and

we find ourselves thinking, feeling, and responding in new ways.

The history of science is filled with such cycles of change, as Thomas Kuhn described in his classic 1962 book *The Structure of Scientific Revolutions*.[1] When we're ticking along within an established paradigm (a given model of reality), we feel we've got change under control. We can predict what's going to happen, and when something doesn't go the way we expect, we can usually find a way to make it fit our theory. If we don't like the direction of change, we can make things take a different course, like diverting a stream to water some crops.

But as we go along, we come to the limits of a model. Anomalies start appearing—situations that our paradigm can't explain or help us resolve, no matter how hard we try. Perhaps we find that, by diverting a stream, we've made a mess of the ecosystem, destroying the habitats of the birds that eat the bugs on our plants, not to mention depriving our neighbors downstream of water. Or, if our paradigm doesn't sensitize us to these issues, perhaps we come to the waters of the Mississippi or even the ocean, and our best methods for controlling streams don't work. Somehow, somewhere, reality breaks through our paradigm's limits, and when it does, beefing up the old paradigm won't help.

That's when we have to ask ourselves whether the old paradigm's way of responding to reality—in this case, trying to control streams— is the best response. Is our paradigm barking up the wrong tree? Imprisoning people in crisis, for instance, comes to mind as a wrong tree that our current social paradigms are madly barking up. This response calls in the cavalry to eliminate the troublemakers, instead of first understanding the processes going on and then working for mutual good, which usually involves self-examination and self-transformation on all sides. If we've tried one response for all it's worth and things still aren't working, it's time to change models.

This is the beauty of paradigm cycles: we're not stuck with one. Life's experiences chip away at the most entrenched ways of thinking, loosening their hold on us and launching us into new cycles. We seek a new paradigm, build new ways of living based on it, come to its limits, and then

1. Thomas S. Kuhn, *The Structure of Scientific Revolutions* (Chicago: University of Chicago Press, 1970).

embark on another paradigm shift. Whatever other cycles of change we may experience, we can be sure we're at some phase of the paradigm cycle—personally, socially, culturally, and globally.

Through these cycles, we take with us what we've learned, but we also integrate it with a more encompassing framework. For instance, the emerging paradigm of restorative justice carries along from the retributive model a deep concern for the safety of citizens. It shares a commitment to social order by reducing or ideally eliminating crime. But it addresses these concerns not just in the short-term frame of emergency restraint but more in the long-term frame of prevention by restoring broken relationships, healing traumatized psyches, and transforming social systems so that we don't produce new generations of unhappy, desperate, violent, soul-damaged people. The valid concerns of the contemporary paradigm of justice are not only embraced but also heightened on the new restorative model.

What spurs change cycles, though? Why can't we just stay "as is"? Again, we experience cycles of change because that's reality's nature, and we're part of reality. We're moving with all that is, or rather, all that is moves, and we express that moving, because we can't get outside it. Cycles of movement are our nature and being. Even God may well be subject to reality's change nature.

That's an odd way of speaking, though, unless by "God" we mean something like physicist David Bohm's concept of the holomovement.[2] The holomovement signifies "all that is" engaged in a continual process of self-expression. The whole is an unbroken unity, and yet it's not static. Reality is always evolving and coming into being, and yet from another view, it operates as a complete and coherent whole. Paradoxical as it seems, there are reasons to assume that this is how reality works—not only spiritual reasons but also reasons from physics. The universe hangs together as a coherent unity, and yet it's also moving in constant flux.

To try to identify the most fundamental phases of reality's changing

2. See David Bohm, *Wholeness and the Implicate Order* (London: Ark Paperbacks, an imprint of Routledge and Kegan Paul, 1980), especially 150–157 and chapter 7, "The Enfolding-Unfolding Universe and Consciousness," 172–213. Also see David Bohm, *Unfolding Meaning: A Weekend of Dialogue with David Bohm* (London: Ark Paperbacks, 1985), chapter 1, "The Implicate Order: A New Approach to Reality," 1–32.

nature, Bohm discussed the holomovement's cycles in terms of two processes: unfolding and enfolding.

(1) The *unfolding phase* brings the unseen whole into specific, tangible expression. To use Bohm's terms, unfolding draws out the implicit or "implicate" order—order that's embedded in the whole but unseen to us. In its unfolding side, the holomovement manifests itself in time, space, and consciousness through forms we see and experience, including our own forms. These visible forms are the "explicate" order of nature, society, and the world. The explicate order is all the stuff of life.

(2) The *enfolding phase* reintegrates the explicate order with the whole context. Whatever goes on in the explicate world has a meaning and value within a larger process. Forms don't come into expression and then get stranded out there on their own, alone and lost. We're always embedded in the whole and can't get outside it. The holomovement's process is our process. By revealing everything as moving within the whole, enfolding reintegrates "the many" with "the one," affirming how everything has its own meaning and importance within the larger dynamics.

To use an analogy, the unfolding phase is like our writing this book, making a hidden order of ideas floating around in collective consciousness explicit. The enfolding phase is like your reading it, because then you integrate what's expressed with all that you know and have experienced. You put this book back into some sort of whole meaning that is greater than this book but that is also somehow enhanced (hopefully) for your having read it. Enfolding completes the cycle. It brings everything back to the core idea that we're all participating in the holomovement and can't get outside it.

Linking Bohm's ideas with the two sides of change, we can say that unfolding brings development, a coming together of things to reveal new forms of wholeness. Enfolding, on the other hand, brings disintegration. The view of forms as separate entities dissolves as forms reintegrate with their whole context. All the trappings that go with the appearance of separate forms start falling away. Enfolding is like death, not the meaningless annihilation concept of death, but death as Rumi described it, namely, as coming home to who we are by reuniting with the whole, our origin and essence, leaving behind anything we don't need.

Development and disintegration are equally "necessary" and "always connected," according to mystic teachings, because they're two phases of one process, like breathing in and breathing out. We could think of the one process as "life," "evolution," "consciousness dynamics," "spirit, soul, and psyche birth"—or perhaps as "cooking up some meaning-filled, order-expanding worlds," and, at least in these parts of the galaxy, we have a messy enough kitchen to show for it. Words don't do the trick in describing holomovement processes, but they get us thinking.

However we characterize the process, it has these two phases, and if we understand them as complementary—as working together as two facets of one process—it's easier to deal with them. As the second root principle states, "Both of these kinds of change are necessary and are always connected to each other." Together they create the cycles identified by the third root principle.

Unfolding and enfolding describe cycles of change from the per-spective of the holomovement, the whole. But we're not the whole, which means we don't have the whole view. We don't see things as God sees them—one of the more tedious features of being human. Because our perspective is limited, we don't see the whole order moving through the phases of change, which means it's easy for us to get bewildered and lost. We get caught up in the midst of change—standing in the middle of a storm rather than watching the weather channel's radar tracking of it as we sit snugly on the couch.

From our "coming-to-you-live-from-the-storm" perspective, we see things *coming together* as development and then *coming apart* again as disintegration. Even if we sense the holomovement at work, the storms of change can seem scary and chaotic. We feel as if we work like hell to build things up, only to see them all fall apart.

That's how change gets a bad name, since, however much we may welcome development, disintegration—the coming apart of things—throws us for a loop. Dissolution is like cleaning up after cooking or like discovering the anomalies that catapult us into a new paradigm cycle. We know we're moving into a phase of intense change and not the phase where the course is clearly charted. Things we've worked hard to create in our experience start passing out of it.

Hindu philosophy emphasizes the disintegration phase through its symbols of destroyer deities. Perhaps the most famous of these is Kali, a consort and incarnation of Shiva (Shiva represents a core aspect of the Godhead, perhaps comparable to the Holy Spirit of the Christian Trinity). Kali is depicted as blue-black and wearing a necklace of skulls, and she's in charge of dissolving and destroying. For all her fearsomeness, however, Kali is revered as a manifestation of the Divine.

Nor is this devil worship. Kali is also known as the Divine Mother. She embodies the wisdom that giving birth also means removing whatever isn't integral to the new stage. Kali's job is to clear the space for something new to emerge. If the old isn't first cleared, the new can't develop. When a baby is born, for instance, all the paraphernalia that kept him or her alive in the womb must dissolve—the water, the placenta, even the umbilical cord must go. If a baby doesn't leave the womb, he or she will die. Similarly, pain in the body suggests that a body's healing system is working overtime trying to remove dead cells, clearing the space for new tissue to grow—a fitting image for Kali's meaning.

Clearing away—releasing old forms—isn't evil; it's a cycle of reality. Although we naturally grieve the passing of old familiar models and ways of life, grief is part of dissolution too, working to restructure our emotions and psyches in response to change. Grief is how we let go while also taking with us the good, integrating it with our being. Alongside grief, we sense the value of this phase to some larger process, even if we're not sure what it is.

The real problem we have with the coming apart of things is that, like the wrathful, scowling, skull-adorned Kali, it's not pretty. Few people warm to it, and no wonder. It's painful, confusing, totally disruptive to all that we've established, and disorienting. Dissolution thrusts us into the uncertain and unknown and, as far as we can tell, makes a complete mess of our lives.

Even in somewhat predictable ways, we experience dissolution as deranging. For example, when teenagers want to move beyond their child/dependent/obedient role so they can develop a more adult, autonomous, responsible identity, both parents and teenagers have their less-than-charming moments. Learning to be autonomous and responsible involves making some fairly stupid decisions along the way. Dissolving old roles in family systems isn't fun.

Indeed, "misbehaving," "acting out," "self-sabotaging," and even predatory crime all function on the dissolving side of change. Something isn't working, some paradigm needs to be uprooted, and the behavior shouts this message. When a pattern or structure needs to be dissolved, if it doesn't "come apart" one way, it's going to come apart in another—more publicly and messily, with a roar rather than a whisper.

The key is learning to embrace dissolution, to value it for what it is and to go with it, to allow it to work in our lives, painful, challenging, and rending as it is. Ideally, as soon as we get the message that it's time for dissolution, we can engage in the process—whether it's restructuring belief systems, laws and policies, habits, businesses, relationships, families, marriages, or social, economic, or religious practices. The less we resist dissolution and embrace it as a natural and needed process, the less we experience it as traumatic. Even walking would be agonizing were we to stiffen our bodies and tense all our muscles, trying not to change our position. We need to let our spirits go to move with change, for then it's least painful. Moving with dissolution, we allow it a place in our lives as something that's reality-based, destructuring though it is. It's part of our built-in change cycle, which means it's for the good. It keeps us connected to our most fundamental life process—the holomovement at work.

That's the ideal, but it's hard to practice. When our lives kick into this phase, no matter what triggers it, changes come so fast and furiously that we have trouble processing them all. Big changes work this way, and the bigger the change, the more dissolution goes with it. But at least we have a sense of what's going on. No matter how traumatic it feels or how confusing it becomes, we're not out of reality's order. Some change cycle is at work, not on the sidelines but center stage. Reality is unfolding its whole-connected story through us and our lives, but it's on the reintegrating side. We're being reintegrated with a larger order than we were experiencing, which means the more narrow order we were accustomed to is being called to shift, to destructure so a wider order can unfold. It's natural, it's logical, but it's also hard and often painful.

A close friend in grief over her dog's death—coming on the heels of divorce, the death of both her parents, and the dissolution of her professional group practice—said that the experiences, painful as they were, put her in touch with what's most important in life. The dissolutions focused her entire being on real values, grounding her in a way that was profound. Change—big change, in-your-face change—has that effect.

Nor does the dissolving side of change mean we'll lose all the good we've gained from earlier cycles. In paradigm change, we can choose what to take and what to leave behind. Even if we lose all else, what we've learned in our souls comes with us. The character we've shaped need not be lost. Amid the upheavals, the disintegration phase is actually full of promise for what's to come, because it clears the way for adventures that start with individuals but expand to the whole culture and, because of connectedness, to the whole world.

Social Systems and Our Changing Relation to Them

These two phases of change shed light on our evolving relation to our social structures. Social systems do two things for us: they both support our development and resist it. This sounds worse than it may be. We experience an analogous relation to the earth when we walk on it: the ground supports us but resists us too, in that our feet don't sink through. Sand is more difficult to walk in precisely because it offers less resistance.

The support side, like the development phase, we understand and welcome. Again, it's the resistance side that we find more difficult, because of the fear and pain involved. It's harder to see how resistance helps us because of all the "coming apart" that it triggers. And yet we know that without resistance, we wouldn't launch into the next stage. We'd drift along "as is," whether the status quo serves our development or not.

For all its confusions, resistance helps us know ourselves. We may not know what we want in life, but we have a sense of what we don't want. We feel where we don't fit, and the experience of butting up against obstacles makes us confront who we are, what's ours to do, and our capacities for change. We forge our identity out of the struggles we have with resistance.

Because of this dynamic, we tend to sort the universe into "us" and "not us." Positing a "not us" serves learning. If we want to explore ideas, it helps to talk to people who think differently. The Dalai Lama says that he learns more from his enemies than from his friends. Bumping up against someone who doesn't see things as we do accelerates learning, because it precipitates change. We're forced to reconsider how we think—to challenge our assumptions, to revise them, or even to give them up. Inevitably, our perspective expands.

Social systems function as the "not us" that we share in common, though we each experience this "not us" differently. Ideally, the "not us" of our social institutions gives us enough support so that we grow and develop, but it also gives us enough resistance so that we're challenged to stay flexible, to rethink our ideas, to test what works and what doesn't, and thereby to let Kali loose on our personal paradigms, dissolving attitudes we're ready to outgrow.

To suggest an analogy, social systems (at their best) function like an eggshell for a forming chick. Being inside a shell makes a certain stage of development possible. Nor is the shell totally impermeable. It can't be a totally closed system, or the chick would die. The shell needs to let in oxygen but to resist letting the white and yolk spill out. The shell has a tricky role, complicated all the more as development continues. At some point determined by the chick, the shell must break open or the chick will die. If the shell is too soft, it will break prematurely, but if it's too hard, it won't break at the right moment.

Paradigms function similarly. They provide a matrix for development, a supportive womb for certain ideas, theories, methods, and practices—indeed, for a certain phase of consciousness—to develop. They do this by resisting nonconforming perspectives, explaining them away as unsupportable or irrelevant. Paradigms tell us where to put our focus, which is exactly what we need. We can't focus on everything at once. Paradigms sift and sort the "bloomin' buzzin' confusion," to use philosopher William James' phrase, so that we focus on those areas of connectedness that seem most helpful, meaningful, interesting, and otherwise germane to where we are.

But there's a price: we don't focus on other connections—our paradigms resist our doing so. Even when anomalies build to crises, paradigms can be tough eggshells to crack.

So, too, for social structures: they provide a cultural womb for raising children, expressing our talents and abilities through work, enjoying life through communities, creating just societies, and doing all the things that fill our lives with meaning. For our own growth and happiness, we need social systems to provide cycles of support and resistance, but like the chick, we're the ones to say when it's time for a social-system shell to break, so we can move beyond a given stage. If a system no longer serves us—if it even threatens to smother us—we have to break it open. It's time to ask Kali to help us do some dissolving, or if we prefer Kuhn, to do some paradigm shifting.

Whether social systems are serving or smothering us depends on where we are in our change cycle. But where are we? In the midst of change, we're not sure. On top of that, how does our personal change fit within larger, collective cycles?

The third root principle acknowledges that these questions, as critical as they are, aren't easy to answer. The perspective of "us" is too limited to see what's going on with "not us" or how we fit in: "Sometimes it is difficult to see how a particular change is connected to everything else. This usually means that our standpoint (the situation from which we are viewing the change) is limiting our ability to see clearly."

What do we do, then, especially since we're the ones who must take the lead in breaking through social-system shells? The best response to this quandary comes from a spiritual perspective: we have to trust our own inner guidance. On the deepest levels of our being, "us" and "not us" aren't split. Through our essence, we're connected to all that is, to the one body of humanity, earth, evolution, and consciousness. "Not us" isn't out there; it's "us" too. We're of one movement, participating in a process that harmonizes our changes with the whole dynamics.

Because of this connectedness, the order of the whole is embedded in us, and we can access it from within. Our "soul's code," to borrow psychologist James Hillman's phrase, has a sense of how the whole-meaning moves in us, coordinating inner with outer shifts. It's there to guide us, and its messages come in many forms—through feelings, intuitions, synchronicities, desires, as well as events and our reactions to them. To know when to do what—to develop or dissolve, to stay inside a shell or to peck out—we need to connect with our deep inner awareness, because it has the perspective to sense what's moving in larger change cycles.

The hitch is that our cultural paradigms aren't oriented either to cycles of change or to our following our inner voices in moving with them, and so we're not used to doing this, and we cannot count on society's blessing or help. As a result, we're by and large not attuned to our soul's code or inner knowing. By force of cultural habit, outer concerns take precedence, emphasizing obedience to rules and conformity in pursuing socially accepted rewards. Social strictures and moral conventions drown out inner voices. Even to know whether to peck or not, we must shift paradigms in how we're guided. Inner leadings need to carry more weight with us than conventional wisdom grants them.

Intuition Systems

For thousands of years, cultures around the world have developed systems for calling on our inner resources to orient us in cycles of change. We're not the only culture in history in which it's easy for people to get lost in externals and the change-resistant weight of the status quo. Intuition systems address these problems, helping us get back in touch with what's within, our innate whole-knowing. Modern sciences, or more accurately, aggressively materialist scientists, have dismissed these systems as superstitious nonsense, but then, intuition and consciousness haven't been their focus.

The Chinese *I Ching* means, in fact, the "Book of Changes" and has been relied on for millennia as a rich source for discerning an order of meaning behind changing appearances. Astrology has served as another powerful, cross-cultural symbol system for mapping cycles of meaning, personally and collectively. Indigenous rituals and divination systems use nature—e.g., the four directions, colors, animals, and the elements of earth, air, fire, water, wood, metal—to shed light on the hidden meaning behind outer changes.

In the context of this chapter, we're interested in intuition systems for two reasons. First, we're interested in how these systems work— how they "think," so to speak. We want to know this because we need to explore different ways of thinking about justice—different reasoning processes.

Second, we're interested in where intuition systems apply their way of thinking, namely, to exploring cycles of soul, meaning, and consciousness. We want to know this, because these are the very areas excluded from our current ways of thinking about justice, and yet they touch the essence of human life.

First, as to how intuition systems think, most use a system of symbols that represents cosmic reality and, with it, cosmic order. Assuming that we're made of the whole and mirror our origin, they suggest that the best way to explore the larger order is to explore ourselves. As we do, we'll come to know reality's change cycles from the inside out. We won't perceive ourselves as separate from change or at the mercy of it, as if change is "random or accidental." Instead, we'll feel held in a meaningful order that's unfolding through us and our experiences for our good.

To help us feel how we're intimately engaged with cycles of change, intuition systems offer different symbols for thinking about how development and disintegration operate in our lives. Their images describe archetypal processes, so that we don't have to either reinvent the soul-journey wheel or feel alone in what we're going through. The symbols get us thinking about our lives in terms of universal, core processes, so that we see things in larger contexts and look for meaning beneath the surface of events.

Since meaning is determined by context, intuition systems cast our lives and experiences in the context of universal, whole-oriented symbols. For example, card decks and numerology use numbers, which are universal. The tarot uses universal myths and images: e.g., death, justice, the world, the lovers. Philosopher and mathematician G. W. Leibniz (1646–1716), who introduced the concept of cybernetic systems, observed that the *I Ching*, through its concepts of yin and yang, builds on the universal binary principle—off and on—which has since become the foundation of computer science. Astrology uses the solar and stellar systems—the galactic context in which the earth moves—to symbolize a cosmic order of meaning, while indigenous systems use the entire book of nature and life: the earth, the seasons, animals, plants, the sky and clouds, dreams, everything we experience. For them, the whole universe is talking to us about meaning, and why not? As the holomovement manifests everywhere, it is.

These are whole-minded systems, designed to help us develop a whole-minded perspective. In light of Bohm's ideas, intuition systems map the holomovement's unfoldings and enfoldings as the context for all of life, and the symbols they use provide the tools for doing this.

Now for the practice. Assuming a synchronicity to the whole—a connectedness of meaning that operates everywhere, micro to macro, inside and out, and that's always changing—intuition systems help us explore how a whole-born message might be speaking through the specifics of everyday life. The idea is to investigate cosmic order as it's reflected in our experiences: "as above, so below."

Because their symbols are rich with possibilities, intuition systems don't tell us what the meaning is. Rather, their symbols put us in touch with our own inner resources. They feed our inner reflection with images that can be interpreted on many levels. By triggering soul-searchings, intuition systems spur us to ponder how reality's whole-order flows through our lives (unfolding), and with this awareness, how our lives have a meaning within the whole that we may not otherwise see (enfolding). By engaging us in cycles of inner change, they help us entrain with larger cycles of change at work.

Symbol systems for analytic, rational modes of thinking work similarly, the difference being that their symbols refer not to meaning but to quantifiables, and their thought processes don't use intuition but rational analysis. So what's in common? The way of moving from the whole system to the individualized expression and then back to the whole context.

Mathematics, for instance, presents a system of numbers that covers all conceivable quantities. The numbers and how to combine them are math's elements. With arithmetic, algebra, or some other branch of mathematics, the whole system of calculating can be focused on specific situations: how many bananas are on the table? If we buy this house, how much will our mortgage payments be? How far is it to the nearest galaxy? How many dimensions to this particular universe we're in?

Or consider chemistry. Through the periodic table, chemistry organizes all known chemical elements according to their atomic structure. With a universal system, chemistry gives us a way to understand any specific substance, from a brick to an apple to a cloud. These disciplines use symbols that represent the whole on a given level (math or chemistry), and by so doing, give us the means to understand what's going on in specific instances.

In other words, intuition systems aren't as crazy as the dominant cultural paradigms, both religious and scientific, have made them out to be. They follow the exact logic of unfolding and enfolding: from the whole to its specific manifestations back to the whole again. They simply apply this way of reasoning to nonmeasurable, nonquantifiable aspects of life.

This raises the second interest we have in intuition systems, namely, that they use their way of thinking to map what matters most in life: changes in meaning through personal and social growth. They're designed to shed light on individual and collective consciousness shifts by awakening our innate ability to sense the deeper currents and to move with them.

With our inner link to the whole awakened, the larger order embedded in us talks to us, and we hear it. Intuition systems sensitize us to cycles of change, whether these cycles bring changes in our bodies and psyches, marriages and families, careers, or philosophies and culture. Whatever the sphere, we learn to trust the process—that it's part of reality and that it's not out to destroy us. Whether we're experiencing development or disintegration, we sense how we're connected to processes that are the whole at work and that call us to move with them.

From this whole perspective, intuition systems invite us to explore how our personal changes may be linked to everyone else's. We're all engaged in the holomovement, each in our own ways. By offering a holistic perspective, intuition systems make us conscious of how we're participating in universal cycles. What we're going through is intrinsically connected to what everyone else is experiencing as well, and intuition systems help us see how this works.

Holistic, Cycle-Oriented Thinking and Justice

Thinking in cycles of change makes us rethink our paradigm of justice, because the current paradigm doesn't "think" this way at all. Shifting our philosophy of justice means shifting not only *what* we think but also *how* we think—our reasoning processes. The first two root principles invite a shift from fragmented to holistic thinking, from separateness to connectedness, from thinking in terms of fixed states to thinking in terms of change and processes.

The third root principle pulls it all together by suggesting that our reasoning must continually move from the whole to the part, back to the whole in cycles. We come together in certain ways, which means we come apart somewhat from what we were before, and then we develop in new ways, which means dissolving in other ways, and so on. This isn't about success or failure but simply about our life's process.

As a result, reasoning in cycles is truer to our reality, which means it's more effective in helping us. Understanding cycles of coming together and coming apart, we have more compassion for ourselves and each other as we move through different stages. We better understand what's needed at each stage and how to support what's happening. When someone is going through dissolution, for example, it doesn't help to measure the person against development standards or to try to keep things as they were. A different phase is at work, but just as important. Our reasoning process allows us to think in sync with the cycles we're experiencing. We don't ask that we be somewhere we're not but instead value the phase we're in and honor it by finding ways to move with it.

Applied to justice, when we focus the whole body of laws or whole set of cultural values on a situation, we unfold from the whole to the part, from the general to the specific. That's how we arrive at judgments and rulings. But from a cycle way of thinking, we can't stop there, because that's only half the process. What's missing is the reintegrative side: how do the people, the parts, fit with larger processes? More to the point, how does our view of a specific situation integrate with our larger sense of what society is about, what life is about, and where we want to go with both? Since we're talking about humans and not atomic particles, the enfolding side of reasoning raises questions about meaning and transformation: how can we use the cycles that we all go through to serve a larger purpose of healing and good, which must be their nature to do? That's why we go through cycles: some larger, whole-born, soul-code order is urging itself on us.

The current justice paradigm doesn't "think" this way at all. First, it thinks atomistically in "lone assassins," single, bad people who must be blamed, then removed from society or eliminated altogether. It doesn't see Thomas More's point, namely, that society creates thieves and then punishes them for stealing. If it did, our justice system would work harder to address the system roots of crime. It would figure that, if one person behaves selfishly or destructively, the entire system contributes to this behavior and plays a role in perpetuating it because each part tells us something about the whole. Our justice system would monitor our whole-system connectedness and would spearhead system change when individual pain indicates the need of it.

Second, our current justice paradigm does not "think" from the whole to the part back to the whole with the aim of seeing how situations can turn to create a larger good. It doesn't see individual crises as opportunities for moving through cycles of change into growth and healing. Instead, it "thinks" in boxes for the purpose of putting people in them and leaving them there. Yes, it reasons from the whole body of law (laws, rules, legal precedents) to specific cases, but it does this to place people in preset categories (guilty or not guilty of violating law "x"), so that the machinery of justice can slap on a verdict and move on to the next case—end of story. As historian Vine Deloria Jr. states, the current justice paradigm thinks in "homogeneous solutions," or one box fits all who go in it. It's blind to the uniqueness of circumstances, blind to change cycles, hence blind to the potentials for positive change. The aim is to execute the law according to the boxes, to impose the appropriate punishment, and to do this like a machine.

Third, our current justice paradigm "thinks" blindly and machine-like for a reason, namely, so that justice can be "fair." Justice must be blind to our differences, blind to our growth, inner processes, and meaning. Ignoring all that makes us different presumably means we'll all be treated the same. And yet the reasoning falls short: if who we are is ignored and only the deed acknowledged, who is the justice for? If it is not adapted to us—if who we are is left out—it can't possibly fit us, in which case, how can it be fair? It's not for us but for a box.

Moreover, if who we are is ignored, then how can justice work with us to create positive change? For the current justice paradigm, this isn't the issue. As long as we're being "fair" according to objective, mechanistic standards, it doesn't matter whether the "solutions" do any good—

whether they make people or communities better for it. This is the problem with one-sided thinking. It applies the ideal of fairness in an abstract way, failing to address the larger question of whether what we're doing makes sense in a larger context. Does what we're doing achieve some good beyond adhering to abstract standards?

Fairness is a right ideal, but blind justice doesn't achieve it. Our needs and circumstances vary widely, as do our resources for getting help. Treating a millionaire, an insurance company, a middle-class employee, a young person from Pine Ridge Reservation, and a poor kid off the streets "the same" will not produce the justice we seek, because it's not possible to do, given the realities of differing social, cultural, and economic circumstances.

Challenging the notion that justice can or should be blind, Howard Zehr explores the practical impact of the blind-justice way of thinking. Instead of creating fairness, he argues, it perpetuates inequities, keeping the existing social and economic hierarchies in place:

> Justice is imaged as a blindfolded goddess holding a balance. The focus is on equity of process, not of circumstances. The criminal justice process claims to ignore social, economic, and political differences, attempting to treat all offenders as if they were equal before the law. Since the process aims to treat unequals equally, existing social and political inequities are ignored and maintained. Paradoxically, justice may thus maintain inequities in the name of equity.[3]

What ways of reasoning do we want our justice systems to put into practice? If we don't want justice to be about rooting out the bad apples among us, stereotyping us, labeling us, putting us in boxes, and in the process, ignoring our changing needs and circumstances in order to be fair, then how do we want justice to "think"?

Whatever ways of reasoning we give our institutions of justice, those are the same ways that we'll apply to ourselves and our families, in schools, as well as with friends, colleagues, and coworkers. How we

3. Zehr, *Changing Lenses*, 79.

arrange our formal system of justice affects how we deal with justice issues informally. It sets up a model that we goes with us everywhere.

That's why we need to choose our justice thought processes carefully. Given the force of the restorative justice movement, it's clear that the one-sided, mechanistic reasoning is unsatisfying. What's our alternative?

The American Way

Being American, we look to the judicial model defined in the Constitution as a guide. The Constitution is a profound document, inspired in large part by Native American wisdom and experience. Many Founders, Benjamin Franklin in particular, were inspired by the Great Law of Peace, the democratically principled model of government that has existed for centuries, even millennia, among the Nations of the Northeast.

Most Europeans firmly believed that principled democracy was a noble ideal but impossible to implement, except on a small scale. The Swiss model of a loose confederacy of small territorial cantons was the most that could be successfully ventured, or so they thought. By proving this belief wrong, the Iroquois Confederacy, as it's called, gave many Founders hope that a democratic form of government could work on a large scale and endure through time.

Not surprisingly, the degree of influence of the Iroquois Confederacy on the Founders is a matter of debate, and along predictable lines. Establishment European American scholars minimize the influence, if they acknowledge any at all.[4] To this, John Mohawk responds in his article "The Indian Way Is a Thinking Tradition":

4. Scholars traditionally point instead to John Locke as the leading pioneer of human rights and liberty, overlooking the facts that he was a shareholder in the Royal Africa Company, a major slaving company of the time, and that Locke wrote justifications of the slavery of Africans, using the Bible as one of his sources. Locke envisioned liberty only for white men.

For the American Indian point of view, for whom rights and liberties were not based on race or gender, we recommend several books, starting with two by Bruce E. Johansen: *Forgotten Founders: How the American Indian Helped Shape Democracy* (Boston, Mass.: The Harvard Common Press, 1982) and *Debating Democracy: Native American Legacy of Freedom* (Santa Fe, N. M.: Clear Light Publishers, 1998). *Indian*

As they were standing on the shore watching these people come ashore, the Indians carried with them a tradition of meeting and democracy, of free speech, of free thinking, of tolerance for each other's differences of religion, of all those things which got attached to the Bill of Rights. All those things that we say are truly American were born on *this* soil generations before Columbus ever set sail.

If the Indians hadn't been on that shore, if there had been no one living in the woods, do you really believe that all those ideas would have found birth among a people who had spent a millennium butchering other people because of intolerance over questions of religion, killing people who suggested that the earth was not the center of the universe, burning people who said that the sun was only one little thing in a whole bunch of stars, killing people who said they did not want to send their taxes to Rome? Do you think that that tradition would have found its way, by itself? I think not.[5]

Given the First Nations' alternative to Europe's arrogance of power, racism, sexism, and institutional authority, the tragedy is all the greater that the Founders succumbed to the eighteenth-century European mindset that white, propertied men should have exclusive control of the affairs of state, expressed in the Constitution's exclusion of Native Americans, African Americans, women, children, and landless citizens. To their credit, at least the Founders left the door open through future

---

Roots of American Democracy, edited and introduced by José Barreiro (Ithaca, N. Y. : Akwe:kon Press, Cornell University, 1992), further substantiates the influence of the League of Six Nations and traces the history of interaction between the two cultures. On the creation and history of the Great Law of Peace among the People of the Longhouse up to the present, see Paul Wallace, *The White Roots of Peace* (Santa Fe, N. M.: Clear Light Publishers, 1986, 1994; originally published Philadelphia, Pa: University of Pennsylvania Press, 1946). Current leaders of the Haudenosaunee speak out on their spiritual ideals of government in *A Basic Call to Consciousness*, edited by Akwesasne Notes, 6th ed. (Summertown, Tenn.: Book Publishing Company, 1995).

5. José Barreiro, *Indian Roots of American Democracy* (Ithaca, N.Y.: Akwe:kon Press, Cornell University, 1992), 25.

amendments to right these wrongs. What the Founders produced was not perfect. Even so, a great light, hope, and as yet unattained ideal shine through.

The Constitution begins with the famous system of checks and balances among the three branches of government—the legislative, executive, and judicial, set up in that order by the first three articles. This is more than a bureaucratic flowchart. It represents a way of reasoning about justice, and if we muddle it up, we miss how our system of government is designed to "think." When branches get confused about their own functions, they try to do each others' jobs, leaving their own functions undone. Violating the Platonic philosophy of justice built into the structure of the Constitution, the different branches don't do what's uniquely theirs to do.[6]

As far as we can tell, muddling happens with all three branches. In passing laws requiring mandatory sentencing, for example, the legislative branch tries to tell the judiciary how to do its job. But the judicial branch has its own murkiness of function.

Specifically, if the judicial system is simply a matter of mechanically fitting people into preset legal boxes and passing sentences accordingly, why would we need a judicial branch at all? It's a mechanical exercise. With legal machines, the ideal is to leave as little room for judgment as possible. Why wouldn't the legislative (Article I) and executive (Article II) branches suffice? On the box paradigm, the legislative branch creates the boxes for society, while the executive sees to it that everyone goes in them and stays there. What then do we need a judicial branch for?

Sensing a lack of distinct function, the judicial branch has gradually assumed powers of the legislative, in that a judicial ruling comes to function as if it were a law. Courts make decisions about abortion, corporate monopolies, the legality of income taxes, school segregation, and virtually all social issues. These decisions come to function as law, standards that are binding.

But is this a good method? Is the judiciary where we should be

6. In our discussion of the reasoning process embedded in the structure of the Constitution, we are indebted to Christopher Largent, a philosopher, scholar, and Denise's ex-husband, for he spent a great deal of time studying this subject.

establishing such de facto laws? Many judgeships are not elected but appointed offices. The process of arriving at these decisions is not democratic. But even more, the method is not appropriately universal; it's specific, namely, a specific response to a specific case. A ruling is not a law, because it is a ruling about a specific and ultimately unique situation.

True, legal precedents have their value; like laws in general, they mean we don't have to reinvent the legal wheel every time a similar case comes up. And yet it's dangerous to have rulings stand in as laws. They weren't designed to be such. The two thought processes—one for formulating general laws, the other for passing rulings on specific cases—must remain profoundly different. The pressure of turning rulings into laws or treating them as if they were causes the judges to disregard the uniqueness of specific situations for fear of setting a bad precedent. When that happens, the individual pays the price. The "justice" that people receive is not for them or adapted to them but for some abstract, hypothetical "other" in the future.

Hampered by precedent concerns, the justice process cannot "unfold" from the whole system of justice all the way down to the specific case. Instead, its reasoning processes get stuck at the level of generality and can't go beyond it. The result is what distresses us in the culture: an abstract notion of justice but an actual experience of injustice in relationships, situations, institutions, and court decisions—all in the name of justice. Bound by legalities and precedents more than by a mandate to create human well-being, those working in the justice systems find themselves unable to create justice—i.e., to offer an experience for everyone involved that feels like the real thing, case by case.

To be a separate branch, the judicial must "think" differently and independently; otherwise, it easily slips into the mindset established by the other two branches, and then what good is it either as a check on them or as offering something distinct? If a dictator type in charge of a family, school, government, or business allowed an independent judicial system that genuinely thought differently, it would challenge unjust rules and tyrannical policies for executing them, and the dictator model could not stand. That's the power of a true judiciary. And that's why, when it's compromised, we should worry.

Indeed, many people are worried, for our courts have not acted with this independence for a long time, perhaps not since Chief Justice Marshall opposed President Andrew Jackson's forced march of Native Americans to Oklahoma, which President Jackson did anyway—an impeachable offense infinitely worse than presidential indiscretions. To avoid such standoffs, presidents and other executives pick candidates for judgeship on whom they can rely to back them up—an "old boy's club" co-opting the system of checks and balances by turning the judiciary into their political backfield. The constitutional spirit of checks and balances, intended to create independent thought in the service of justice and the common good, is lost.

What then is the unique job of our judicial system? What is its constitutional calling? And what is a distinctly judicial way of thought and reasoning?

The Haudenosaunee Way

Our Constitution's link to the "People of the Longhouse" or Haudenosaunee (the Onondaga, Seneca, Mohawk, Cayuga, Oneida, and Tuscarora: the League of Six Nations) lends remarkable insights into the judicial branch, its role, and its distinct reasoning processes. Unlike European political philosophy, indigenous philosophy seeks not only equal representation but also equal participation of gender in their system of government—and precisely for the purpose of creating a system of checks and balances.

Because of differences in roles and responsibilities, the genders think differently. Whereas men attend to the business of today, women, given their child-rearing roles, typically have an eye to the future. The Great Law of Peace expresses this priority: "In our every deliberation, we must consider the impact of our decisions on the next seven generations." By integrating women into their system of self-government, the Haudenosaunee use gender differences to incorporate genuinely different ways of thinking into the everyday workings of government. How? In several ways.

Since the inception of the League of Five Nations (perhaps 500–1000 years ago, but also perhaps much longer), both women and children have voted—that's a given—and mothers vote additionally on behalf of their infants. By contrast, in the United States, the Nineteenth Amendment granting women the right to vote didn't pass until 1920, and though Senator Robert Kennedy advocated lowering the voting age, children and teenagers still cannot vote, although their future is at stake.

But beyond representation, the Haudenosaunee's entire judicial function is entrusted to women, specifically to the clanmothers. The Haudenosaunee system of checks and balances builds on a balance of gender perspectives, granting women the power to nominate leaders, to check male leadership, and to impeach men if need be. Men serve under the watchful eye of women—the wise elder clanmothers, who hold foremost in their minds the well-being of future generations. The male way of thinking takes the lead, while the female way of thinking reflects on what is wisest long term, interjecting caution, restraint, and redirection when necessary.

Both practical wisdom and a wider, more holistic philosophy underlie this choice to include both genders in government. Rupert Ross gives an image of the Aboriginal approach to gender balance in the traditional custom of wives walking twelve paces behind their husbands—an image that makes any feminist's hackles go up. But all is not as it seems, as Rupert Ross discovered. From his European categories of hierarchy, Ross naturally assumed that this indicated an inferior status for women, until he talked it over with an Ojibway friend:

She began by asking me to remember where those old people had spent their lives, to imagine walking a narrow trail through the bush with my own family. She asked me to think about who I would prefer to have out in front, my wife or myself, to be the first to face whatever dangers the bush presented. In one way, she said, it could be compared to wartime. "Where," she asked, "do you put your generals? Are they out front or are they in the rear, where they have time to see and plan and react?"

Viewed in that way, things appeared to be the opposite of what I had first supposed. Instead of occupying an inferior position, the woman was seen as the organizer and director, while the man out front was counted on for his capacity to take action under her direction.[7]

Still thinking in hierarchy, Ross then suggested that women are the generals and men the foot soldiers. His friend explained that this was not it either. Hierarchy is a European model, not theirs. According to Aboriginal philosophy,

all things have a purpose, and unless these are fulfilled, the strength of the whole is weakened. The jobs of the husband and of the wife were just that, their jobs, assumed on the basis of their having different skills and abilities—different *gifts*—none of which had to be compared with each other in terms of worth or importance. Comparison itself was seen as a strange thing to do.[8]

We can't imagine a better expression of what Socrates and Plato may have been driving at in *The Republic*, when they suggested that justice means all of us doing what's ours to do. If for some reason we don't, the whole system suffers and drifts out of balance.

What holds for families also holds for communities, the state, nation, and world. We're all needed, as are our distinct gifts and contributions. Excluding women, more than half of the population, from the process of self-government has been as unwise as it is unjust. Our government has suffered from a one-sided perspective in the extreme.

Gender Differences

Unfortunately, this balance of gender in government was too much for our Founding Fathers, steeped in patriarchy as they were and enjoying absolute legal control over women, whose status under English common law was as male-owned property. John Adams summarily dismissed his wife Abigail Adam's eloquent letter appealing to him that he "Remem-

7. Ross, *Returning to the Teachings*, 52.

8. Ibid., 53.

ber the Ladies." She asked that women be given liberty from their husbands' unlimited power over them—"That your Sex are Naturally
Tyrannical is a Truth so thoroughly established as to admit of no dispute." She also argued that women should receive equal rights and representation in the government—"we are determined to foment a
Rebellion, and will not hold ourselves bound by any Laws in which we
have no voice, or Representation."[9]

Indeed, this difference on equal gender representation and participation between the Great Law of Peace and the U.S. Constitution may
well be one reason that the former's influence on the latter is so seldom
acknowledged. Had it been more widely known, surely white women
would have been inspired to lobby for the rights and responsibilities
that Indian women exercised.

The power of women in First Nations is illustrated by a famous
story about the 1804–1806 Lewis and Clark expedition, when the
"Corps of Discovery" struggled over the wintry Rocky Mountains and
stumbled weak and starving into a Nez Perce community. The expedition carried with them great wealth in guns and supplies, which the
chiefs and warriors noticed. The Nez Perce men made the no-brainer
business decision to kill everyone in the expedition and claim their
goods, when an old woman heard of the plan and objected. Apparently,
she had been kidnapped by another tribe and sold to some whites, who
fortunately had treated her well, until she found her way back to her
own people. Because the whites had been kind to her, she argued, the
Nez Perce should be kind to these white strangers. She saved their lives,
for on her say-so alone, the community reversed its decision and instead
fed the white strangers and let them stay as guests through the winter.
Had her single female voice not been honored by the chief and all the
warriors, costing them as it did great material wealth, the Lewis and
Clark expedition would have disappeared without a trace.

The choice to exclude women from government and to reject
women's lead in the judicial branch has affected the evolution of how we
understand justice. Not only has the message gone to all women that

9. Philip B. Kurland and Ralph Lerner, ed., *The Founders' Constitution*, Vol. 1: *Major Themes* (Chicago: University of Chicago Press, 1987), 518–519, see also 520.

their perspectives have no place in government, but also our judicial systems have been deprived of the unique thought processes that women bring to justice. As it turns out, women conceive of justice differently from the way men do—a pattern the Haudenosaunee put to good use. Women can provide the truly different ways of reasoning that a judicial branch requires to be an effective check and balance for the other two.

Carol Gilligan's 1982 landmark book *In a Different Voice: Psychological Theory and Women's Development* explores this difference. She found that male psychologists, notably Lawrence Kohlberg, defined justice according to male standards (white European male, at that), never considering that there could be any other, and then in their studies judged girls' developing sense of justice to be deficient. It did not occur to them that girls and boys might think about justice in different but equally valid ways. Judging girls to be deficient on a male scale is like saying an orange is deficient because it isn't red like an apple. Obviously, women psychologists could just as easily judge boys' developing sense of justice to be deficient when measured by female standards. The better approach would be to investigate the differences and explore how both might be needed to create fair and balanced relationships.

What is the difference between men's and women's concepts of justice?

Before we go further, we're moved to weigh in with those who believe that what's characterized as men's or women's views is largely influenced by how the culture raises men and women to think. Yes, there are biological differences, of course—who has children and raises them, as well as who has how much of which hormones—and the roles that go with the biologies influence how we think, as the Haudenosaunee observed. But cultural variations on how gender differences are handled—how we're raised to respond to our biological differences—suggest that cultural programming is a major player here.

Beyond both biology and culture, though, individual men and women can and do think differently from their gender's patterns. We respond to family and cultural influences in our own ways. We cannot predict from biology or culture how a given man or woman may think. For instance, although men's views of justice traditionally fit the retributive model and women's the restorative, the new field of restorative justice is being pioneered by both men and women. So much for people being stuck in gender patterns.

Since men control our judicial systems, though, men's traditional concepts of justice are what dominate our institutions and cultural beliefs. According to this model, justice is a game of following rules and rewarding or punishing people accordingly with blind impartiality. Its dispassionate legalism inspires the campaign crowd-pleasers to "get tough on crime!" or to pass the "three-strikes-and-you're-out!" laws or to champion the death penalty. On the traditionally male view, justice is an abstraction: a strict standard of universal principles that admits no exceptions—"the rules are the rules"—never mind who made them and stacked them to favor whom. Real people with real needs and circumstances are secondary to meeting abstract legal requirements. As philosopher Alan Ryan put it, "judges and rulers must 'do justice though the heavens fall,'" not allowing personal worth to enter into their decisions. The law is the law—that's the male model.

In the culturally male view, the moral problem of justice is "how to exercise one's rights without interfering with the rights of others."[10] This is important because men's primary concern in personal development, as the culture defines it, is to develop personal autonomy as a separate identity. John Wayne style, the self-made man doesn't need anyone else, making intimacy and interdependence unnecessary or even threatening to that attainment.

"Needs," in fact, becomes a bad word. If we need something from someone, we can't be separate and independent. And if others need us, they become a burden, creating a dependency on us, which again compromises our separateness. The natural flow of mutual help and support in relationships within a context of mutual respect and freedom gets gummed up by the agenda of maintaining separateness. More than that, we pretend that we don't have needs, that we're self-made and independent, self-contained floating islands. The businessman's boast of making it on his own ignores the contributions of many people on his way to the top.

10. Carol Gilligan, *In a Different Voice: Psychological Theory and Women's Development* (Cambridge, Mass.: Harvard University Press, 1982), 21.

This male perspective causes us to act in the world of connectedness as if connections don't exist except to be exploited. Small wonder that we organize our justice systems around the problem of how far people can go at individuating themselves into increasing separateness without getting into trouble by hurting someone else. The questions for justice then become ones of how much hurt can we tolerate from separateness, and which hurts are so bad that inflicting them counts as crimes.

Built into this model is the further assumption that there's one correct judgment that can be made about who's right and who's wrong, who went too far, who did what to whom, and who should pay. There's little allowance for differing points of view, each having its own validity. On a male model, saying that one person's view has truth to it directly implies that another's view, if different, must be false. One party must be judged right and the other wrong.

Women, by contrast, develop their sense of justice from a primary concern for connectedness: how are we related, how can we nurture good relationships, and how can we avoid harming them? Justice isn't about separateness but about interdependence and acting responsibly mindful of our connectedness. As one young woman put it, justice is about "how to lead a moral life which includes obligations to myself and my family and people in general."[11] Gilligan goes on to say, "Thus while Kohlberg's [male] subject worries about people interfering with each other's rights, this woman worries about 'the possibility of omission, of your not helping others when you could help them.'"[12]

Framed in the context of connectedness, women's sense of justice is about caring for people and attending to their needs, even if it means bending the rules. A rule constructed for one circumstance may not apply to another, and even if it does, it may not serve human good, in which case the point of following rules is defeated. Rules don't exist for themselves but for us. When they cease to serve us, it's time to devise new ones.

Because women tend to believe that helping people is more important than letter-of-the-law obedience and correctness, they're likely to

11. Ibid., 21.

12. Ibid., 21.

seek innovative alternatives to the standard black-or-white, guilty-or-innocent dilemmas that traditional justice poses. These alternatives involve talking things out, arriving at mutual understandings, and finding solutions that strengthen personal well-being and relationships. What good is following the letter of a rule if it damages a relationship? Again, we have rules to protect relationships. When they fail to protect, rules lose their legitimacy, and we're no longer bound to follow them. It's time to find our own way.

For women, therefore, justice isn't an abstraction imposed on us but something that's worked out in specific interactions, with each case having its own character and subtleties. Justice is a response to our changing experiences that's focused on healing what's gone wrong, restoring broken relations, and making things right all around: win–win rather than win–lose. If our priority is on taking care of our connected worlds, win-lose doesn't work; it divides us and creates hostilities. To strengthen our connectedness, win-win is the way to go.

As to the assumption that there's one right answer when it comes to justice issues, women don't buy it. Because being in relationship is their primary concern, girls are raised to be more attuned to others' points of view. They grow up mindful that there's more than one "truth," one perspective, and that each view has its own truth and validity. What's principled and noble to one person is seen as cowardice and base to another. Even if we agree on principles, how we apply them varies. Women's response to these fundamental differences is not to judge the different views but to understand them in their own contexts and according to their own reasoning processes, to value them for what they are, and to work with them as resources for expanding our ways of thinking. Women's aim is to incorporate differences in a more diversified perspective. Judging who's right or wrong is antithetical to this process. Gilligan writes:

> Sensitivity to the needs of others and the assumption of responsibility for taking care lead women to attend to voices other than their own and to include in their judgment other points of view....The reluctance to judge may itself be indicative of the care and concern for others that infuse the psychology of

women's development and are responsible for what is generally seen as problematic in its nature.[13]

Whereas Kohlberg ranked the two perceptions of justice in a hierarchy, with men's view superior and women's inferior, Gilligan sees them as connected and complementary (in this case, both psychologists thinking consistently with their genders):

While an ethic of [fairness] proceeds from the premise of equality—that everyone should be treated the same—an ethic of care rests on the premise of nonviolence—that no one should be hurt. In the representation of maturity, both perspectives converge in the realization that just as inequality adversely affects both parties in an unequal relationship, so too violence is destructive for everyone involved.[14]

The genius of the Haudenosaunee is that they integrate these two perspectives in their system of government, which means they don't see justice as we do in the West, namely, as exclusively male defined. By allocating issues of rights, equality, and impartiality to the legislative and executive branches (the men's strength in their system of self-government) and issues of care for connectedness, nonviolence, and the nurturing of life into the future to the judicial (the women's strength), they achieve a balance of perspectives in their reasoning processes.

For them, justice can't ultimately be about rights and revenge—"If you hurt me, I [or the state] have a right to hurt you back"—because that concept nearly annihilated their cultures centuries ago when it led to all-out intertribal wars. What justice is there in fighting, misery, and death, even if we do these things in the name of justice? We can't create a just world if we kill each other doing it. Through hard experiences, the Haudenosaunee learned that real justice has to do with building relationships and caring for people, the community, and future generations. For this, we need men's and women's perspectives operating in balance.

13. Ibid., 16–17.

14. Ibid., 174.

If we think about what the legislative and executive branches under the U.S. Constitution are supposed to do, this allocation of different justice thought processes makes sense, whether it's individual men or women who fill the offices. Thanks to the First Nations of the Northeast, we have a structure of government that has the potential to incorporate men's and women's perspectives in a balanced way.

Whoever works in the legislative and executive branches needs to exercise more of what's associated with male qualities and a male way of thinking about justice, e.g., in terms of universal principles and rules. The legislative branch is charged with the responsibility to pass laws that support our rights and establish fairness and equality in how we conduct our lives. The Bill of Rights, for instance, is part of our legal corpus, and the Nineteenth Amendment had to be approved by federal and state legislatures. Fair taxation is a congressional issue, as are regulations that establish fair business practices—practices that balance the rights of owners, workers, consumers, fellow species, and the earth.

The executive branch is supposed to execute the law impartially, not favoring one group over another, but working to establish equality as the foundation of a free society. Rights, fairness, and the impartial execution of the law: these male-oriented values form the constitutional mandate for the first two branches.

If that's so, then the issues of rights and impartial execution are well covered by the first two branches. These male-oriented concerns are already addressed. We don't need the third to do the same but to contribute something different that complements the other two.

To this end, whoever works in the judicial branch—man or woman —needs to exercise more of a female way of thinking about justice, e.g., with a focus on care, compassion, helping to restore people and relationships, meeting human needs, assisting us through change, and bringing the whole body of law and resources down to where we are, case by case, with the overriding purpose to serve, help, mend, and better our lives. The judgment that's required isn't organized around blaming or punishing but around deciding what's most mutually beneficial —what can bring the greatest healing and good to everyone involved. Women's ways of thinking about justice reason not from laws but from wisdom and compassion, an open mind and an open heart.

Justice and Cycles of Change

Combining men's and women's approaches, we gain a sense of justice that supports us through our change cycles, which is precisely what we long for. When we think of justice that's inspiring—justice that makes us happy to be part of it—we think of justice that has a heart, that sees our needs and responds to them.

If a child breaks a rule, for instance, we don't want to see blind, mechanical punishment exacted. We want to see a parent or teacher help the child, so that the child learns why it's better not to do "x" for real-world reasons. We want a justice that shows us how to use all experiences—especially the mistakes, misunderstandings, and conflicts—to enhance our relationships, rather than polarizing them into good guys and bad guys, the self-righteously superior and the shamed lesser beings, punisher and punished. When we raise children, we know this. We want to educate, train, nurture, and love them, not to keep score on them.

If our children become addicted to alcohol or drugs and steal as a result, we don't want them jailed. We don't believe that that's a solution, for the obvious reason that it doesn't address the addiction. Rather, we want them healed by both dissolving whatever issues are creating addictions and developing whoever they're meant to be, so they can find jobs—and lives—that suit them. Not only are they happier, but also they're not driven to steal again. We want our society to work, and soul-nurturing justice makes that happen—not by punishing us but by affirming our innermost need to be true to ourselves and to go on our soul's journey.

This view of justice creates a happy society because it calls us home to living who we are as beings of change. The logic is simple. If we're stuck living as no more than shadows of ourselves, something is wrong with how we've structured our lives. Our ability to move with change has been disrupted. We've needed to dissolve some aspect of ourselves or of how we were connecting, but for whatever reason, dissolution doesn't happen. Or we've wanted to develop, but again for whatever reason, we can't find the means to do it. Our cycles of change go on hold. When we can't peck out of some shell, instead of developing, we start dying, and then we're not happy.

When we're not happy, we can't think straight, and we find it difficult to appreciate more than our own perspective. That's when we act badly, when hurts and injustices occur. Instead of hurting us back for these actions, a model of justice organized around healing and promoting human good takes a practical, problem-solving approach, focusing on causes and solutions. It adopts reasoning processes that serve healing. First, it investigates causes: why we're not moving with our rhythms of change, which gets into personal histories, family dynamics, economics, career, and workplace conditions, societal structures, religious beliefs, and cultural philosophies. Second, it explores solutions: how to help us reconnect with our soul's path on all the levels that this involves, from physical health and finances to emotional well-being in relationships to dreams, aspirations, longings, and inner growth. When justice is organized around securing happiness and supporting our whole-being evolution, we're happy.

For this to happen, we need justice on our side and working for us. Naturally we want justice to uphold rights and fairness, but we also want it to include care, sensitivity to our struggles, compassionate support each step of the way, and forgiveness. Once we change and do what we can to make things right, we don't want to be bound to past errors. Indeed, holding errors against us prevents us from moving beyond them. That's why we need justice to focus on healing our woundedness, which is the source of doing harm, mending our relationships, and supporting us through transitions.

In other words, we want justice to help us create happiness by helping us be happy with ourselves and each other. Blame and punishment don't inspire happy self-acceptance, nor does making miserable people more miserable create a happy society. We have to get real about what we're doing with justice—what we want it to do and whether the methods we're using can possibly achieve what we want.

Justice guided by the aim that each of us be who we are and do what's ours to do satisfies our longings for a nurturing justice, because the model centers on our good and well-being. It's got the right aim. The Confucian text *The Great Learning*, which we quoted in chapter 2, states clearly that a nurturing model of justice builds the health and happiness of society on *our* health and happiness. Society becomes truly just when its ways of reasoning help us grow into living our souls, our meaning, and our calling in life. That's a big aim, one worthy of justice.

The narrower aim of determining the "truth" of who did what to whom and punishing people accordingly misses the mark. There's no model for adapting to our changing needs, nor is there any effort to move with natural growth and healing processes. Neither is there a priority on creating a just world, nor any vision of how to do so.

Even so, how to implement a nurturing model of justice remains unclear; we don't know what it might look like. Virtually all our experiences of justice have been shaped by one-sided, male-oriented, legalistic, retributive thought processes. We need to "dissolve" our habits of thinking about justice to make the mental space for exploring a feminine, clanmother approach.

Drawing on women's views of justice makes exploring a nurturing model easier, though, since we all know women. Some of us even are one. Granted, female biology is no guarantee of a nurturing consciousness, but women's roles as mothers offer clues about how to support change in human development.

For example, a mother's justice is completely organized around supporting the good and the growth of the child. That's the purpose behind every decision she makes, every attitude, her entire approach to the child down to each specific interaction. To this end:

- A mother doesn't hold mistakes against a child but keeps the focus on teaching and guiding, helping the child to take new steps and to release existing patterns as the child is ready to outgrow them.

- A mother "reads" her child by observing and listening to him or her, trying to understand what's going on with the child from his or her perspective.

- Instead of imposing rulings, a mother first gets the full picture of the child's processes and then tries to work with the child to find and pursue the next step.

- When some sort of discipline or restraint is required, a mother does not discipline to inflict hurt or pain but to help the child break away from a destructive habit or to protect the child from doing or receiving harm.

Granted, it's not easy. Not all mothers learn it. In the name of what's good for the child, mothers can become domineering, controlling, manipulative, and overbearing. When this happens, mothers don't trust the innate growth principle—the holomovement unfolding its own unique expression—within the child, so they interject their own agenda, as if they could stand in for the child's whole-born being. That's not a good choice. It's not the response of a wise clanmother either, someone who has seen enough children grow and blossom into their uniqueness through their own winding paths to trust the process.

What does this model look like in practice beyond the example of mothering? It's already being actively applied. As we've mentioned, the fields of restorative and therapeutic justice have developed victim-offender mediation programs, healing and sentencing circles, family group conferences, and drug courts to pioneer justice practices that heal both individuals and relationships.

Yet these programs only scratch the surface of what's possible, designed as they are to deal with the special cases of some criminal or blatantly destructive behavior. Justice in our lives is infinitely more than putting us back together after we're broken. It infuses our entire experience, expressed in how we interact with ourselves as well as with each other at home, at work, and in the community.

Given this wider context, the possibilities for practicing a nurturing model of justice are unlimited. A new model of justice is bound to spur change in families, schools, businesses, and courts, as well as in our own psyches. Again, it's already happening, and for the practical reason that a nurturing model of justice works. We just don't realize that it's justice being redefined. Good therapy, for example, seeks not to blame or punish us for our problems but to help us heal our pain, deepen our self-understanding, and facilitate our self-acceptance. It helps us come home to who we are and do what's ours to do. Good therapy is actually restorative, therapeutic justice at work in the fields of mental and emotional health. We just don't call it that.

Management practices offer another example of how restorative justice can work in life. According to the top-down, autocratic model of management, it's perfectly just for management (the higher-ups) to be treated and paid one way and for workers (less-higher-ups, staff, and

bottom-rung folks) to be treated and paid another. But the double standard leads to a breakdown of connectedness, manifested in, among other
things, a loss of mutual respect, which in turn leads to unhealthy, unpro-
ductive behaviors on all sides.

Over the last four or five decades, management practices have been
shifting to both a more equitable (male) and a more nurturing (female)
model of workplace justice. In practice, this means honoring the knowledge and creativity that each person brings to the enterprise by engaging them in the flow of knowledge and decisionmaking. People are
valued for their contributions and allowed to develop their abilities
within the business structure—the essence of Platonic justice. They're
acknowledged as integral players in the business system. No participant
in the enterprise is stuck in a box that warrants his or her contributions
being dismissed. The more fiscally progressive companies have even
shifted to profit sharing and employee ownership. And it has paid off:
productivity and quality go up.

The model of real, nurturing justice has been used to save companies—businesses, plants, and factories—that were either in bankruptcy
or headed for it. For instance, the General Motors (GM) plant in Fairmont, California, was the worst and least productive plant in the country, whether measured in absenteeism, product quality, or volume of
cars produced. When the factory's management was turned over to Toy-
ota, a company that operates according to a philosophy of worker em-
powerment rather than worker domination, the employees were treated
according to a more respectful, affirming model of workplace justice.

Under the reorganized company of New United Motor Manufac-
turing Incorporated (NUMMI), the plant quickly turned around and
became one of the most productive, even without the benefit of updated
production equipment, such as robotics. The shift came entirely from a
shift in management philosophy and hence in employee attitudes—a
different model of workplace justice. The change was so remarkable
that GM invested four billion dollars to develop the Saturn line of cars
produced on the same principles.[15] Nurturing, soul-honoring justice

15. See Paul S. Adler, "The Time-and-Motion Regain," *Harvard Business Review*,
January 1, 1993, reprinted in *Quality Digest*, April 1993. See also *Business Week*,
March 16, 1987, 107; and April 20, 1987, 57.

works, both for souls and for finances.

In short, a justice that's responsive to us and adaptive to our changing needs makes sense. Is it just to expect the ones in crisis to adapt to a powerful, rigid structure? Shouldn't it be the reverse—that the more powerful adapt to help the weaker, that the system possessing might and resources adapt itself to assist the ones in need? Governments are our servants—a driving conviction behind the American Revolution. If so, then justice and its institutions should be organized around the purpose of helping us.

To do this, true justice must embrace our change cycles and respond to them. It must respect both developing and dissolving processes and find ways to assist us through both without judgment, blame, or punishment. The ideal of justice is to help us birth our being, and this involves change—messy, confusing, conflicting, and painful as change cycles can be.

Plato expressed the adaptive quality of true justice through the idea of moderation, the third virtue. Blind impartiality is not moderate; it's extreme, harsh, and oblivious to our needs during change. It executes legal justice "though the heavens fall."

Moderation, by contrast, seeks a middle road, one that aims to advance the good of everyone involved. Since this can be pursued in many ways, the path of moderation isn't cut and dried. It's uncertain, ambiguous, tentative, experimental, a matter of feeling our way along and doing the best under the circumstances. Moderation doesn't see things in black or white, right or wrong. It allows many perspectives, each of which has its own truth. Moderation creates the mental space to ponder the totality as best we understand it, allowing that our views are always changing.

As a result, moderation seeks not perfect justice but working, in-the-trenches justice—a greater mutuality of respect, understanding, care, and support that emerges through the unpredictable course of personal change. Justice built on moderation doesn't work perfectly all the time for all people, but then our current system scarcely works for anyone if measured in positive personal change and healing.

Instead, moderation seeks the best that can be done under the circumstances, given our limits and frailties. Until we develop healing methods equal to dealing with extremely wounded, violent people, this may mean emergency restraint—locking people away for a time, so that they don't do violence to others. What moderation rejects is the policy of making emergency measures the norm for millions of people who are not dangerous but lost and trapped in patterns of pain and trauma. Mandatory imprisonment is an extreme use of the lock-up "solution," not a moderate use. In place of blanket solutions, moderation seeks to apply the greatest wisdom and compassion to each case. To do this, moderation seeks balance. It balances who we are now with who we've been, our histories, as well as with who we may become. Moderation sees us as changing beings, moving in many contexts and verging on many possible futures. Instead of imposing fixed judgments, as if we'll never be other than who we've been, moderation honors our innate potential to grow in ways we've never imagined.

Similar to the way intuition systems think, then, Plato's value of moderation weighs the whole and adapts it to the individual case. Applied to justice, moderation operates from the widest sense of justice: justice that balances men's with women's views, rights and fairness with care and compassion, outer with inner concerns, but especially the search for truth with the search for the good. Moderation brings it all to bear in the quest to do what's most healing, transforming, and restorative for each person and each case, and then it evaluates what's done in the larger picture of serving human and planetary good.

But is this doable? What does it look like in practice? Can justice really give us all these things we want—and need—from it?

≈ EIGHT

The Seen and the Unseen

The seen and the unseen. The physical world is real.
The spiritual world is real. These two are aspects of one
reality. Yet, there are separate laws which govern each of
them. Violation of spiritual laws can affect the physical
world. Violation of physical laws can affect the spiritual
world. A balanced life is one that honors the laws of both of
these dimensions of reality. —*The Sacred Tree*

He came to our Iroquois lands in our darkest hour, when the
good message of how to live had been cast aside and naked
power ruled, fueled by vengeance and blood lust. A great war of
attrition engulfed our lands, and women and children cowered
in fear of their own men. The leaders were fierce and merciless.
They were fighting in a blind rage. Nations, homes, and families were destroyed, and the people were scattered. It was a dismal world of dark disasters where there seemed to be no hope.
It was a raging proof of what inhumanity man is capable of when
the laws and principles of life are thrown away.[1]

THE PERSON who came to the Iroquois many centuries ago to
end this social catastrophe is described as a prophet and a
philosopher, Deganawidah, called "the Peacemaker" and sometimes
"the Messiah." How did he do it? Not with force, intimidation, or even
personal charisma but with a message of peace to be won through justice,

1. Oren Lyons, "Land of the Free, Home of the Brave," in *Indian Roots of American Democracy*, ed. José Barreiro (Ithaca, N.Y.: Akwe:kon Press, Cornell University, 1992), 30–31.

an ideal he put into practice through the Great Law of Peace. How then did he persuade a people locked in rage, hate, violence, and mutual destruction to go for it? By beginning "the great work of healing the twisted minds of men":[2]

> He argued that we can create a world in which people look to thinking instead of violence and created the council of the Five Nations as a place that sits under a tree, protected by the law, and around the idea that the chiefs hold their hands together to do clear thinking about the welfare of coming generations, of the people of this earth.[3]

Thinking—something we can't see or touch—transformed their world from a hell of mutual annihilation to an advanced democracy. The Peacemaker established "a tradition of responsible thinking" that treats justice as a core principle of life. This justice isn't a fixed body of written laws but a consciousness of what justice means and a culture-wide commitment to living it:

> The Iroquois tradition of law is a tradition of responsible think-ing. It is not something written in paragraphs and lines because it doesn't matter whether the letter of the thing is right. The questions that have to be put before the people are *what is the thinking? Is the thinking right?*[4]

Responsible thinking uses our intelligence to create a world where everyone feels not only fairly treated but also confident about being able to resolve conflicts peacefully and respectfully. We each experi-ence things differently—that's not only natural and good but essential to creating a rich, diverse community. Justice gives us methods for

---

2. Ibid., 31.

3. John Mohawk, "The Indian Way Is a Thinking Tradition," in *Indian Roots of American Democracy*, 27.

4. Ibid., 23.

negotiating our way to a shared understanding and mutual tolerance, so that our differences don't lead to conflicts and abuse:

> [The Peacemaker] said human beings have the capability of thinking, human beings can reach the conclusion that peace is a more appropriate state of being than war, and that all human beings who are capable of thinking will want to find ways to reach peace and the absence of violence. He said that peace is not only the absence of violence. He said peace is arrived at through the conscious and energetic struggle by human beings to use their intelligence to negotiate a place in which all injustice has been spoken to, and all persons feel that they have been treated fairly. When we create that reality, a reality in which all people can say that no one in their society is abused, we will have reached a state of peace.[5]

At the end of the previous chapter, we wondered whether justice can give us all the things we want and need from it. In light of what the Iroquois experienced before and then after the Peacemaker's work, it seems that nothing else but justice—the justice that values each of us for who we are, that treats us all well and fairly, and that protects all creatures from abuse—can give us a happy, peaceful society. This understanding is the Peacemaker's most enduring gift.

What an odd gift, though. Justice is invisible and intangible: unseen. It's not anything we can point to and say, "There it is." It's no-thing (not a thing, not an object), but it's everything that makes relationships, families, communities, and society good. It's an idea, a way of understanding life. More, it's a philosophy of who we are and what it is to be together in society and on earth.

It's also an interactive gift. The gift of justice can't be given unless we take it in and let it percolate through our lives and psyches, changing us as it goes. Even simple, everyday brushes with justice have a transforming effect. Something as basic as being heard—as speaking our truth and having even one person listen and acknowledge it—is an

5. Ibid., 23.

experience of justice that can change us. We don't feel as tossed aside or insignificant. In societies that think about justice, unseen justice makes each of us feel seen—and heard, the original idea of giving someone "a hearing."

On a level beyond everyday experiences, justice challenges us further. It calls us to rethink our categories and reexamine our pillars of life: What really sustains us—the seen or the unseen? What makes our lives good, happy, and worth living? Plato's fourth virtue challenges us to look at this precisely because justice is an idea, something intangible.

Through justice, therefore, we arrive at the larger philosophical question posed by the fourth root principle. What role do the seen and the unseen play in our lives? We need to think about this, for it may be that our cultural worldview doesn't have much place for the category to which justice belongs. If we dismiss the unseen from our lives, we dismiss justice with it. This being no small issue, we're going to take our time walking around it.

The Pursuit of the Seen

In our ordinary consumer consciousness, we've come to think that the things we can see—people and possessions—make life good, and the unseen isn't as important. Having a good family and owning good houses, cars, and clothes, which we gain by having good jobs: these matter.

Honestly, we find ourselves thinking this way too, at least the part about liking a comfortable life. We'd love for everyone on earth to have happy, meaningful relationships; a beautiful, comfortable place to live, enough food and clothing; satisfying jobs; schedules that include useful productivity, challenge, rest, play, more play, time for meditation and contemplation; and whatever else we may need to be who we are and to do what's ours to do.

While we're at it, we'd love the earth to be clean and beautiful, with ample forests, wildernesses, wetlands, lakes, streams, and oceans preserved as safe, clean habitats for plants and creatures to thrive in. We want all creatures, humans included, to have the full support of their environments. Who doesn't want this?

The trick is making it happen. Obviously, the way we're going at it isn't working out as well as we'd hope. We thought we were building a good life together, and now we're discovering more messes than we can count. Globally speaking, for example, only a few are getting the goods. Vicki Robin, co-author of *Your Money or Your Life*, cites a 1998 United Nations human development report stating that "the world's richest 20 percent consumes 86 percent of the world's resources."[6]

On top of imbalances in how the seen is distributed, the ways we've been getting the tangibles are costing the earth a fearful price. How do we bring back a plant or animal that has gone extinct? How do we replace a rainforest that has taken centuries to grow—forests on which global weather patterns as well as the planet's supply of oxygen depend?

Whereas the Iroquois faced a social catastrophe, today's crisis is, among other things, an environmental catastrophe, evident as close to home as our own bodies. Millions of us breathe air officially classified as unsafe. The assurances we get from corporate-paid scientists that ingesting "x" amount of toxins is okay lack objectivity. Too many times they've dismissed dangers that later proved real. For folks trained to do time studies, their confidence is anomalous, considering that this is the first time humans have collected such a bizarre soup of chemicals in their bodies.

Consider, for instance, sexual dysfunctions. Dr. Theo Colborn believes that the rapid decrease in the sperm count and increase of male impotence across species directly relate to a group of chemicals now referred to as "hormone disrupters."[7] Some male alligators are even losing their penises—their male organs are shrinking away—and they're starting to grow female organs instead. If we keep going as we are, Colborn fears, neither we nor any other species will be able to reproduce.

This is not a fame-seeking alarmist speaking but a grandmother worried about her grandchildren and great-grandchildren—the kind of woman the Iroquois listened to. Even if there's the remotest chance that

6. Vicki Robin, "Is simplicity necessary in this era of abundance?" *Christian Science Monitor*, November 1, 1999.

7. Theo Colborn, *Our Stolen Future: Are We Threatening Our Fertility, Intelligence, and Survival?—A Scientific Detective Story* (New York: Dutton, 1996).

our chemical industries are unwittingly turning the planet's males into females by bathing them in an estrogen-mimicking soup, we should rethink our course. As a response to patriarchy, we're impressed with Mother Nature's power to make a point, but changing the money-and-power-driven, hence seen-only categories might be preferable to having male equipment become as scarce as hen's teeth. We write this from both a man's and a woman's point of view.

Examples of unhealthy patterns passing for life as usual can be multiplied, since we each have our favorite rants. Suffice it to say, something is missing from how we've sought the good life, and the lack of it has allowed our thinking to grow twisted.

At this point, we'd be tempted to launch into a well-worn tirade of what's wrong with humanity that we've made such a mess of things. East and West, ancient and modern, the general logic has been, if we're lost, we must be losers. The logic is tempting, and it's easy because then we're not called to action—to heal ourselves and to transform our ways of structuring societies. If our species is an innate mess, what's the use?

Oddly enough, this isn't the response that many indigenous traditions have to our species' more insane behaviors. It wasn't the Peacemaker's response, at least, and for good reason. What's to be gained by making us feel terrible about ourselves and guilty just for who we are? Why reduce our totality to how we behave at our worst, that is, when we're most traumatized, afraid, insecure, or depressed? Moreover, what's the benefit of one-upping the species by trashing it? According to the Peacemaker's teaching, these are divisive mental habits, and they contribute to twisted, us-vs.-them thinking.

For our own sanity's sake, we must keep alive the vision and hope of ourselves as more. If connectedness holds at all, we're in this together. We each have a role to play, something to contribute. Justice is about creating a place where we can each do what's ours to do—the core message of Plato's *Republic*. When we put our minds and energies to good use, we fulfill who we came here to be. Then we're happy, and our thinking doesn't grow twisted.

What's not so clear in Plato's work is how to make the shift. In his cave allegory, the person who left the cave, saw the sun, and walked among real people (as opposed to shadows of them) had a terrible time when he returned to the cave dwellers to tell them what he'd experienced. The shadows they saw on the cave's wall were their only reality, and they weren't budging just because of some guy's personal experiences—"You can't trust anecdotal evidence, you know."

With this allegory, Plato describes the power of "the seen" to block our minds from considering anything more. What we see becomes everything, and we assume nothing else exists. The suggestion that we're seeing only shadows and that what's unseen could give us a very different understanding doesn't seem as compelling as what our eyes report. Mesmerized by the visible, we don't suspect that maybe we're not getting the whole story.

Socrates' message was political dynamite for those who'd rather we'd accept the face-value version of events and not look deeper. But the discrepancy between the seen and the unseen isn't limited to politics; it's everyday life. If we stop with the seen, we don't have an accurate picture of anything. Swedenborg used acts of friendship to illustrate: are kindnesses done to get something in return, or are they gifts? Unless we consider what's unseen, we can be misled, even about ourselves. The unseen intent makes all the difference. "A thousand people can behave alike—that is, can do the same thing. . . . Yet each deed in its own right is unique because it comes from a different intent."[8]

In other words, what we see means nothing without an unseen framework to interpret it. We see a person plunging a knife into another: is it murder, surgery, autopsy, or a movie? To grasp the seasonal sight of plastic-armored men slamming into each other with thousands of people sitting around doing nothing to stop the conflict, we need the invisible concept of a "game" called "football." An alien visiting earth without the proper unseen categories might scratch his or her head (or whatever he, she, or it scratches) over the behavior and phone home a bizarre report about earthling behavior.

Ignoring the unseen, we're like the alien. Seeing injustices everywhere and all through history, we get mesmerized by what we see and then draw one-sided conclusions. Instead of considering the unseen

8. Emanuel Swedenborg, *Heaven and Hell*, trans. George F. Dole, The New Century Edition of the Works of Emanuel Swedenborg (West Chester, Pa.: The Swedenborg Foundation, 2000), §472.

context, we start thinking that some people aren't good at anything but profiting from abuse and exploitation, and before we know it, we're wondering if people in general aren't that way. We're back in a trashing mode—based on what we see.

One of the gifts of indigenous traditions is their ability to stay in balance, not to swing to extremes. The reason we fall into polarized views, they suggest, is that we focus only on what we see of ourselves and humanity. Our de facto philosophy is that invisibles aren't as important as visibles: that ideals, values, and intuitions aren't as important as "facts," for instance, or on a more mundane level, that making money is more important than attending to unseen factors such as ethics, rights, and fairness, webs of connectedness, or future consequences. Our learned response, which has become automatic, is to side with the seen and discount the unseen. (By that logic, what's on television is the most seen; therefore, it must be the most true and important.)

Having trained ourselves to think this way, we're fooled by our own theater of shadows. We see the rapist/murderer; the money-obsessed businessperson; the hypocritical religionist; the cranky, power-wielding bureaucrat; the angry street kid; the cold, control-freak authority; the abusive police; the ego-driven politician; or the con artist. Or we see ourselves afraid and struggling to pay the bills—stressed and reactive at work and unpleasant to those we love at home. We see these things and stop there.

The Power of the Unseen

What's missing from our thought processes is the unseen. We don't look beyond the visible, yet what's invisible powerfully shapes both what we see and how we see it. For example:

- What complex histories, unseen to us now, lie behind visible forms and behaviors?

- What unspoken family and cultural taboos, judgments, and expectations sit heavily on us, impeding our freedom to move with change?

- What messages do our social, educational, economic, business, religious, and political systems send through their attitudes and policies?

- Behind that, what philosophies, ideas, and values guide us in setting up our lives and institutions?

- What larger issues of development and evolution are we working out both individually and as a species?

- What's going on soul-wise with our longings for meaning and often-denied souls' callings? Where do our loves lie, and are we free to pursue them?

- What about the unseen spiritual dimension, which includes guides, angels, past lives, future time lines, higher selves, and a higher power or whatever we sense as God?

All these unseen factors—from the mundane, psychological, and societal to the philosophical to the nonordinary and transcendent—are unseen, yet they're powerful in shaping human experience. Indeed, barring pole shifts or asteroids hitting the earth, they're the most powerful factors in human life. Swedenborg argued that the inward (where we interact with the unseen) is vastly more powerful than the outward (what we see), precisely because the inward is the source of the outward.

Peter Senge, business consultant and author of *The Fifth Discipline*, argued similarly.[9] Trying to solve outward problems (events and crises) isn't half as powerful as trying to change the less visible patterns of behavior that generate them. In turn, trying to alter behavior patterns isn't nearly as powerful as changing the even less visible systems, paradigms, and structures that produce the behaviors. The deeper we go into the unseen, the more potent and effective our efforts are.

This only makes sense. All that we see of human beings and societies distills from the unseen. What is a car, for instance, but something created from engineering knowledge and ideas? What's on television but ideas that people translate into images? What's a relationship or family

9. Senge, *The Fifth Discipline*, 52–55.

but invisible bonds of love, respect, and affection—and complex histories of screwiness and pain too? What's a war but an invisible quagmire of hostilities, crossed ambitions, memories of past hurt, and fears of future harm? What's a job but a construct of invisible assumptions about what's useful and money-making? Speaking of which, what's money but an invisible agreement about a measure of value? In financial markets, what are futures or stock options except ways to capitalize on the unseen—the more unseen, the more money to be made? For that matter, what is a culture but a complex set of invisibles: philosophies, values, ideas, shared memories, histories, traditions, and aims?

Our lives are chock-full of invisibles—indeed, they're entirely shaped by them—and yet our cultural habit has been to ignore the unseen or to downplay its role.

That's an unfortunate belief-system, in our view, because it clips our powers to change. If we don't like where our unseen team is taking us, we can change it. To exercise this power, though, we need to recognize the unseen, acknowledge its influence, and then take stock of what's there. As long as we're mesmerized by the visible, we don't do this.

Believing we're at the mercy of externals, our minds have little creative to do. We feel trapped in a no-option way of life. Instead of enjoying a healthy, conscious, creative relation to the unseen, our minds play the "seen-only" game, which allows us nothing more to do than manipulate visibles: "I have no choice but to do business this way!" "I must take revenge!" "I must make that person love me and do what I want!" Buddhists describe this way of thinking as "grasping" and "clinging," and it causes suffering.

Indeed, the seen-only model colors how we think about everything. We regard humanity in seen-only terms because that's how we think about reality. What is racism or sexism, for instance, but a mindset that stops with the seen? What is speciesism but the same? It assumes that humans are superior and free to abuse animals simply because they look different and don't use our language. What if forests and oceans could talk back? Even a simple "Ouch!" or "Back off, buster!" or "What were you thinking?" from a swamp or stream might inspire a different relationship.

It's ironic that a seen-only way of thinking blinds us to what we're doing to our bodies, each other, animals, or the earth. Why wouldn't a seen-only view make us more sensitive to them? But it's actually logical. If we rely on the seen, we're bound to have a partial view.

From the visible-only perspective, it's as if we see a single frame in a movie. Insofar as we think that what we see is all there is, we're tempted to conclude that we saw the whole show. If we don't temper this freeze-frame partiality with some conceptual framework to broaden it— to clue us in to the larger reality—we end up with a chronically one-sided, or in the Peacemaker's terms, "twisted" mind. What we don't see doesn't exist, and the fraction of the universe that we do see becomes everything.

If we limit ourselves to the observable, believing that's all there is, our minds won't be able to "think responsibly," not because we don't want to, but because responsible thinking must take into account a host of invisibles: unseen futures, unseen webs of connectedness, unseen possible consequences, unseen options, as well as the core stuff of philosophy—the unseen ideas, values, qualities, principles, and paradigms that steer our course. None of these is tangible, but each is essential to making wise decisions. Unless we're in the habit of taking the unseen seriously, it won't occur to us to think about these things. That's why, if the observable is all there is for us, our perspective becomes dangerously narrow.

Thinking about Unseen Justice

To untwist our minds and think responsibly, we need intangibles to expand our ways of seeing, so that we open ourselves to what we haven't seen or even to what cannot be seen. We can never see, for example, what makes a poem or music beautiful. We can read words or hear sounds, but beauty is intangible. Neither can we see how other beings think or feel within themselves—their own inner experiencing—and yet we must grant this intangible reality in others if we're to have a relationship with them. We can't see truth, love, creativity, or justice either, and yet we need these values in our lives to be happy and to create a good society.

As we open to the unseen, it's a new world. Because of its vastness, the unseen inspires humility as well as joy and hope in the possibilities revealed. Socrates believed that the beginning of wisdom is knowing that we don't know. What we see and know is tiny compared with what's unseen and unknown. Realizing this is the beginning of wisdom—and of thinking responsibly.

Consider, for example, what happens when we ignore the intangible called "justice." Our worlds may not have much justice in them simply because we don't think about it, at least not as much as we think about the weather or groceries. We put time into things we can see—gathering "facts," statistics, and profits, or adhering to visible norms and traditions.

Consistent with this cultural bias, when someone is harmed, we inquire about "seen" factors: did someone break the law or not, and if we can prove a person did, how should he or she be punished? In other words, who did what to whom, and who pays? We settle for thinking about justice in tangible ways—as everyone getting his or her due—and then we try to further visible-ize this concept of justice by instituting laws, rules, regulations, penalties, and punishments. Justice lies "out there" as an external, measurable thing.

Fully occupied with what's visible, we don't ask whether the visible measures we're taking address the less visible roots of hurt and unhappiness: do punishments resolve the unseen dynamics that lead to harmful behaviors? Does using authority to intimidate people and inflict pain on them change them for the better? Offenders may change in the ways we'd hope, but they may also become more resolved not to get caught next time and more clever about how to commit crimes by learning from fellow inmates. A model of justice centered on the visible doesn't call us to think about justice in larger or more profound ways.

Insofar as we pass over the deeper issues, we don't wrestle with what justice means as an ideal—as a healing, restoring, protecting force in society. As a result, we don't think about what bringing these unseen qualities into our justice systems might look like, which means we're not inspired, for example, to put much public money into drug-and-alcohol treatment centers, even though untold millions of potential offenders could be treated, untold lives of addiction, prison, or early death averted, and untold drug-related crimes prevented.

   This situation reflects a public choice based on how we think about justice. Healing and transformation are invisible processes, less measurable than lengths of time in prison. We stop with visible-ized justice— "justice has been served" with sentencing and imprisonment—which means we don't engage in a consciousness of justice that's more.

   We can all think of people who've pushed us to a deeper sense of justice: friends, family members, teachers, or associates. Historically, many people's lives have inspired us to expand our views of justice to include invisible values. The Peacemaker and Socrates, of course, but also Muhammad, for whom social justice is a major driving concern; suffragists such as Lucretia Mott, Elizabeth Cady Stanton, and Susan B. Anthony; abolitionists such as Henry David Thoreau, Harriet Tubman, and Frederick Douglass; the many great chiefs and leaders of the First Nations, Tecumseh, Chief Joseph, Black Kettle, Sitting Bull, Big Foot, to name a few, all seeking principle, peace, and justice where there were none to be found; Mahatma Gandhi and his work of nonviolent noncooperation with evil, as well as the truth-telling African American leaders Carter G. Woodson ("the father of black history"), Rosa Parks, Martin Luther King Jr., Malcolm X, Malidoma Somé: these are a few of the people whose struggles with justice as more than "the seen" come to mind.

   We remember and honor such people—each of us having our own list—precisely because they thought about justice in life-transforming ways, seeking harmony and happiness by first changing our consciousness of justice. Justice needs to be alive among us, they reasoned, because it's the backbone of human life. The more the invisible idea of justice lives among us, the more healthy visible society will be. Without it, we don't last long.

   During the 1950s and 1960s, Martin Luther King Jr. modeled such a consciousness, vowing to work "until justice rolls down like waters and righteousness like a mighty stream."[10] He challenged the nation to think about justice through the civil rights movement, and his work stands as a cultural turning point. People began to look beyond skin

10. Martin Luther King Jr. was paraphrasing from the Bible the prophet Amos (Amos 5:24). This quote is engraved on a fountain in front of The Southern Poverty Law Center in Montgomery, Alabama.

color (seen forms) to a common humanity (an unseen concept) and hence to honor the rights and dignity that go with being human (also unseen).

King's active consciousness of unseen justice changed how we see things. What before was accepted as a fair and just arrangement of racial separation and inequality shifted to a perception of systematic injustice and gross wrong. He led the nation to look beyond bodily and cultural differences to the unseen world of justice, and the seen world now looks different because he did.

In 1971, lawyer Morris Dees founded The Southern Poverty Law Center in Montgomery, Alabama, to continue this kind of active thinking about justice. Dees recalls the case of nineteen-year-old African-American Michael Donald, who was murdered by James Knowles and others acting for the Ku Klux Klan. On behalf of Michael's mother, Beulah Mae Donald, Dees sued the Klan and won $7 million in damages for her, bankrupting the Klan and requiring that the deed to its central office building be transferred to Mrs. Donald. Dees comments:

> One of the most memorable and dramatic moments that I've ever had in a courtroom was at the end of the Donald trial. I finished my closing arguments. The Klan lawyer finished his, and James Knowles, one of the defendants, stood up and asked the judge if he could say something to the jury.
>
> He walked over in front of the jury and said, "Everything that Mr. Dees said we did, we did." He said, "We did it at the direction of those Klansmen sitting right over there, those leaders." And he turned to Mrs. Donald. He said, "Mrs. Donald, I've lost everything I've ever had in my life, my home, my family. I'm in prison for life. I'd like to ask you if you could find it in your heart to forgive me."
>
> And she kind of rocked back in her chair, looked at him in front of that jury and said, "Son, I've already forgiven you."[11]

11. Lawyer Morris Dees speaking on a videotape entitled "Seeking Justice," produced by The Southern Poverty Law Center, 400 Washington Avenue, Montgomery, AL 36104, tel. (334) 956-8200, website: www.splcenter.org.

From racism and hate to remorse, from murder to accountability and rights defended, from pain and outrage to forgiveness: the experience of justice brought a shift of consciousness. Something unseen—justice—operated as a healing force, touching each person differently and altering the future in ways we can only imagine.

By contrast, when we settle for visible justice as all there is, justice ceases to be a dynamic unseen presence—something that continually challenges us to think beyond current social conventions and appearances—and instead becomes a "letter of the law" affair, a routine application of law and precedent. Justice stops living for us, because we stop engaging with its unseen power to call us to soul searching and transformation.

Two Worlds and We Need Both

Because our visible-only ways of thinking about justice stem from a deeper visible-only cultural philosophy, we come around once again to the issue raised by the fourth root principle: how did the category of the unseen drop out of our lives, and why is it missing from our reasoning? If we reject the category to which justice belongs, then our insights into justice will fall short of what justice can be. The problem is that, culturally speaking, we've haven't yet found a healthy balance between the seen and unseen.

From the standpoint of not only many Aboriginal philosophies but also many mystical teachings, that's dangerous, because the seen and the unseen are two faces of one reality. We need both to negotiate our way through life. Dropping either one out of our lives throws us badly off balance, personally and culturally. The question we asked earlier—what really sustains us: the seen or the unseen?—is a trick question, because both do. As long as we're walking around in time, space, and bodies, we don't do well if either gets short shrift.

Unfortunately, cultures that have been subjected to heavy doses of control-oriented paradigms have found a balance between the seen and the unseen elusive. We say this because we suspect that, if we keep these two in balance within ourselves, we're a force to be reckoned with. When we're rooted in our inner authority and creative about exploring outer options, the unseen and the seen work together in us, and we're less likely candidates for being thrown off our center and controlled from without.

If, however, we sacrifice one for the other, we hobble along with one-legged thinking, and we're more easily swayed by money, authorities, experts, the weight of the status quo, or the pressurings of others. We lose our bearings. And yet we're confronted with trade-offs all the time: if we try to make things right externally, internally we pay the price with emotional suffering. Or if we try to live from our inner truth, then we meet external disapproval or a financial void.

Either way, we end up being not as strong within ourselves, mainly because we sense—and rightly so—that we're missing something essential. Nor does it matter which is denied. Disconnecting with either the seen or the unseen clips our powers.

Unseen-oriented cultures tend to denigrate the visible world as an unspiritual place inhabited by low lifes. We're here because we need to be cleansed by suffering or to burn off karma through hard experiences. Only then can we earn the right to inhabit the spiritual world beyond. The material world is regarded as a lesser reality unworthy of respect, and life here means basically doing time. Whatever belongs to the visible world—the earth, women, children, animals, bodies, sexuality—doesn't count in the spiritual scheme of things and so should be treated with disdainful domination.

Given this perspective, we look the other way on social oppression and don't put energy into social reform, because we figure misery and injustice are par for the course. What more can we expect from such a place, inhabited as it is by creatures such as we are? Escape from this world rather than its transformation seems the ticket—both preferable and more easily accomplished.

More popular today, however, is the opposite view which denies the invisible side altogether, a trend led by reductionist science, a school of science that reduces everything to physical processes. We're atoms and chemicals, nothing more.

According to this cultural choice, the visible world is the only reality. If visibles are all there is, then why bother with invisibles? They have no "sense content" (we can't observe or measure them); therefore, they have no objective meaning. Because intangibles are viewed as entirely relative—that is, whatever anyone thinks they are—they command little respect. In the seen-oriented definition of truth and validity, intangibles don't count.

This can be a liberating cultural choice insofar as it pulls the rug out from under religious dogmatism. And it makes a good point: we need feedback on our thoughts and imaginings. The unseen cannot be whatever we say it is—entirely relative or all made up in our heads. Yet denying the invisible altogether doesn't address the issue of how to go beyond subjectivism. Instead of rising to the challenge of thinking clearly, intelligently, and nondogmatically about the unseen, empiricism runs the other way, refusing to think about it at all.

Because all thinking involves unseen elements, by refusing to acknowledge this dimension, empiricism ends up simply exchanging one dogma (unseen-only thinking) for another (seen-only thinking). While many scientists continue in the tradition of open inquiry, others embrace reductionist materialism as a way to shut down thought. Science goes into the business of policing what's thinkable: only what's seen—measurable, subjected to statistical analysis, or replicable under laboratory conditions—can be reasonably discussed.

With what result? When invisible ideas such as justice lose their place in our thought processes, society drifts into rule by raw power—visible might makes right—which is one of the cultural crises we're facing. In the courtroom, Capitol, or corporate boardroom, money talks, and the more money, the more compelling the argument. It buys presidents and congresspeople. It controls the media. It dictates the start and duration of wars. It makes the majority of decisions—personal, educational, business, political, and environmental—in our culture. Only our trust in intangibles can challenge this hegemony, and if we've lost that, what recourse do we have?

Both ways of thinking are one-sided, and both disempower us, lopping off our access to reality as more than one dimension. For example, siding with the unseen—whether as a religion or as an intellectual or political philosophy—cuts us off from the grounding feedback that the seen offers. We're tempted to slip into an in-our-heads absolutism, expressed in judgmentalism and self-righteousness. Given the emphasis on the unseen by many religions, it's easy to go this way.

But the imbalance soon shows itself in unhealthy behavior. We neglect our visible selves and core needs, and before we know it, we're out of touch with our real-life experience, hence also with our truth. Self-care is seldom a priority, and self-deception slides in. Instead of living from where we authentically are as human beings in human bodies and relationships, we try to practice an ideal of what we think we should be. It doesn't work, not because we shouldn't pursue ideals, but because we need our whole selves to do it.

Without our wholeness, it's easy to drift into hypocrisy, addiction, or even cruelty in the name of being spiritual—the very things we dislike about religiosity. We can think of families where religion is used to shame and control people—"If you love me, you will practice my concept of morality and spirituality." We can also think of the centuries of Inquisition in Europe, with all the suffering caused by imposing a fixed notion of the unseen. Or we can consider the truly sick, evil behavior of the invading European-Americans toward the First Nations, done by self-righteously religious Christians. In the name of ridding the land of heathens ("the only good Indian is a dead Indian"), they slaughtered peaceful, treaty-protected, sleeping communities, including women and children, and then mutilated their bodies, turning body parts into trophies. Then of course there was the "peculiar institution" of slavery, inhuman and brutal, carried on for centuries by churchgoing Christians who inflicted this evil for personal profit, even righteously claiming they were doing slaves a favor by exposing them to Christianity.

We know enough about self-hate and how it gets projected onto out-groups to recognize the process in such blatant forms, and we know enough about Christianity's historical rejection of both the body and human sexuality to venture a guess as to where such a violent load of self-hate might have originated. Yes, there was raw greed for land and money, but there was also a profound illness manifested—a harvest of centuries of rejecting the seen for the unseen.

Coming from a professional background in science and engineering, Swedenborg was a sharp critic of unseen one-sidedness. He insisted that spiritual insight means nothing if it's not wedded to life and actions. The seen part of us keeps us humble and honest about our spiritual pursuits. It inspires compassion, a sensitivity to how difficult life can be, a deep attunement to pain, and an awareness that "there but for the grace of God go I."

Francis Bacon offered an analogy for how we get stuck in one-sided thinking. We make idols of either the unseen or the seen, both of which prevent us from clear, scientific, i.e., holistic thinking. If we make an idol of the unseen, he wrote, we become like a spider, spinning webs out of our heads that ensnare us. No matter how exalted our ideas, we have to venture out of our heads occasionally and check what's going on in experience. Otherwise, our mental webs are woven of fantasy. Joined with the seen, fantasy webs inspire creativity, but on their own, disconnected from the rest of life, they trap us in illusions. Being one-sided, they fail to connect us with multileveled reality.

If, in Bacon's analogy, we make an idol of the seen, we become like the ant, collecting bits of information about things but never having the unseen tools to put them all together in a meaningful way. We get lost in data, swamped in information overload.

Thinking one-sidedly, whichever side we choose, gets us in trouble not only because it makes us fanatics but also because it diminishes our power to interact with reality in all its dimensions. It disempowers us, and as a result, both ways of thinking one-sidedly flirt with fatalism—the notion that our course is fixed, that we can't change our future, and that we must simply accept our lot in life. One-sidedness traps us in no-option mental habits.

Seen and Unseen: One Process

East and West, we're prone to lapse into variations of either/or thinking about the seen and the unseen, and whatever we hear on this subject gets filtered through the same old one-sided categories. Because of these cultural habits, it's hard for us to think in genuinely unified, dimensionally integrated terms.

The fourth root principle, while acknowledging the distinctness of the seen and the unseen with laws appropriate to each, treats the two as intrinsically related, and that's the key. We can't side with one to the exclusion of the other, because reality—our reality too—is both.

Violating the laws of one affects the other. Because the two dimensions interconnect and move as one, we need to acknowledge how they're working together in us and in our shared evolution.

Perhaps that's why the indigenous teachings underlying all cultures have become so compelling for many people today. Predating "dominator societies," to use Riane Eisler's term,[12] they seem to experience reality more dimensionally and holistically, with the seen and the unseen operating in greater balance. We can't replicate these ancient ways of thinking. Indigenous European teachings have long since been utterly wiped out. But from those ancient wisdom traditions that remain, we do want to learn, so we can strike a balance between the seen and the unseen that's adapted to where we are. In a sense, the Aboriginal vision of multidimensional continuity sets the goal, and we have to figure out how this perennial philosophy makes sense to us now, given our current cultural experiences.

How then can we reconceptualize the seen and the unseen, so that we attune ourselves to the intrinsic balance between them? This question raises the issue of philosophy—how we conceive of reality. If reality is neither all seen nor all unseen, how is the universe constructed to integrate both? And since we're all part of the universe and made of it, how are we constructed so that both live in us in balance?

We're not looking for final answers here. Given the rate of change, it's hard to imagine what "final" anything would mean. On top of that, the concept of "final answers" is a troublemaker. By definition, it shuts down free thought; for, if we have things all figured out, why think further? It also incites battles over whose answer is the officially final one. All we're looking for is a good working model—some conceptual framework that helps us feel more at home with the different dimensions that make up our lives.

Investigating how the seen and the unseen operate as a seamless unity takes us back to physicist David Bohm, who tackled this issue head-on. We keep returning to his model because it offers one of the best modern frameworks for thinking about mystical, holistic, and spiritual ideas. And no wonder. Bohm started from the core assumption that reality is unified

12. Riane Eisler, *The Chalice and the Blade* (New York: HarperCollins, 1987).

and whole. There's something coherent going on that embraces all that is, matter and mind, atoms and consciousness, seen and unseen.

Not that the whole is monolithic—the same for everyone. Reality appears differently according to the differences in our perspectives. Our islands of everyday normalcy float in a sea of infinite possible worlds, such as might stretch the imaginations of Gene Roddenberry, Jim Henson, or their ancient storyteller counterparts. Yet no matter how diverse, reality is ultimately one and operates as such: that's Bohm's premise. There's an underlying unity that makes things hang together.

Bohm's model doesn't assume a static whole, either. The holomovement is dynamic and flows throughout, spurring change everywhere. Reality is like a super hologram that's continually moving, and, as in a hologram, each individual process mirrors the whole dynamics. To experience any part is to experience the whole from a specific perspective, since nothing can be outside of it.

What we experience as separate parts, then, isn't separate at all but the whole in action. Each aspect reveals the whole through its own form, path, and expression. There's both mind-boggling diversity and compelling unity going on at once, since each part has no existence apart from the whole's workings. That's why, for many spiritual traditions, each life is sacred and not to be abused. To do so is to abuse the reality that's our reality too.

Being dynamic, the holomovement has many levels of expression, which brings us to the seen and the unseen. They're not two separate realities but two manifestations of one process, as the fourth root principle suggests. The seen is the manifested order of the whole, whereas the unseen is its hidden order.

Using Bohm's terms, the unseen is "the implicate order": what holds implicitly within the whole but eludes form. The seen is "the explicate order": what's become explicit or manifest and perceivable. It's all the holomovement going on, but from our perspective, we experience the process as these two broad dimensions.

In elaborating these terms, physicist Will Keepin brings out that, of the two, the implicate and unseen is the greater and more powerful. It's the primary phase, because it's the formative one—the unlimited ground from which visible, hence more limited forms come:

It's tempting, perhaps, to think of the explicate order as the primary reality, and the implicate order as a subtle secondary reality. For Bohm, precisely the opposite is the case. The fundamental primary reality is the implicate order, and the explicate order is but a set of ripples on the surface of the implicate order. So, that which we can see and feel and touch is merely the waves on the surface of reality, which is the vast ocean of implicate order.

Another way of possibly thinking about this is in terms of the good old television set. The implicate order is essentially all the programming being broadcast at any given time, and the explicate order is what's on the screen at a particular time. So, the explicate order is but a narrow window on what's actually there— a tiny little part that's manifest on a sea of possibility—and the full reality exists in the implicate order.[13]

The seen and the unseen, explicate and implicate, can also be likened to theater: only a few people are on stage at any given time. The rest of the actors—not to mention the stage crew, writers, director, and producers—are off stage, unseen by the audience. Would an audience really want to see, for example, all the telephone conversations coordinating the production and performance, the hours that go into writing the play and pounding out the script, all the arrangements that have to be made, all the time and energy that go into sewing costumes, constructing sets, and memorizing lines, or all the rehearsals?

As far as the audience is concerned, theater is 99 percent unseen— not counting the unseen meanings that we derive from the play itself, which is the point of doing it in the first place. To reduce the entire theater company to the visible actors on stage would ignore the larger production process without which there would be no actors, no story, no performance, and no meaning.

As in these different examples, what we actually see depends on us and our perceiving, filtering faculties. The unseen, implicate side

13. William Keepin, "Astrology and the New Physics: Integrating Sacred and Secular Science," *The Mountain Astrologer*, no 58 (August 1995): 16–17. This magazine can be ordered from TMA, P.O.Box 970, Cedar Ridge, CA 95924.

includes vastly more. Our eyes simply aren't set up to see more, or the script we're following doesn't put the entire theater process on stage all the time. In the television example, what appears on the screen depends on our channel surfing among all the possibilities being broadcast at a given time. We choose—or our makeup as human beings chooses, as the philosopher Kant argued, or our culture chooses, or our family chooses, and on and on—from an unseen reservoir that's greater, packed with both realities and potentialities. We don't choose everything about what comes into the world of the seen, of course, but we choose more than we realize.

That's true collectively as well as personally. Collective choices about how we manage education, food production, or waste treatment affect what forms come into expression from the unseen. Combustion engines, for instance, aren't mandated by God or physics; they're a collective choice, that is, a choice made by a few automakers and oil companies on behalf of the rest of us. From all the possible ways of moving things around, this form is chosen. There are countless alternatives for managing energy and transportation; but, to find these alternatives, we have to go into the unseen and choose differently.

In other words, we have a say about what comes into form. The more we go into the unseen to explore its rich reservoir of potentials, ideas, and wisdom, the more we participate in reality's theater process, and the more choices we have about what comes on stage. Because reality is both seen and unseen moving together, ignoring either narrows our powers to shape reality as we know it.

Protecting the Seen with the Unseen

How does all this boil down to telling us something useful about justice? If who we are has its roots beyond our visible forms in an unseen order, then the job of justice is first and foremost an invisible one, namely, to attend to what's invisible among us, harmonizing us on our intangible side: our minds, feelings, emotions, psyches, values, principles, and philosophies. By helping us honor meaning as it flows through our lives, justice strengthens the unseen ground from which our seen lives take form. We're coordinated from our souls, from the unseen unity that includes all of us, and this invisible foundation makes our visible worlds naturally more just.

Without this foundation, justice degenerates into being defined by whoever has most power to say what it means in the worlds of the seen: might makes right. The unseen foundation of justice slips away, and we sense its absence immediately. No one feels happy or safe, and no relationship feels trustworthy. This is a key to what justice does: it protects us. The unseen protects the seen by creating an invisible context that affirms who we are and excludes harm.

Given the power of the implicate order, the formative ground from which everything comes, the further justice reaches into the unseen to create harmony among us—reaching into our souls and core philosophies—the more protection we have. Indeed, no visible protection can equal it. Justice's unseen protection makes us safe in ways visible protection never can, because it makes the need for outer protection obsolete. Correlatively, the more visible protection we require, the less unseen justice there is present among us, and the less safe we are.

On whatever levels justice operates—visible or invisible—Socrates believed that its protecting powers should be something that we experience as good. Even if justice must occasionally dispense a bitter pill—like a drug court requiring random drug testing or the police and courts restraining harmful actions by intervening—justice shouldn't be all bitter. Our primary experience of its protecting power should be as a positive, supportive presence in our lives.

Rewards and punishments don't measure up on this scale. We don't feel protected but threatened. In the name of justice, the potential for hurt hangs over us. If justice means protecting us from harm, how can it do this effectively when its primary mechanisms generate so much harm along the way? Rewards and punishments harden us to each other and put walls between us. Sensitivity, fellow-feeling, generosity of spirit: such qualities have no place in competitive, punitive worlds.

Justice conceived of as protecting us in doing what's ours to do doesn't have this hardening, embittering effect. Quite the opposite. When we think about justice in ways that affirm who we are, what comes on stage in our lives is affirming too. The unseen context created by our philosophy generates worlds in which we each feel genuinely respected and nurtured. We honor individuals and groups for who they are, no matter how different from us they may be, and we honor our natural environment as more than a source of either profits or potential dump sites. Unseen justice inspires us to seek a respectful balance with everyone and everything. It creates a gentle world, and the more just, the more gentle we and our worlds become. There's no need to be aggressive, manipulative, defensive, or armored.

Not that soul-based justice forces us to behave one way or another from without, externally. We're not talking about laws and enforcement here, nor are we talking about refereeing a contest among competing and conflicting rights. Rather, we're talking about justice on a more formative level—the presence of justice in consciousness before we ever start thinking about doing this or that. In Bohm's terms, we're thinking about justice in its implicate order.

At an implicate level, justice operates in our consciousness as an unseen starting point before we make decisions and act. This foundation of justice in philosophy is what the Native elders were trying to show Rupert Ross—that justice starts with our cultural paradigm. It grows from how we understand ourselves and the universe.

When our core philosophy affirms the sacredness of each life, it provides the common ground of intention, again, something unseen but nonetheless palpable in our interactions. Moved by a philosophy of mutual respect and support, we naturally treat each other well. We may not understand the concept as it applies to each situation—who does?—but we nonetheless intend to practice justice in all our relations, fully aware that we may not do it perfectly. When harms occur, our intentions move us to make things right, as best we're able.

The result is just worlds. In just communities, for instance, people don't have to lock their doors, fence and gate their communities, or worry about their children being kidnapped. They don't do business in exploitative ways, which means they don't have to draw up contracts that cover every conceivable circumstance or devise laws to prohibit every imaginable violation.

Granted, given where we are in personal, social, and cultural evolution, laws play a vital role in maintaining justice. We're by no means advocating that we dispense with laws as yet. Founding Father James

Madison said, "If men were angels, no government would be necessary." Our wings need growing time, and until we're more fully feathered, laws are necessary.

Rule by law functions on many levels. Restraint is the most immediate level, serving as it does to prevent harm. On this level, laws protect our relationships from the pre-law models of "might makes right," abuse re-enacted, or escalating cycles of revenge.

As we develop our sense of justice, the character of laws shifts. We use laws not only to restrain harmful actions but also to help us do things creatively and constructively in society, like setting up businesses or arranging our exchanges so that they're fair and flow in easy ways.

When it comes to the Great Law of Peace or constitutional law—a much more profound sense—the laws aren't designed to restrain harmful actions or even to organize daily affairs but rather to provide a framework for evolving creative, trustworthy, self-governing social, economic, and political systems. These laws create a context that protects the evolution of human society to more just and creative forms. They instill principles in consciousness that then guide us in whatever we do.

On all these levels, though, law as something written and seen depends on the unseen consciousness of justice to do its job. Without that, laws are utterly ineffective. Historically, First Nation peoples made treaties assuming a shared consciousness of justice—a consciousness Euro-Americans lacked. Consequently, the treaties have been broken and violated, still today as Native lands are used as dump sites for toxic waste, plundered for their resources, or sought for dam projects. Without a consciousness of justice, laws are no protection, not for any of us. When finding loopholes and ways around the law becomes one of the highest paid professions—i.e., when "monied might makes right" is the de facto cultural philosophy—law is virtually powerless, and no relationship is safe: "Trust no one." In *Reason for Hope*, primate researcher Jane Goodall writes, "Real change will come only from within; laws and regulations are useful, but sadly easy to flout."[14]

All we can do then is work to change consciousness. Pushing to

14. Jane Goodall, with Phillip Berman, *Reason for Hope: A Spiritual Journey* (New York: Warner Books, 1999), 270.

change laws can be a way to do this, but it's the consciousness shift that's most effective. When justice lives in consciousness, just and trustworthy relations emerge naturally, with or without laws to support them. We treat our family and friends with kindness and respect, for example, not because a law compels us to do so, but because we love them and would never wish to do otherwise. We want their happiness, and affirming them in doing what's theirs to do is the best way to support it.

Unseen justice turns out to be the most powerful protection we can have. And it's free. It's something we create (or not) every day in our dealings with ourselves and others. When the power of justice dawned on the First Nations of the Northeast, they stopped slaughtering each other and followed the Peacemaker's advice to build their visible societies on this invisible idea.

Protecting Property: Scene-Only Justice

If the job of justice is to protect, then what exactly do we ask to be protected? As we discussed in chapter 1, the Euro-American model calls on justice to protect private property. And it's a legitimate concern. We need to feel safe in our personal, physical environment, and protecting private property is how we've chosen to address this core need.

Yet focusing justice's protection powers primarily on private property leads us in short order to "scene-only" thinking. Several millennia of limiting justice to contests over which property should belong to whom has not produced a just world. The model lacks too much of justice's unseen context to pull it off. Fairness, an idea of the unseen, gets drowned out by greed, an obsession with the seen.

Reducing justice's protection powers to defending property is like marking off sections of a stage and telling a theater company to fight over who gets to stand on which spot. Far from protecting the meaningfulness of what goes on in theater, the model inspires turf wars. Some actors may want more of the stage than they could actually stand on. Or they may want center stage: "Location, location, location!" We'd get action, but we wouldn't have a play. The meaning that's supposed to unfold in theater wouldn't happen.

So, too, some meaning beyond property is supposed to unfold in human experience, yet concerns over our visible forms can divert us from it. Organizing our lives around getting property and protecting it, we forget to use the seen to tell a more meaningful story. Why? Because our concept of justice has given us a bum steer: it says the more property we acquire, the more we're getting our just deserts—our fair place on life's stage. Justice must involve more than protecting property, because we as human beings involve more.

Meaning: Humanity's Implicate Order

Starting with the seen to create justice doesn't work, because it misses what's most essential to humans: meaning. To work for us, our model of justice must take into account what matters to us. Meaning is our implicate order, our sense of who we are and why we're here. It's the vast, unseen reservoir out of which our lives take form. Meaning is how the whole manifests through everything that's us: our feelings, aims, longings, perceptions, and sense of purpose. It's the hidden organizer of our lives, yet like justice, it's invisible. We see evidence of it in how we focus our time, thoughts, and energies, but meaning itself remains unseen.

In *Creating Sanctuary*, Sandra Bloom explains how even our sense of safety comes from our sense of meaning. If we feel meaningfully connected to our world, we feel safe. That's why we're always looking for the meaning of things—why humans are "the meaning-making animal." We need a high level of meaning to get out of bed or walk down the street without being scared. Bloom writes:

> Most people base their sense of safety in the world on a sense of meaning that they have derived individually from their own experience and from the social milieu of which they are a part— their gender, their family, their community, their ethnic group, their racial group, their religious community, their national group. Man is the meaning-making animal. All of our cultural achievements are directed at making sense of the world we live in and of each other.[15]

15. Sandra Bloom, *Creating Sanctuary* (New York and London: Routledge, 1997), 71.

When bad things happen and we can't make sense of them, our sense of meaning is shaken. If we lose our connection to meaning altogether, we lose our reason to live. We become self-destructive, or our immune systems weaken. We need meaning in our lives as much as we need food, clothes, and shelter.

In his classic book *Man's Search for Meaning*, psychologist Viktor Frankl tells how he discovered this in the Nazi concentration camps in which he was imprisoned.[16] Frankl observed that the prisoners who stayed connected with their inner meaning survived, whereas those who lost it fell apart and died, although they may have been physically stronger to begin with. The ability to find meaning and live from it, even in the face of the worst conditions, made the difference between life and death.

Because meaning speaks to who we are and what we're here to be and do, meaning and justice go together. In Bohm's terms, meaning is our implicate order—the formative ground from which our lives take shape. Accordingly, justice must reach into these unseen levels of human life in order to do its job of protecting our visible expression. To feel safe and secure in the world, we need justice to protect our meaning.

Maybe that's why Socrates and Plato came to the understanding of justice that they did in *The Republic*. We can't have justice without thinking about personal meaning, because that's the cornerstone of human life. Justice as a human affair must be about humans, and if we're about meaning, justice has to be about meaning as well. Our meaning has to count for something. It has to be worth honoring and protecting; otherwise, we don't feel valued, which means we don't feel we're being treated rightly or fairly. We feel expendable, worthless—precisely the unseen context that sets the stage for unhappiness and crime.

By protecting our meaning in life, justice protects society. We're all needed not as robots or clones of some preset image but in our own special meanings, which change and develop. Our very differences make society healthy, because then societies have more resources to respond to crises and evolve. To protect society's health and ours too, justice must protect our different and individualized meanings.

16. Viktor E. Frankl, *Man's Search for Meaning* (Boston: Beacon Press, 1959).

Two Models of Justice: Two Models of Meaning

The two contrasting paradigms of justice—justice as rewards and punishments and justice as protecting who we are and supporting us in doing what's ours to do—address meaning issues differently.

The reward–punishment model of justice defines meaning in terms of the rewards or punishments we receive. Since our meaning depends on our being able to prove either that we've earned rewards or that we don't deserve punishments, the model sets us up to be stressed and defensive. Our worth isn't a given; it hangs in the balance. With our best intentions, things may not work out as we hoped. Our efforts can be misconstrued, especially when everyone else is angling to get rewards and avoid blame and punishment too.

Mayhem follows. Sometimes things work out, and we go into astonished ecstasy. But other times, things go from bad to worse. Either we don't receive the rewards we feel we deserve, or we're unfairly punished. Innocent people frequently go to jail; since 1973, eighty-two people later proven innocent have been put on death row.[17] Those involved with dispensing both rewards and punishments are neither omniscient nor infallibly just. Consequently, as long as our meaning in life depends on externals, we never feel secure.

But honest mistakes aren't the only problem; the entire system of rewards and punishments can function unfairly. From our own experiences, we know that the best people don't always get rewarded, nor do the worst thieves, abusers, or con artists in positions of power get restrained. Aggressive personality types elbow their way to the top, while less assertive though often more competent people go unnoticed. White-collar drug dealers, bribed politicians, and corporate raiders drive Mercedeses, while people doing good for their families, communities, society, and the earth struggle to pay the bills.

What's going on here? Why is a culture so committed to rewards and punishments so unable to allocate them justly, especially since that's the purported point of organizing life this way? According to the fourth

17. Stacy A. Teicher, "Making amends for jailing the innocent," *The Christian Science Monitor,* October 14, 1999.

root principle, there's no mystery here. When justice is reduced to set-tling disputes over visibles, justice can be externally manipulated, so that those most adept at manipulating appearances determine who gets what. The best spin-doctors or most outwardly powerful get the reward and avoid the blame; hence, they define justice as it's actually experienced. The larger context of unseen principles and values that would prevent such abuse has been excluded from how we think about justice.

Justice rooted in the unseen deals with meaning differently. Human worth—indeed, the worth of all life forms—is a given, a starting point. No one has to prove this. We're all the holomovement expressed, so we each have a place that's ours in the big picture. All our presences need to be felt, and our voices heard.

By not budging from this premise, soul-honoring justice supports our efforts to connect with who we are and do what's ours to do—to make the best use of our talents. Far from judging, condemning, or excluding us, justice helps us discover how profoundly we belong—how we're needed precisely for who we are. From the mystic perspective as well as from David Bohm's, we wouldn't be here if we weren't needed; that's why we've been called into being.

Meaning, then, isn't contingent on externals, even though external conditions matter. For example, those who love to study whales or teach children don't care about having a million dollars or living in mansions filled with servants. Attending to such things would be tedious distrac-tions, as many lottery winners have discovered. We do, however, need the wherewithal to do what we love and feel called to do—we need the education, funding, network of colleagues, and means of living that our endeavors require. Meaning-centered justice works to make this hap-pen—to structure societies so that they support us in pursuing our life's meaning.

But what social structures do this? A meaning-oriented model of justice doesn't seem to fit any of the conventional categories—not social-ism, communism, or capitalism—though it would share similarities with each. Similar to socialism and communism, this model seeks a balance in how the seen side of life is managed—our physical, educational, finan-cial, and other tangible human needs—for only through balance can all needs be met. What sense does it make to over-meet a few people's needs by under-meeting everyone else's? Meaning-centered justice seeks a balance not to inflate state power over individuals but to enrich society by helping everyone do what's his or hers to do. That's what we like about the ideals of socialism and communism, distinct from the twentieth-century corrupt, control-addicted practices of them.

What we like about capitalist theory—again, distinct from the twentieth-century corrupt, power-warped practices of it—is its accent on freedom and the individual. Meaning-centered justice depends on these values entirely. Who else knows what's ours to do but we ourselves? Even our parents and spouses can't decide this for us. And how can we find our calling except by exercising freedom—a freedom that we don't have as long as we're bound by wage slavery, the curse of capitalist societies?

None of these systems have a good track record of helping us do what's ours to do. Neither have they actually created the balanced societies they aspire to. Nor, for that matter, have any of them forged a balanced, respectful, sustainable relationship to the earth and future generations. Meaning-centered justice proposes that we evolve social systems that don't yet exist on earth and for which we haven't yet developed adequate social structures.

Despite their current nonexistence, though, such models seem to be part of our shared vision of our future. In all the *Star Trek* series and films, no one worries about money. If it exists, it's not on people's minds the way it is now (except for the merchant Ferengi or some old-school Klingons, of course). Projecting several centuries into the future, we assume all beings will be valued for who they are. Money no longer calls the shots; individual needs and qualities do, or on a larger scale, concern for the general welfare does. If we need education, we get it, and not by putting ourselves or our parents in debt. Society needs us not angry, lost, and penniless but in full possession of our minds, hearts, and talents—and fully motivated by our sense of meaning.

Henry David Thoreau closed his famous essay on "Civil Disobedience" with imagining a state that truly honors the individual. Clearly he did not see our current majority-rule form of government as the pinnacle of evolution in social structures:

I please myself with imagining a State at last which can afford to be just to all men, and to treat the individual with respect as a neighbor; which even would not think it inconsistent with its own repose if a few were to live aloof from it, not meddling with it, nor embraced by it, who fulfilled all the duties of neighbors and fellow men. A State which bore this kind of fruit, and suffered it to drop off as fast as it ripened, would prepare the way for a still more perfect and glorious State, which I have also imagined, but not yet anywhere seen.[18]

Protecting Relationships by Changing Cultural Patterns

Personal meaning doesn't happen in a vacuum, though. It emerges in the context of relationships, which means justice must protect relationships and all kinds of them. Indeed, we depend on justice to protect all the relationships that make life on the planet possible, for without justice, relationships don't last long. People don't drop nuclear weapons on each other, for instance, unless some injustice is afoot. Socrates observed in the opening pages of *The Republic* that even thieves must practice fairness in their relations with each other, or they could never get any proper thieving done. Relationships must be patterned on justice, or they don't work.

Insofar as our cultural philosophy focuses on individuals as separate atoms, we've overlooked the influence of relationships. In current justice systems, the offender acting out his or her traumas on others is brought to trial, whereas the cultural paradigms and institutions that contribute to traumatizing mental and emotional habits go unquestioned.

If we want justice in society, we must address our patterns of relating, especially when their very structures make our relationships a source of pain. For example, power imbalances court the abuse of power, and when it happens, injustices occur: the less powerful are not free to be who they are or to do what's theirs to do. This experience produces

18. Henry David Thoreau, "Civil Disobedience." The full text of this famous essay is readily available on the Internet on various university and other library web sites. A simple search of the author and title will suffice.

trauma, because it sends a message to those in the one-down position that denies their identity, worth, and even existence. Trauma researchers Sandra Bloom and Arnon Bentovim observe that, given the amount of trauma in our multicultural history as well as in many lives today, our psyches and societies become organized around it: "Trauma can become the central organizing principle for human thought, feelings, behavior, and meaning."[19]

How can this be? Our society looks so "normal." We appear to be functioning and getting the jobs done. Well, yes and no. Not all trauma is visible. Most of it is carried in our emotional structures, and most of it starts when the unseen context of justice is lacking in our relationships. Whether we're talking about intimate family relationships, relationships at work, or relationships between groups in society, when we don't have a true model of justice to protect us, we fall into habits of relating that communicate subtle and blatant hurt. Even with the best of intentions, relationships devolve into contests for control, manipulation, or domination, because we don't have the unseen justice context to keep us on track. Before we know it, none of us feels free to be who we are or to express our truth. Our relationships start feeling like psychological prisons, and we find ourselves functioning as either inmates or jailers to each other.

Resentments and frustrations build, which lead to hostilities. The potential for positive partnering, not to mention genuine intimacy, diminishes, while the potential for hurt mounts. We know we're unhappy and contributing to others' unhappiness, and yet we don't know how to change things. As Peter Senge wrote, "Structures of which we are unaware hold us prisoners."

That's because the patterns aren't personal in origin; their roots lie in cultural systems—established beliefs, traditions, and institutions. Many of these cultural patterns are instilled through child-rearing methods. In her book *For Your Own Good*, recovery researcher Alice Miller explains how traditional child-rearing rules epitomize injustice and model it in the parent-child relationship. The inherent power imbalance gives rise to abuses of power. Children receive the message that who

19. Bloom, *Creating Sanctuary*, 72.

they are is somehow flawed or unacceptable and that they must become what authorities tell them to be in order to become accepted. This isn't basic discipline; it's a toxic message that erodes self-worth and self-acceptance. After years of this message beyond what's needed to prevent food fights or children from playing in the street, we lose confidence in doing what's ours to do and believe instead that we should do what others expect. A pattern of self-rejection is implanted in us, and we find it hard to be who we are in relationships, much less pursue our life's callings.

To create justice in our relationships, we need to change these cultural patterns, and the response that works is the Peacemaker's—building a new consciousness of justice.

A more human justice doesn't call down abstract concepts of who deserves what, as if it's ours to balance the cosmic scales of rewards and punishments. If we believe in a judging God (and we personally have our doubts—some version of God, yes; judging, no), we must also believe that the job is taken, and that humans are not God's equal. We no longer believe that kings and their courts are God's chosen representatives for judging people on earth. Neither do we believe in human infallibility, which balancing something as important as the divine, cosmic, or human scales of justice would require. If there are divine scales of justice and if some divine being has a direct hand in righting them, then it's comforting to believe that God, and not we, maintains their ultimate balance, albeit on levels we may not see.

Entrusting God's job to God, we're free to evolve a notion of justice that we're more fitted to doing something about. We give justice—and hence ourselves—the job of protecting the fundamental human needs for security, meaning, and self-worth. Associating justice with supporting, nurturing, and caring for each other instead of judging, condemning, and excluding each other moves us in this direction. We think of justice in more humane terms, and by so doing we make a paradigm shift in our core philosophy of what it's all about.

Millions of people around the world are already making such a shift. On personal levels, the rules of child-rearing and schooling are changing to reflect a truer justice, one that honors children as individuals deserving of respect. Few parents these days can stomach raising children by the traditional book, and religions no longer preach "spare the rod and spoil the child." *Hinduism Today*, for example, regularly runs articles opposing corporal punishment and exploring alternative models of parent–child relationships.[20] Discipline isn't used to inflict hurt but simply to intervene on destructive behavior and to support growth beyond it. Parents want methods more consistent with nurturing a child's self-worth and potentials.

These developments reflect a commitment of adults to resolving their own inner pain and fragmentation. Across society, we're learning how to heal the trauma of injustices carried within our emotional structures, so that we don't perpetuate these patterns in our dealings with others. We're trying to make soul-destructive cycles stop with us by learning new ways of being with ourselves and consequently of being together. Gandhi entitled his autobiography *The Story of My Experiments with Truth*. He used his own life as an experiment for learning about justice, and then he applied what he learned to changing Indian society. So too, we're shifting paradigms by using our own psyches and lives as our laboratories, and then we're asking our cultural belief systems and institutions to change with us.

At the forefront of this paradigm shift is the restorative justice movement, questioning as it does the old judge-and-punish model and proposing instead a spectrum of relationship-restoring methods. Independently and around the globe, therapists, social workers, lawyers, judges, prisoners, and prison guards are abandoning retribution in favor of healing. They're working to identify soul-damaging patterns and to engage people instead in experiencing their souls' meaning and potentials for change.

The paradigm shift in our cultural philosophy of justice is well under way. It's happening in our personal lives as we heal from the trauma of injustices, shift our emotional structures to reflect a greater self-justice,

20. *Hinduism Today.* The entire July 1998 issue is devoted to this subject, the lead story being, "Corporal Punishment: Shall We Be Tough or Tender with Kids?" There are also articles on this subject in the July 1997 issue, "To Beat or Not to Beat?" and the May/June 2000 issue, "No Spanking." See Resources at the back of this book under "Newsletters, publications, and information" for further information on *Hinduism Today.*

and consequently change our models of relating. And it's happening in our more formal models of practicing justice in society, as we use broken relations as opportunities for personal transformation as well as for addressing the larger system sources of pain.

Using the Unseen in Everyday Life

To ground this chapter about the seen and the unseen, we'd like to explore how the two work in everyday life when we're faced with conflict. How does a soul-honoring model of justice use its unseen powers to protect our relationships when they're strained to breaking?

Let's first recap the territory. The fourth root principle states that the seen and the unseen, as two aspects of one reality, must be kept in balance. We need both to create a good life. We know the seen; it's in front of us all the time. The unseen is the context we bring to it, and that's what justice offers. Belonging to the category of the unseen, justice is a way of understanding who we are in the big picture and how we can live happily together. It does this by affirming our innate worth and potentials for change. A justice that shames or demeans us—that treats us as less than who we are—is not true justice but a shadow of it. It's shadow justice because, by reducing us to right or wrong actions, it omits our unseen side and so fails to do us justice. Whole justice treats us as whole beings, seen and unseen both, which is the only way to treat us fairly.

But how do we practice this in the trenches of everyday experience, especially when conflicts arise? How do we create space for the unseen to come in and transform our experience of the seen? How does the unseen protect the seen in the midst of disputes, when everything about the seen appears to be falling apart?

We'd speculate that all restorative justice practices, and certainly the ones we've studied, operate on the fourth root principle of uniting the seen and the unseen dimensions and keeping them in balance. Specifically, they unite the seen and unseen dimensions of who we are, bringing more of our meaning as human beings to the negotiating table. The practices that we'd like to use as examples have become almost universally recognized as effective for conflict resolution, namely, the methods outlined in the book *Getting to Yes: Negotiating Agreement Without Giving In*, written by Roger Fisher and William Ury of the Harvard Negotiation Project.

Fisher and Ury present their ideas clearly and compellingly, and we highly recommend reading their book. Here, we'd like to suggest that these methods have the power they do precisely because they use the unseen to create a context that protects the seen. Their methods reinforce the teaching of the fourth root principle, namely, that only by keeping the seen and unseen in balance can we work out fair and just resolutions to conflicts, and thereby protect the good in our lives.

Fisher and Ury pose the dilemma we've all faced in conflicts. Do we take a "hard" position and refuse to budge until we get our way, invariably damaging our relationship with the other? Or do we take a "soft" position and yield for the sake of preserving the relationship, only to discover that the "resolution" doesn't work for us, which puts us back at square one? Neither strategy works, they explain, which is why they propose an alternative, described as "principled negotiation." Right away with the term "principled," the unseen comes in.

Fisher and Ury present four methods for principled negotiating:

(1) separate the people from the problem;

(2) focus on interests, not on positions;

(3) invent options for mutual gain; and

(4) insist on using objective criteria—principles instead of power—for arriving at decisions.[21]

What's the logic here? If we start with the seen—the situation presented to us of entrenched opposition—there's no way out. What's visible is fixed, set by hard and fast boundaries. The only way to get things moving is to introduce perspectives that carry us beyond the seen to the unseen, to the realm of not-yet-recognized realities and potentialities. But how do we break the mesmerizing fixation on the seen, the very

21. Roger Fisher and William Ury, *Getting to Yes: Negotiating Agreement Without Giving In* (New York: Houghton Mifflin, 1981), xv; 2nd ed. with Bruce Patton (New York: Penguin Books, 1991).

perspective that keeps us locked in deadening win-lose or even no-win models?

(1) *Separate the people from the problem.* We start by expanding our awareness of the people involved. We see them not as opponents first but as people first, fellow humans possessed of many dimensions to their being, including potentials for change, growth, and healing. When we're in the midst of conflict, the warm, rational, fair-minded, honorable, even basically human side of the idiot so-and-so definitely qualifies as unseen.

Conflicts narrow our views of each other, since it's easy to identify ourselves and others with whatever positions we're taking. We forget that we're people with feelings, dreams, and challenges before we're men or women; black, red, yellow, or white; conservatives or liberals; management or labor, Catholic, Protestant, or Jewish, that is, "us" or "them." Seeing all parties in narrowly defined ways, we can't imagine being together happily. When we're not open to each other's greater reality, we become trapped inside how we appear on the surface.

Fisher and Ury break the seen-only mesmerism with the simple insight that we're more than the stereotypical images we present. Hidden in our pasts are stories that reveal how we've come to where we are and that shed light on why we think and act as we do. Unseen in our futures are potentials for developing, transcending our current views, and experiencing each other differently. And here in the present, we each have resources, talents, and abilities that surpass the role of defending this or that position. All this remains invisible to those whose encounter with us is through a polarized situation.

The trick lies in realizing that, whereas a position is fixed, we're not. Because we're more than the positions we assume, we can move and shift; and as we do, our perspectives on ourselves, others, and problems change. By acknowledging what's unseen about us, we're able to engage more sides of us than those that lead to deadlock. In other words, when we use a model of justice that affirms who we each are in our fullness, we do greater justice to each other, and as a result, we're more able to resolve our differences.

In *Reason for Hope*, Jane Goodall tells how she dealt with impasse when she met with scientists involved with animal testing. After touring the hellish conditions of animals used for testing at the federally funded laboratory SEMA, Inc., in 1987, she found herself turning to this method. Sickened and reeling from what she saw, in tears as she reached her fingers through the bars to the chimps caged in the dark, she was at a loss for words. She writes of this experience:

> When I emerged from the underground lab, shocked and sad, I was taken to sit at a table with SEMA and National Institutes of Health personnel. I realized that everyone was looking at me, questioningly. What on earth could I say? And then, as so often happens when my mind goes blank, words came.
> "I think you all know what I felt in there," I said. "And since you are all decent, compassionate people, I assume you feel much the same." They could hardly contradict.[22]

After affirming the unseen side of the humans present, she spoke to them about the unseen side of chimpanzees, not visible from the traumatized, severely depressed, drugged chimps locked in cages:

> I talked about the lives of chimpanzees in the wild, their close family ties, their long and carefree childhood. I described their use of tools, their love of comfort, the rich variety of their diet, and some of our recent insights into the workings of the chimpanzee mind. Then I broached the idea of a workshop, a meeting at which biomedical scientists and veterinarians and technicians from labs could discuss, with field scientists and ethologists and animal welfare advocates, what could be done to improve conditions for the lab chimpanzees.[23]

By appealing to what's unseen about humans and animals, Goodall used the unseen to change the seen. In her work around the world, instead of accepting polarized positions, she believes in trying to connect the unseen minds and hearts of people with the unseen character of animals:

22. Goodall, *Reason for Hope*, 213.

23. Ibid., 213.

[A] question I am asked repeatedly is: How can you keep calm when you go into an animal research lab? How can you stop yourself from yelling and shouting and accusing everyone of cruelty? The easy answer is that the aggressive approach simply doesn't work. In addition, while some people are, unfortunately, sadistic, most people who are cruel to animals simply haven't understood their true nature. They don't believe that any animals, even those with complex brains, have minds and feelings and emotions similar to ours. It is my task to try to change their attitudes in this matter; they will not listen if I raise my voice and point an accusing finger. Instead they will become angry and hostile. And that will be the end of the dialogue.[24]

If we're working for change and transformation, separating people from the problem is the strategy that works. Granted, it may take a saint or divine intervention to pull it off sometimes. In the absence of those, we can boost our resolve by remembering our goals. If we want to blame the jerks and fight from moral or personal outrage, we can go for it and nail the suckers—and keep fighting, since nothing will change. But if, as Jane Goodall observes, we're seeking some real shift in consciousness and hence in how we're structuring our lives together, we need to grant ourselves and others the space to move beyond our current positions. Acknowledging what's unseen about everyone involved is a good place to start.

Criminologist John Braithwaite applies this method to criminal justice practices. In his book *Crime, Shame and Reintegration*, he explains the need to separate the criminal from the crime.[25] Criminals are people with stories too. Indeed, classifying them as "criminals" mistakenly identifies people with their actions, reducing them to their crimes. We're more than what we do, and we can become yet more—all of us can. We need to make this distinction, for otherwise we label others as miscreants—"bad people"—and ostracize them. The stigma hangs over

24. Ibid., 270.

25. John Braithwaite, *Crime, Shame and Reintegration* (Cambridge, UK: Cambridge University Press, 1989).

them for life, preventing them from moving on and leaving the persona of "thief" or "druggie" behind. We trap them inside the very image that we—and most likely they too—wish to see changed.

Not that we turn a blind eye to crimes. Braithwaite recommends that we shame the act but not the actor. Stealing and killing are wrong, shameful deeds. But the people who have done these things are not shameful beings. As a result, it's their destiny as far as justice is concerned to heal from whatever drove them down that road. As they do, they develop other dimensions of who they are and can be reintegrated into society.

Indonesians, who inherited European law from Dutch colonial rule, have a tradition that welcomes home someone who's been in prison. Herman Bianchi explains:

> [W]hat happens when a man has been in prison for two, three years, still today, when he comes back into his community? It's a big feast. They put tables on the street, and they make a lovely meal. "You are the prodigal son. You have done the duty of penitence, and now you're back, you're again with us." . . . Now, the Indonesians did not understand imprisonment, but, all right, let's try to diminish the consequences of imprisonment by receiving the man back into his community. They say, "You are our brother again. We love you again." That's something beautiful. That's *adat* [the Indonesian word for the feeling of justice beyond legislation].[26]

The need for transformation and reintegration holds true whether the killer is an eleven-year-old African American boy, a tobacco executive, a pharmaceuticals manager who uses political clout to push dangerous drugs on to the public, an auto manufacturer who authorizes the production of unsafe cars, or a government official who, at the behest of corporate powers, wages overt or covert war on countries to get control of their resources. On this list, only the street kid gets the label of "murderer."

26. From David Cayley's interview with Herman Bianchi, "Justice as Sanctuary," *Ideas*, 27 October, 10 November 1997, ID9743 (Canadian Broadcasting Corporation), pages 3 and 14, respectively.

The point is that we need to have everyone engaged in healing traumas, twisted minds, and broken hearts, so that society receives the best use of our talents and energies. Instead of ostracizing those who have harmed others, whether they wear Gucci suits, white lab coats, uniforms, or Salvation Army specials, we need to help them rejoin society—not just in a physical way but in a mind and heart way.

Connecting with the unseen dimensions of who we are is our way back, and it's the way of true justice. By not losing sight of the unseen dimensions of ourselves and others, we protect our powers to resolve our differences and join in transformation. We open ourselves to working together as human beings who may have more similar interests than we imagined, which leads to the next point.

(2) *Focus on interests, not positions.* Positions are fixed: "I want that person jailed!" "I want $300,000 for my house and not a penny less!" "I'm taking two suitcases no matter what you say!" But behind our positions lie interests—concerns about what we really want and need. Fisher and Ury explain, "Your position is something you have decided upon. Your interests are what caused you to so decide."[27] Whereas our positions speak to "what" we want, our interests speak to "why"—the reasons that led us to choose one position over another.

If we start with our positions, we start with the end of our reasoning processes, our conclusions—what's visible in the present. Yet we spend our lifetimes mulling over our concerns and reasons, which distill into positions as we go. Our processes of arriving at conclusions remain invisible, but they express something about us. When our end-of-reasoning positions clash, it's because our unseen sides don't jibe, at least not as our positions narrowly present them.

Shifting the focus from positions to interests creates an opening. Because our positions don't express all the interests that we have, we need to look past them to the wider domain of what we're feeling in order to find common ground. Humans share many interests that we'd all grant as being legitimate. For example, we all have interests in happiness, security, health, freedom, and love. We may not agree on how to fulfill these interests, but we can join with others in holding them

27. Fisher and Ury, *Getting to Yes*, 41.

and respecting the presence of these interests in others.

By acknowledging each other's interests, we expand the possibilities for meeting them, because we go deeper into our unseen experience. A position charting only one way of meeting interests presents a tiny window on what we're thinking. Sharing our interests with each other opens the view, revealing more of where we're all coming from, and this wider perspective gives us the space to be flexible and find alternatives. Some part of us that we ourselves may not have known can hold the key to resolution.

Learning about each other's concerns and reasoning processes makes us think about situations in new ways. Fisher and Ury offer a simple example:

> Consider the story of two men quarreling in a library. One wants the window open and the other wants it closed. They bicker back and forth about how much to leave it open: a crack, halfway, three quarters of the way. No solution satisfies them both.
>
> Enter the librarian. She asks one why he wants the window open: "To get some fresh air." She asks the other why he wants it closed: "To avoid the draft." After thinking a minute, she opens wide a window in the next room, bringing in fresh air without a draft.[28]

By exploring our interests together, we're able to do greater justice to each other. We develop the art of "thinking with" others—and they with us—thereby creating a new default mode from the old habit of "thinking against" each other.

That's why the media's proclivity to frame issues in polarized positions is unhelpful, however sensational the arguments they create. Polarizing the public mind into opposing positions shuts down thought, for once we've sided with a position, we're prone not to think about the subject further in any deep or open way. Neither do we think of our opponents as real people. They become the "other," people for whom we have diminishing respect.

28. Ibid., 40.

Polarizing the public mind is also an effective way to make us think that problems are insoluble—that mutually beneficial solutions can't exist. Debating positions ad nauseam, we start believing that humans can never get along, and nothing can ever be resolved. We review the positions (usually not more than two or three), observe the mutually exclusive nature of them, and despair of finding solutions that would be workable for everyone. Intentionally or not, we condition ourselves to think that win-lose is inescapable and win-win a pipe-dream.

No wonder conflict resolution is a new discipline; it's a new concept. Whereas positions are seen and heard, interests are unseen and unexpressed. As such, interests can easily slip to the periphery of consciousness, lost in the shuffle of positions. Following a trail of positions, we lose touch with whether our positions are in fact serving our interests. Indeed, we can find ourselves sacrificing real interests—in being happy or experiencing joy in life, for example—for the sake of maintaining positions that don't serve us.

In the case of victims of crime and their families, for instance, their interests involve needs for safety; for physical, emotional, and psychological healing; for putting their lives back together; for financial and medical needs; for feeling good and safe about their communities; perhaps for learning how to deal with police, lawyers, courts, hospitals, insurance companies; and so on. Victims have many personal and practical interests, few of which are met by a position that seeks revenge on the one or ones who hurt them.

This is why restorative justice shifts the focus from revenge positions to addressing the practical interests of victims. As a culture, we spend billions to preserve the punishment position, while very little to address the interests of victims, offenders, and their communities in healing.

In short, interests expand the possibilities for resolving conflicts, because they point us deeper into who we are. We share more of ourselves and experience more of others, and this deeper connection gives us more to work with. By shifting from seen positions to unseen interests, we find formerly unseen possibilities for resolving our conflicts—the next method.

(3) *Invent options for mutual gain.* We all love to come up with options beyond what's obvious, because it engages our creativity, and it also

inspires freedom. In the moment of discovering an option that works for everyone, we realize we're not locked in to how things appear. Perhaps we felt trapped, and then suddenly we began to see ways to resolve differences that hadn't been apparent before. We shift from impossible to possible, and it's pure joy.

Beyond the moment of solving this or that problem, though, we realize that we can be so much more than we thought. We get locked in certain ways of being, but we don't have to be so defined. Exploring options is really about allowing ourselves to be more than we imagined we could be—doing justice not only to ourselves but also to our potentials. This is what inventing options for mutual gain calls us to do: to let ourselves change.

We're familiar with inventing technological options. For example, physically carrying a letter from one place to another is no longer the only way to communicate with people at a distance. We now have telephones, telexes, CB radios, answering machines, faxes, e-mails, satellites, cell phones, and who knows what else on the horizon. Over the past century, we've wrapped our minds around inventing physical-world options that were previously unimagined.

Faced with conflicts, we're challenged to bring this same inventive spirit to working out our relations with each other: person to person, gender to gender (men have more than Mars in their natal charts, and women more than Venus), group to group, labor to management, management to board, business to business, nation to nation, species to species, species to planet, and who knows what else. What we see of how humans interact—especially the control, manipulation, possessiveness, competition, polarization, defensiveness, mutual distrust, hostility, jealousy, and violence—does not exhaust the possibilities of how we may be together, any more than paper and envelopes exhaust the ways of communicating.

Fisher and Ury offer many helpful aids for pushing beyond the seen to unseen possibilities. They start by suggesting what does not help us to invent options. We get stuck in single-solution thinking, they say, because of four habits,[29] all of which cause us to spin our

29. Ibid., 57–59.

wheels in the narrow channels of the seen and not go beyond them.

First, we bring in judgments prematurely and don't give ourselves enough brainstorming time. Brainstorming is our direct, nonstop flight to the unseen. We need to allow ourselves time to roam the unseen and not be too quick to settle on solutions.

Second, we assume the end result will be to settle on a single answer that doesn't change, so that's what we seek from the start—"the one, right answer." Yet neither creativity nor life works like this. Every "solution" is a stepping stone to a new problem. Solutions are never fixed or static. A solution doesn't mean putting things in a box and having them stay there. The unseen that we're missing here is life's process, which is ongoing change.

Third, speaking of box-thinking, we assume "a fixed pie" or "fixed sum" game: "Either they get the deal, or we get it, but we can't both get it." "Either I control and love you, or I reject and hate you—no third option." It's the either/or, "all or nothing" model. In this case, the unseen that's missing are the countless ways of working things out beyond two extremes.

Finally, we're hampered by us/them thinking: "Solving my problem is my problem, and solving theirs is theirs." We're just learning that someone else's problem is our problem too, and that one-sided solutions aren't the solutions they seem. What's missing is an understanding of our unseen connectedness—that in the web of our relatedness, anyone's hurt is our hurt too.

Loosening these habits, we invite the unseen into our problem-solving processes to help us generate options that we never imagined. The unseen gives us the resources to become genuinely creative with our lives and the difficulties that arise.

Again, at its core, inventing options means exploring different ways of being who we are and doing what's ours to do—of opening ourselves to our own unseen potentials. The more we're creative with ourselves, the more options we can discover for what we can create together. But how do we make good all-around decisions about where to go or how to change?

(4) *Insist on using objective criteria—principles instead of power—for arriving at decisions.* The previous three methods balance the seen and

the unseen by bringing in more of the unseen. The fourth method balances the seen and the unseen by making us more savvy about the unseen. Not all that's unseen is good or helpful. In fact, much that's unseen can be a disaster. We protect the seen—in this case, our efforts at resolving conflicts—by keeping the wrong unseen concerns out and bringing the right ones in. The question is, which is which?

According to the fourth method of principled negotiation, wrong unseen concerns don't pertain to the problem and throw us off track. For example, fears about who wins and who loses, who is or will be more powerful, or who will come out looking better don't pertain to the issue at hand. They're extracurricular, so to speak. They're not the subject but side issues, yet we can become more emotionally caught up in them than in the issue at hand.

Other concerns that throw us off arise from power imbalances among the people involved. Insofar as these concerns predominate, we don't feel free to make good decisions. When might makes right and pressure, manipulation, and coercion determine decision-making, how can wise decisions be the result? "Who is more powerful?" is no philosopher's stone; neither are more subtle forms of coercion, such as using emotions, tears, guilt, threats, or ultimata to force a decision. Deciding things according to who exerts the greater pressure fails to address the real concerns involved. Good decisions don't come of it, because the actual issues remain unsolved. Hence, Fisher and Ury's motto: "Never yield to pressure, only to principle."[30]

Indeed, many unseen concerns qualify as irrelevant, and it's the job of justice-thinking to weed them out. Fisher and Ury pose an example of a conflict between a contractor who is building a house for someone for a fixed price. The contractor and the owner disagree about how deep the foundation should be, a depth unspecified in the contract:

> What if [the contractor] offers to hire your brother-in-law on the condition that you give in on the depth of the foundations? You would probably answer, "A job for my brother-in-law has nothing to do with whether the house will be safely supported on a

30. Ibid., 91.

foundation of that depth." What if the contractor then threatens to charge you a higher price? You would answer the same way: "We'll settle that question on the merits too. Let's see what other contractors charge for this kind of work," or "Bring me your cost figures and we'll work out a fair profit margin." If the contractor replies, "Come on, you trust me, don't you?" you would respond: "Trust is an entirely separate matter. The issue is how deep the foundations have to be to make the house safe."[31]

What right unseen concerns do we invite in? Logically, those that pertain to the problem. The best way not to get sidetracked, Fisher and Ury recommend, is to work out situations on their merits, attending to the substance of the differences and then basing a decision on mutually acceptable criteria. In other words, we need to stick to the real-life issues at hand—and the big unseen of who we are is always part of it—and avoid getting lost in irrelevancies.

Criteria for doing this can be found in adhering to standard professional practices or objective rules in a field. It can involve identifying principles that both parties agree to or submitting ourselves to standards of reasonableness gauged by some third party. Or it can mean developing methods that both sides regard as fair. These are all different forms of unseen values. What we're looking for in the quest for mutually acceptable criteria, shared principles, or objective standards is an expression of justice, as best we understand it.

Ultimately, the right unseen categories open us to who we are. We are our own most right unseen category, because no matter what we're dealing with or who, we're wrestling with some issue that relates to our self-awareness. Right unseen categories widen our perspective of ourselves and hence of who we can be together. Using a soul-oriented model of justice, we resolve differences on the overall principle that decisions should help each of us connect with who we are and what's ours to do. The right unseen stuff catalyzes our change processes in these directions, making us jump levels in self-awareness, deepening our awareness of others, expanding our options for personal change, and

31. Ibid., 90–91.

strengthening our powers to undergo transformation. This is justice at work as a commitment to us as whole, unfolding beings, and it's the epitome of right unseen stuff.

From saving a society from self-annihilation to saving our relationships when they fall apart in conflict to saving ourselves from self-rejection and loss of meaning, justice can be a mighty force for good in human life. Its unseen quality only increases its power, because then it's universally available. Without justice's unseen protection, we make a mess of things and have no clue how to right them.

If your mind is anything like ours, though, this cannot be the end of the journey. We've just begun to think about justice differently. Many questions either remain or arise as a result. With justice, we have a tiger by the tail, and this creature has only begun to stretch her mighty legs.

In the next chapter, we'd like to consider a major objection to the way we've been discussing justice: does it really work in creating just worlds, or does it cause suffering instead?

NINE

A Call to Soul and Healing

O NE OBVIOUS OBJECTION to the paradigm of justice we've been exploring is that it's so individualistic that it leads straight to anarchy. Well, it does, and it doesn't. Anarchy has two opposite meanings, one inspired that serves as a beacon for personal and cultural transformation, the other grim, violent, and a highway to suffering.

Idealistic anarchy has drawn stellar advocates over the centuries: William Godwin (Percy Bysshe Shelley's father-in-law), Pierre-Joseph Proudhon, Leo Tolstoy, Oscar Wilde, Henry David Thoreau, countless artists and poets (e.g., Gustave Courbet, Georges Seurat, Robert Henri, Herbert Read), Aldous Huxley, Paul Goodman, as well as Mahatma Gandhi. Indeed the civil rights movement of the 1950s drew inspiration from anarchist philosophy, namely, a conviction in the worth of all individuals regardless of race, in the fallibility of governments to honor this worth appropriately, and in the right of individuals to peacefully oppose unjust treatment by society, the state, and their laws.

These thinkers and activists did not identify with the prevailing mindsets of their societies. Faced with the discrepancy between their inner truth and outer norms, they believed that "Soul-force," to use Gandhi's term, should have ascendancy over the "brute force" of established social, economic, political, religious, as well as family institutions. The way things are should not coerce us into compliance or conformity, if we're called to see things differently.

This doesn't mean that visionary anarchists think that we as individuals are perfect or infallibly right. We're not, nor should we expect ourselves to be. But we do have inner voices that are here to guide us. We carry within a wisdom that comes from who we are as the whole expressed, and these roots in reality—roots that we all possess by virtue of our existence—speak a truth that both we and our communities need to hear.

Neither are these voices calling for destruction. As anarchists of this type often observe, at our core we all want the same things—happiness, freedom, love, peace of mind, well-being, soul, and meaning. In our essence, we're connected by our shared rootedness in the whole, and these values describe different ways of experiencing our being as the holomovement expressed. Through them, we feel connected both to who we are and to what's greater than us in ways that feel right and good, as well as fulfilling.

As we go along, we bring our inner voices to our shared systems and ask that they change to reflect our growth. We ask that social structures be open to our perspectives or at least not rally to shut us down. If we see ways to restructure societies that further human happiness and planetary good, we ask that social systems consider our concerns and, if they see flaws in our proposed remedies, come up with something better. When outward structures resist change, idealistic anarchists seek nonviolent means for making the voice of individual soul and conscience heard.

We do this not en masse but one by one, individually. Change occurs, visionary anarchists believe, as we each think for ourselves, speak our truth, walk out from under oppressive models, and assert our freedom to follow our own light. Individuals lead society. As we awaken to who we are and claim our power to pursue our life's course as we see it, we are our own best hope for making this new millennium a dawning of freedom, justice, and joy.

Then there's the other anarchy, the nasty one, whose negative reputation eclipses in the public mind the insights of these visionaries and reformers. We're referring, of course, to anarchy as chaos created by individual acts not only of violence but also of greed, selfishness, domination, and exploitation, all of which bring untold suffering.

Whenever idealistic anarchy finds expression, this destructive image rears its ugly head, as it logically would. It raises the fear we all have that, if we express our individuality, we won't create justice but a nightmare. What about people who believe it's theirs to do terrorism, as anarchists of a desperate bent have believed? Or in more general terms, what guarantees that my doing whatever is mine to do won't make your life hell, or vice versa?

Whether we embrace the idealism of the first anarchy or fear chaos from the second would seem to hinge on whether or not we believe individuals are innately good—or at least good enough not to make hell on earth. If we're not good by nature, Plato's justice falls somewhere between a utopian pipe dream and a formula for social madness. Human nature is posed as the crux of the matter, and the argument that's used to dismiss individual self-government as the way to justice and social harmony is that we humans are a mess.

As arguments go, this isn't a hard one to make. Who hasn't seen the news? Who hasn't read history? Who hasn't been hurt by people? Frankly, we find the argument troublesome beyond our comfort zone because it is so persuasive. Even Socrates had a quaking reaction when faced with an especially fierce argument, so we're allowed our tremblings over this one. Indeed, if you've been worried all along about anarchist tendencies in this philosophy of justice, we marvel that you've stayed with us. Equally amazing and fortunate for our shaky stomachs and wobbly knees, we have a response.

To start, we want to reflect on the realities of anarchy, the chaos and dark-night version, that is, and what actually causes it. Our suspicion is that human nature is taking it on the chin, when something else is the culprit. Not our nature but the models we use to channel it cause suffering.

The Anarchy of "Might Makes Right"

Are we sure we don't already live under nasty anarchy's chaos far more than we realize—that our current models of philosophy and culture don't create precisely what we most fear? Specifically, the model of "might makes right," which functions as the de facto rule in social, corporate, political, and international spheres, is a potent chaos maker. How could it do otherwise? The model appeals to coercion and violence outright as its prime threats, threats which are carried out liberally to back up demands.

The twentieth century witnessed continual outbreaks of violence around the globe, all generated by a few in power attempting to control the earth's resources and dominate its people. Centuries before that, the "might-makes-right" model swept the American continent with the arrival of Europeans, almost totally annihilating Native peoples and cultures for the purpose of stealing their land and resources. "Might makes right" enslaved Africans, killing millions in the process. Every continent has horror stories, though, with "might makes right" at the middle of them. Today, "might makes right" ravages the earth, as if laws of nature, biology, and sustainability don't hold. It also roams the globe searching for the poorest, least protected populations to exploit in virtual slave labor. Thanks to this paradigm, we've reaped a full harvest of violence, injustice, and suffering down through history. Even though these evils aren't being done by lone assassins or bombers but by individuals in governments and corporations, it's nasty anarchy nonetheless, full blown and causing chaos and suffering—a breakdown of order.

But not only in national and world affairs is "might makes right" a doorway to suffering. In marriages, families, schools, communities, and religions, intimidation is often used to make us hesitant to speak our truth and to prevent us from following our inner guidance. We learn the rule of might in our earliest experiences, which is how it becomes the primary model we know. Children face it daily with bullies and sometimes with parents and teachers who use their authority in bullying ways. The rhetoric of freedom and equality is laid over an unrelenting childhood experience of "might makes right."

Whatever other chaos follows—as it does on any number of levels—the core effect is psychological and emotional anarchy. We live under the rule not of soul-respecting justice but of the most controlling personalities, those most skilled at shaming, instilling fear and guilt, imposing judgment, pressuring, or otherwise manipulating psyches and emotions. We learn not to trust anyone, believing that contests of might are never far away.

From marriages and families the model spreads to businesses, professions, and governments. We think that the way to make things run well is to control them, to apply force, coercion, and intimidation. The more control we exert, the greater the order and success we achieve.

Building on this premise, the most aggressive types dominate a group's dynamics, largely because of their readiness to use pressure backed by threats of creating pain. Either we fall in line, or chaos follows, whether as an emotional meltdown, a ruthless "re-org," or a forced, no-win, all-or-nothing "choice." Our culture offers a smorgasbord of blatant and subtle methods for getting our way by throwing our weight around, often with the support of moral, religious, business, and social belief systems.

This is the kind of anarchy we don't want, and it's everywhere. It's the anarchy not of living by individual conscience but of just the opposite, namely, of being controlled from without. We think we reject anarchy, and yet we embrace the philosophy that creates it.

That's because we're culturally ambivalent about the model: we don't like "might makes right," especially when we're on the receiving end, but we're afraid it's how the "real world" works; worse, we're afraid we need the model to maintain "order." So we grudgingly accept it and tolerate its consequences. Because of our compliance, the model "works," or at least appears to. Those most skilled at exerting pressure have their way. "Nice people finish last." Power talks, and heavy-handed threats bring the desired results. The ways might-minded people frame situations and the spin they give things tend to stick, usually because the trauma surrounding their assertions burns their perspectives onto everyone's psyches. Their games become the games we play, and their rules hold. "See," we tell ourselves, "'might makes right' is just how things are. We can't do anything to change it."

If we're one of the "nice people," that is, one of those not emotionally wired to be aggressive, we slip into the role of enablers. Fearful of pain let loose, we appease, cajole, tiptoe around, bite our tongues, sacrifice ourselves, react instead of act, stuff our feelings, hide our truth, whisper our frustrations to other enablers, and hope the fury will blow over until the next crisis, believing we haven't much power to do otherwise. We enable the model instead of challenging it, though it costs us in self-worth, the freedom to speak our truth, and happiness.

We've accepted this arrangement and given our energies to keeping the model going because we're raised to function this way. Adjusting ourselves to external might is the profile of a model child, student, spouse, employee, believer, or even citizen. Culturally, we don't learn how to deal in open, healthy ways with those who use, in Fisher and Ury's terms, pressure rather than principle. If we did, we'd know that pressure never works as a solution—that it prolongs and even exacerbates problems, because it fails to address the real concerns involved. Back to the *Titanic* metaphor, the captain could decree that there is no iceberg, but it wouldn't make the iceberg go away or stop the ship from sinking on hitting it.

Given the nature of the might model, how could fear and chaos not follow? Might has no inner *logos*, no corner on justice, truth, or the good. It offers not the slightest promise that human relationships will be handled in wise, fair, mutually beneficial, or genuinely problem-solving— i.e., principled—ways. All that control can promise is that it will be used in the interests of those who possess it.

As to who we are—our nature—a might model describes us in terms that necessitate external control, namely, as separate selves locked in conflict, an issue we've discussed throughout this book. Being separate makes us vulnerable, and so we're driven to finding big sticks to protect ourselves from all the other scared, separate beings. Comparing sticks and using what sticks we have to our cleverest advantage become the rules of action and the organizing principles of human affairs. If this is who we are and nothing more, then we do indeed need to be controlled from without to prevent us from killing each other.

Small wonder that we've witnessed the drama of dictators in family, political, religious, and corporate life. Dictators and demagogues are the direct manifestations of our cultural philosophy. We think we need them—more, that they're our saviors, especially if we think they're benevolent and exerting their force for the greater good. If "might makes right" were not our cultural paradigm, power-driven types wouldn't get to square one. As it is, if we don't agree with the model— if we think individual soul and conscience should have a say in challenging the rule of might—then we're the ones charged with being the dangerous anarchists, the ones threatening social order.

It's not our cultural habit to describe the model in such bald terms, though. We dress it up so that it sounds good. In government, for example, the concept operates as majority rule: those who are mightier in numbers can do what they choose. It sounds like "power to the people," and compared with monarchies or dictatorships, it is, especially when democracies work according to principles, integrity, and a commitment not to power but to the general welfare and to future generations.

Without a firm commitment to such principles, though, democracies play with anarchic fire. Sheer majority has no principle of fairness inherent in it, which is why mob rule doesn't inspire confidence. If it did, why would we need a constitutional Bill of Rights to protect the minority against it? We need safeguards because majority rule is by no means just. It may reflect collective wisdom and the melding of individual consciences, and we hope it does; but it may also reflect collective prejudice, greed, ignorance, or rumor-driven hysteria.

Or worse. Appeals to majority rule may, in fact, cover a corrupted democracy, one in which wealthy factions have usurped control. In *The Republic*, Socrates and Plato argued that this inevitably happens to democracies—that powerful vested interests take over them, which is what we face today. Financial might has virtually reduced the democratic model to a quaint delusion, useful only in keeping the public's focus off what's really going on. We tell ourselves that we have a democracy, that "might makes right" isn't the rule, that our government runs according to principle rather than pressure, that money doesn't buy elections or sway decisions, and that the media who report what's going on aren't owned and controlled by a few corporate conglomerates. Why?

Because we can neither process the implications of things being otherwise nor figure out what to do about it should the worst be true. Might-wielders have developed clever skills of deception over the centuries, and "we the people" seem ready to believe them. Not that we're pointing fingers; we know the impulse: "What can we do?" haunts us all.

The Power to Change: Calling Our Souls Back

Yet we actually do have powers we don't realize, namely, to shift models and choose a different script. Plot lines and scenarios—this money-driven scandal, that backstabbing power struggle, those behind-the-scenes connivings—aren't the issue. Outer dramas are effects, not causes. Neither are people to blame. Not the actors of this script but the script itself, the model, is faulty. That's what sets the course, inspires the motives, and choreographs the actions. What needs to change is the philosophy, and that's in our power to do.

In other words, the alternative to tolerating bad anarchy is to name the model that's causing suffering and to identify how it works—or more accurately, fails. We can stop believing that "might makes right" is our ticket to social order, because it's just the opposite. We can expose the model's link to interpersonal misery as well as to a history of injustice, devastation, and unhappiness. And then we can reject the model, chaos-making that it is.

So yes, nasty anarchy is a problem: it wreaks havoc at all levels of human society. But Plato's model—or Gandhi's or Thoreau's or that of mystics—isn't what's behind it. Individual conscience is not causing all this suffering. What creates social misery is the very thing that vision-ary anarchists argue against, namely, control by force, whether it's emo-tional, physical, political, racial, bureaucratic, military, religious, or financial. Visionary anarchists oppose the rule of might wherever they find it for a practical reason: beneath a controlling personality is a psy-che that's out-of-control, one that's drowning in trauma, soul lost, and desperately seeking to control externals in order to save itself, to find security and meaning.

The psyche issue turns out to be the crux of the problem: it's not only why we have "might makes right," but also why the sane alterna-tive of changing models has been so devilishly hard to implement. Because the might model has dominated so many cultures and so much of human history, not only controllers but all of us suffer the soul loss and trauma that come from living under "might makes right." We lose touch with our inner compass, and when we do, we lose access to every-thing we need to break the cycle.

We lose, for example, trust in ourselves and our inner voices, because we've been raised to place greater trust in external authorities, tradi-tion, and the status quo. We lose access to our inner resources, which include our powers to think freely and to change and grow as a result. We lose our sense of meaning as something that's ours to develop. Under a model of control, meaning is defined externally in terms of rewards and punishments, expectations, "shoulds" and "oughts." What comes from within is regarded as suspect, precisely because it may not conform.

To change models, we must first change ourselves. As the Ojibway elders of the Hollow Water community explained to Rupert Ross, if we want to stop nasty anarchy, which in its broadest definition includes all crime, we need to go on the healing path.

In other words, we need to reconnect with our souls and regain open access to them. We need to rekindle trust in who we are, trust that a deep wisdom lives in us and can guide us. We can conceive of our essence broadly as the holomovement expressed, and we can also recognize its presence specifically in the feelings we have, pleasant or painful, joyful or angry. We carry a soul core in us that's our link to all that is and hence our source for truth, meaning, and potentials for change. Our deep reality won't go away just because the might model decrees it to be off limits. The icebergs that are our souls' truths don't disappear so easily, and the ships that are our lives and societies will sink if we ignore them and keep crashing into them as a result.

Granted, reclaiming ourselves is utterly subversive to the might model. It's true anarchy, but it's not destructive. It's what we must do to lessen and ultimately end suffering. Without reclaiming ourselves, we hurt from "might makes right" more and more, but all we can think of to deal with nasty anarchists are might-model methods—counterforce, threats, intimidation, defenses, fighting back, emotional violence—more of the same. We become what we oppose. Reconnecting with our souls is the only way to break the cycle and make a true shift.

The four Platonic virtues—those that we discussed in part 1 and have been using all the way through—call our souls back. They urge us to bring our inner realities to the forefront of our lives, so that we can benefit from their power and guidance. The virtues also connect us with meaning—how we're connected to more than the seen. Balancing inner and outer, the four virtues engage our souls to the fullest. They help us access and then exercise our whole nature. How?

Wisdom calls us to see ourselves within the big picture—who we are and why we're here—and then to apply this vision to our lives with prudence, careful thought, knowledge, skill, and mindfulness. We're more than the slices of us that social demands and expectations allow.

Wisdom invites us to inquire about our whole being: what's going on with the unseen side of us—our souls, transformation processes, and quests for meaning. Do the outer patterns of our lives support what's meaningful to us, or do they undermine it? What do we really care about, and what are our options for expressing our caring in life? The socially "correct" channels by no means exhaust what's possible.

In other words, wisdom calls us to step back and consider our lives in a wider perspective. It's easy to get lost in expectations and stuck in routines. We forget that we're here for some soul purpose—something that excites us and fills us with joy. Wisdom reminds us that we're more than we appear. It helps us keep returning to the soul quest and framing experiences in this deeper context.

Courage gives us the strength to change when our souls call for it. With courage, we step out of the box of cultural beliefs and conditioning. We dare to suspend our participation in institutionalized roles, demands, and expectations. It takes courage to follow our own light—lots of it. We need fortitude to hold our ground, whether it's to stand against dominant mindsets, to depart from what already exists and to create something new, or to continue within existing structures until our souls tell us to move. Both routes take courage, a willingness to surrender to inner guidance.

We gain courage and fortitude by looking beyond the visible, for then we're not as overwhelmed by the weight of established forms. No matter how mighty the visible seems, the invisible truth of our souls is more. That's because our souls draw on a wisdom about what's good in the bigger picture that our outwardly oriented personalities can't see, and this soul-grounded wisdom gives us the courage to move with change as best we know how.

Moderation tempers and softens us. Visionary anarchists have patience, because they know soul-change is at the root of everything, and it takes time. We can't heal traumas in a day. Neither can we abandon overnight models, however self-destructive, that we've been raised to accept and relied on our entire lives. Change does happen, because it's the nature of reality. There's no avoiding it. But it involves cycles and processes which must be worked through step-by-step, personally and collectively.

Moderation gives us an understanding of change and a compassion for ourselves and others as we move through its processes. Change is neither easy nor quick. Some changes take generations. Guided by moderation, we learn to nurture soul-good from the inside out gently and with grace, whether it's easing us or thrusting us into new cycles.

During intense periods of transition, moderation gives us temperance, a nose for the middle way, especially when everything about a situation would push us to extremes. Faced with challenges, we don't slash and burn for quick advantage, seeking ends without concern for the consequences of actions. Whereas "might makes right" inspires no awareness of the relations that hold us, moderation keeps in view the connected context, even when we're swimming in confusion and upheaval.

Justice, the fourth virtue, is our souls' home, because it's the essence of justice to honor who we are in our wholeness. Valuing us is what we want of justice and what we expect when justice is truly served. When we watch movies or read novels, we want a character's inner truth to be honored, and when it's misconstrued, we feel some injustice has been done. The job of justice is to hear our truth, to respect our individuality, and to protect our quests for meaning and happiness. True justice is our souls' best friend. It's our guarantee that we can be who we are and explore what's ours to do as we together go through life.

The Mystic Response

What makes mystics so sure, though, that following our souls will bring harmony and happiness rather than suffering? How do we know that exercising our individuality won't hurt someone else? What's the mystic's logic?

The core of mystic reasoning is the conviction in the oneness and hence interrelatedness of all things. Everything springs from a ground of unity, which creates a powerful connectedness among us. Indeed, nothing would exist without this cosmic web, a coherent system that holds everything in its order and calls us into being. Coming from this origin, our souls are whole-connected by nature. According to Bohm and mystics, we are the whole in expression, since nothing can be outside of it.

That's why we're sacred, and everything else is sacred too. We exist within our whole-connectedness, and every facet of our being, inner and outer, is permeated by it. When we follow our souls, connectedness guides us, and we don't do harm.

Granted, in normal awareness, the full implications of how we're connected surpass our comprehension. We make mistakes and stumble over our connectedness. Our lack of awareness, though, doesn't mean connectedness isn't there or doesn't affect us every moment. We don't, for example, know the full marvels of how our bodies function—our DNA and immune systems and all the rest—but our lack of knowledge doesn't mean our bodies are any less complex or that we're less affected by their complexity.

In an article, "The Entangled Universe," biologist Mae-Wan Ho, also a student of quantum physics, writes:

> Think of each organism as an entity that is not really confined within the solid body we see. The visible body just happens to be where the wave function of the organism is most dense. Invisible quantum waves are spreading out from each one of us and permeating into all other organisms. At the same time, each of us has the waves of every other organism entangled within our own make-up.
>
> In a very real sense, no person is alone, no man is an island. We are not isolated atoms, each jostling and competing against the rest in a Darwinian struggle for survival of the fittest. Instead each of us is supported and constituted, ultimately, by all there is in the universe.[1]

As Mae-Wan Ho says, our everything-with-everything entangled being holds not just for matter and objects, the way physicists talk about connectedness, but for living beings as well. Mystics go a step farther to include a profound connectedness within the unseen dimensions. We're connected through our emotions, intuitions, dreams, meaning quests,

---

1. Mae-Wan Ho, "The Entangled Universe," *Yes! A Journal of Positive Futures* 13 (Spring 2000): 23.

and consciousness. We're also utterly "entangled" with the unconscious, collective archetypal consciousness, and the unseen beings of untold unseen worlds. Things hang together, mystics reason, because that's the connected nature of the cosmic wholeness that we're all participating in. We have meaning built into us, a meaning that, based on the ground of unity, links us to everyone, everything, and every event.

Naturally, because we can't see all these connections, we're in the dark about them and the meaning that's unfolding through them. Whole-born meaning weaves the fabric of our lives in ways we can't fathom, and our inevitably partial views of the process leave us confused. Intuition and insight offer glimpses of the larger connections, but these glimpses are incomplete. Neither can we run a test to determine the meaning of some happening; and, even if we could, the meaning would likely shift to incorporate new meanings the next moment. Just as the whole is always changing, so is meaning. Perhaps that's why Pema Chödrön recommends that we embrace an inevitable "groundlessness" to life.[2] If we try to pin down meaning and turn it into a fixed ground, we'll miss what's going on. Our meaning-ground is always shifting because it's like a living, organic being.

Because meaning is fluid, it's full of possibilities. The mystic premise of super-connectedness doesn't imply an order that's predetermined. Math expresses an order, yet we can do infinite things with it. Assuming a meaningful order to life doesn't suggest there's only one possible way for that order to be expressed. Rather, the idea that there is an order frees us to explore possibilities that wouldn't exist were there no order to build on.

Justice works the same way. On the premise that our souls are formed and guided by the holomovement, truly just social orders emerge the more we're each true to our souls, at the same time honoring this mandate in others. In being true to ourselves, we're true to the whole in us, and this harmonizes us with what's true in everyone else.

But how our souls guide us and what we understand as ours to do at each point are open questions. Neither is one way of following our souls

2. Pema Chödrön, *When Things Fall Apart: Heart Advice for Difficult Times* (Boston, Shambhala, 1997), especially 32–37.

right and all the rest wrong. Wandering down dead-ends and doing things that don't work out are all part of it. When justice grows from our commitment to being who we are, it leaves judgments behind. Justice simply calls us to go on the inner journey and follow it, wherever it leads. The very uncertainty of it gives us space to explore what feels right to us at each point. There's nothing predetermined about it.

Because our souls reflect wholeness and connectedness, building justice on them creates a far deeper harmony than trying to impose order from without could ever do. Things hang together from a coherency that creates order the way the trunk of a tree creates order among its branches. It's built in, not imposed. The essence of a twig is to be one with the tree and to move in harmony with it. True, at the twig level, branches seem to be growing every which way, but the connectedness of each twig to the tree gives order. The order grows from within. It's natural, and it fits us.

Egos and personalities can't give us such a natural, easy-fitting order. They're too surface-oriented, too focused on externals—twigs. Our egos want to squeeze us into accepted habits and traditions. Granted, that's precisely the kind of advice we want from our egos. We want them to carve out a place for us in the external world. That's good and necessary, as long as our egos stay linked to our souls' direction and step aside when our souls call for change. When egos dig in, we feel conflict between our ego-made worlds and our souls, and that's painful. But soul pain has its uses. It burns away ego rigidity and resistance, so that our fluid reality can come through.

The mystic's logic is that the more we follow our souls and the less we get caught in egos, the more naturally we move with each other. Our shared roots coordinate our energies, so that we cooperate with each other from the inside out. Guided by who we are on deeper levels, we create channels for our energies that feel right. As this happens for more and more people, tending to the specifics of material life flows easily. We each contribute what's ours to offer, and it works. We get along, and we're happy.

From a mystic way of understanding, this soul-based ground of social order is as coherent and compelling as the system of matter-energy that physicists describe. Compelling is the issue. It's not wise and ultimately not possible to ignore soul and meaning or to try to live our lives without them. This isn't because of a judging or punishing God. It's more about the physics of consciousness. We seem to be built—constructed as human beings—to live who we are and not someone else. We're also built to do this by experiencing meaning in our lives, and if it's not there, we languish as surely as if we starved from lack of food. Meaning is that important. Without our souls' presence in our lives, we shut down. We're not happy, life doesn't seem to hold much purpose, and we become self-destructive.

Consequently, it doesn't work to structure our lives and cultures—religions, businesses, governments, families, schools—in ways that exclude who we most essentially are. According to mystics, our roots in a larger reality mandate our presence in our lives—our whole engagement. If we adhere to our own unseen order, as true justice calls us to do, we'll have anarchy for sure: a complex, changing, nourishing, rich, diverse, living, dynamic expression of who we all are. We'll have bugs to work out and differences to resolve as we go along together, but we can approach these challenges not only with cooperation and creativity but also with a commitment to finding solutions by bringing in more of who we each are, not less.

What Blesses One Blesses All

That's the mystic's logic. But how might we characterize the order that follows from it? Unity, connectedness, soul, and evolving meaning converge in a principle of order that directly offsets the notion of individuality as competitive separateness. As far as mystics are concerned, we're not isolated beings; therefore, the idea that our nature is to struggle for survival by grabbing as much of the pie as we can makes no sense. It can't be our core nature, because it flies in the face of the larger reality that constitutes who we are. If we're shaped by unity, connectedness, and whole-born change, then it must be our nature to move with each other in some sort of mutually supportive harmony.

This mystic sense of a deeper order is expressed in the ancient spiritual principle, "What what blesses one blesses all." Mutual blessing is the ultimate way of things: "all things work together for good," the Bible says. To use the image of a tree, if water falls anywhere on the tree, the entire tree is replenished. What blesses one leaf blesses all. In other words, if reality operates as one, coherent, all-inclusive system and if we all participate in the same system—if we're each the whole expressed—then on some level we ultimately pull together rather than apart.

This doesn't mean we have to agree on things or shouldn't object when someone hurts us. No, that's not it at all. Quite the reverse. The more different we are, the more opportunities we have to enrich and bless each other. Differences in gender illustrate the point: it's nice to have both males and females.

If, for example, our souls tell us to expose "might makes right" in all its destructiveness, then that's what we should do. "What blesses one blesses all" says we help each other by speaking our truths, because that's how we learn. If "might makes right" is a model we humans need to abandon, then all will be blessed by learning this, especially those most committed to that model now. They of all people know that a change of fortune can put anyone on the receiving end of might's fury. A vigorous challenge to the power model is what they need the most.

In other words, we're in this together, and the more we're each true to our souls, the more we'll bless each other by doing so. What's good for one coordinates with what's good for another—good, that is, not on the surface of ego worlds but on the deep, rigorous agenda set by our souls. Our souls are set up to synchronize, complement, and mutually benefit each other, although the ways they do this are far more complex, ambitious, and unpredictable than we'd imagine. Mutual blessing is not about making things come out right according to social expectations or securing material comfort. It's the far tougher blessing of confronting our reality. What can our experiences contribute both to our own souls' journeys and to our collective human evolution—to radical personal and social transformation and to the deep healing of things we'd rather let pass?

Win-win is not, therefore, a fantasy; it's how the universe at its deepest levels is constructed. The closer we're attuned to the unseen—to soul issues and meaning—the easier it is for us to sense the truth of this principle.

This is an ancient version of what we now talk about in terms of systems thinking. Systems operate as wholes or integral processes. Each part isn't a separate thing but is the whole system manifest through a specific aspect or function. As a result, whatever an aspect does from its deepest levels is system-informed, system-guided. The entire system is strengthened when one aspect functions at its best, which, in turn, serves the good of every other aspect.

This system dynamic is great news if the system we're talking about is the ultimate whole, the One of mystic contemplation, or a higher power that operates for universal good. Within the holomovement, there's room for all of us to live deeply and from meaning—room for us to be who we are and to do what's ours to do. Indeed, the whole needs us connected with our souls' callings to operate in all its richness and diversity.

But systems in human society don't have this universally beneficent quality. They're not perfect, and we don't always feel a flow of mutual benefit in them. We've constructed social systems to help us, and some do this better than others. The hope for cultural evolution is to evolve social systems that honor the values of soul, meaning, and purpose for everyone, so that we can live from our souls and fulfill our destinies. In history, such social systems seem to have either existed among certain indigenous societies or been approximated by reforming communities, usually ones with a spiritual focus. The twelfth to thirteenth centuries' Albigensians in southern France come to mind as an example in the West. Gender equality, freedom of thought, nonviolence, and openness in spiritual pursuits were principles put into community practice.

Today, we all feel an intense desire for systems that honor our souls and operate for mutual blessing, and yet we also know that few of the systems we've been raised in fit this profile. Some are so unhealthy that everyone involved experiences them as a source of unhappiness. If our current models of family, school, workplace, political, or even religious systems have a soul-affirming agenda, they hide it well. Setting us free to explore our souls' callings isn't the message we get. Instead, social systems operate by rules that dismiss our inner voices, requiring, for instance, unquestioning obedience. Thinking for ourselves, trusting our inner authority, or exercising the freedom to break with convention and follow our inner light: these behaviors aren't encouraged.

Because we're born into these systems, we internalize their rules and turn away from our souls. It's a life's work to come out from under this early programming, since soul-dismissal is powerfully reinforced by family, school, work, and cultural systems all through life. True justice helps us do this. Transcending as it does this or that social system, it spurs growth beyond conventional forms by demanding that our souls not be dismissed. Who we are is the lifeblood of our systems. We have to be here—fully engaged in our lives and societies—for anything to work. Heeding our souls' callings is how we start to change systems and make them serve our whole being.

Doing this, we bless ourselves, and we bless everyone else too. First, we break the hold of soul-dismissive systems. Claiming our own freedom frees others to claim theirs. Second, we open channels for joy, beauty, freedom, and vitality to come into our worlds. The blessing of our whole-being starts flowing through us, but it doesn't stop with us. It flows everywhere to people and places we'll never know. Connectedness works that way.

Essentially, "what blesses one blesses all" says that we need to be true to ourselves, and we need others to be true to themselves as well for all of us to be happy and functioning in our full capacities. We also need social systems that honor and support these dynamics. We're each what the whole needs now in time, space, energy, and culture. Being less than who we are won't suffice. The more our individual expressions differ, the better for all of us, for then we have a chance to experience through each other what we came here to be and do.

Mid-nineteenth century French anarchist Pierre-Joseph Proudhon presented a version of this principle as "mutualism." He believed that true social order will emerge as we seek our mutual interests, especially our mutual interest in organizing our lives and societies so that we each have a place of value within them. As far as mystics are concerned, that's the destiny for human society. It's justice lived.

If all this is so—if unity, connectedness, and the principle of mutual blessing are true and the deepest order of our being—then why don't things look better than they do? Actually, they could look worse, much worse. If we all truly operated from a model of competitive separateness—out for ourselves only and getting ahead at others' expense—then human society would have long since degenerated into a war of each against all, culminating in complete mutual annihilation.

The point is, we're still here, amazingly. Something in us must be greater than "might makes right" and all the pressures to abandon soul and conscience. Yes, we have fearful problems these days; some people seem more troubled by soul loss and trauma than others, and some of the troubled people hold some dangerously high-level positions. But a higher sense of justice is being born among us, and more of us are seeking to connect with our souls and to confront our loss of soul and inner compass, and we're finding mutual support for doing so. The model of win-lose separateness is losing its hold on the public mind, and the idea that we're connected in ways we never imagined is growing stronger. We're getting the message that mutual blessing within the web of life is not only possible but also essential to survival.

In other words, through personal and cultural paths, we're arriving at the mystic's perspective—and the visionary anarchist's. We're finding that neither individuality nor human nature but the models we use to channel them throw us into chaos, and that we don't have to go there. We can change our models, and as we do, we can shift the ways we focus our energies. Granted, it's a one-by-one, hence invisibly subversive, process, but hidden subversion is the method of choice for mystic anarchists.

As we shift models, we start healing within and getting our souls back, and this process reconnects us with our true powers. We rediscover all sorts of powers within: our power to act from our inner truth, our power to challenge coercive mindsets and institutions, our power to evolve in whatever ways our souls guide us, our power to let our whole-born nature flow through us into our lives, our power to work with others rather than against them, our power to embrace cycles of change, and hence our power to be free as we never imagined—free to be who we are and to do what's ours to do, *and* to be happy and at peace with others as we go.

The challenge that mystic justice poses for us, therefore, isn't to deny our nature for the sake of social order but the reverse, namely, to bring our full nature into our worlds. We need to connect with who we are in our totality, not just in outer ways. Listening to our souls is how we do it. In turn, our souls use the totality of our experience—our thoughts, desires, dreams, longings, relationships, bodies, as well as our loves—to tell the unfolding story of who we are and what the whole calls us to do.

That's why, in following our souls, we can't go wrong. Granted, we can raise the ire of conventional wisdom and social expectation in a flash, we can make mistakes, and we can go through intense, painful, even hellish transformations; but we can't go wrong as far as the mystic order of justice is concerned. One way or another, following our souls opens a window for our core individuality to come through, and that blesses us all.

So what do we do? We get our souls back: that's our first job. It's the mystic way as well as the practical way, and it's the way of justice:

- We do justice to ourselves by engaging our whole being, outer and inner, seen and unseen;

- We do justice to others by honoring their whole being, our connectedness to them, and our whole mutual-blessings dynamics;

- We do justice to our communities and society by giving them what is ours to give; and

- We do justice to justice itself by no longer reducing it to external reward-punishment terms, instead letting it operate as a force for soul, transformation, happiness, and good.

Granted, getting our souls back when our personal and cultural model-habit is to live estranged from them isn't easy. Neither is living mindful of our connectedness when we've been raised and trained to act from separateness. Model shifts and soul journeys entail processes, and long ones. They're also processes we can't do alone, since our souls are by nature connected. Just as our hurt came from beyond us, so must our healing. To create justice in our worlds, we need to go on the healing path, and we need to do it together.

✑ Bibliography

This is not intended as an academic, "cover-all-the-bases" bibliography but as a personal sharing of a few of the books that have contributed both to our process of learning about restorative justice and to our development around the larger issues we've explored. Occasionally, we have supplied information about a book's contents or theme.

Philosophy

Allen, R. E., trans. *The Dialogues of Plato*, vol. I. New Haven, Conn.: Yale University Press, 1984.

Bohm, David. *On Dialogue*. Edited by Lee Nichol. New York: Routledge, 1996.

———. *Unfolding Meaning: A Weekend of Dialogue with David Bohm*. London: Routledge & Kegan Paul, 1985.

———. *Wholeness and the Implicate Order*. London: Routledge and Kegan Paul, 1980.

Briggs, John, and F. David Peat. *The Seven Life Lessons of Chaos: Spiritual Wisdom from the Science of Change*. New York: Harperperennial, 2000. Chaos theory is about the power of self-organizing systems to structure, destructure, and then move to new levels of order. Order isn't imposed from without but emerges from within the elements of the system and their own dynamic interaction. The implications for our worldview—how we understand and experience personal and social change—are profound and still unfolding. It seems to be the deep theory behind a true anarchist philosophy.

Durant, Will. *The Story of Philosophy: The Lives and Opinions of the World's Greatest Philosophers.* New York: Pocket Books, 1991.

Epictetus. *The Enchiridion.* Trans. Thomas W. Higginson. Indianapolis, Ind.: Bobbs-Merrill Educational Publishing, 1948. A little book full of wisdom from this Roman Stoic philosopher, born a slave.

Frankl, Viktor E. *Man's Search for Meaning.* Boston: Beacon Press, 1959.

Goodall, Jane, with Phillip Berman. *Reason for Hope: A Spiritual Journey.* New York: Warner Books, 1999.

Heaney, Seamus. *The Cure at Troy: A Version of Sophocles' 'Philoctetes.'* New York: The Noonday Press, Farrar, Straus, and Giroux, 1991.

Houston, Jean. *A Passion for the Possible: A Guide to Realizing Your True Potential.* San Francisco: HarperSanFrancisco, 1998.

Kuhn, Thomas S. *The Structure of Scientific Revolutions.* Chicago: University of Chicago Press, 1970.

Levoy, Gregg. *Callings: Finding and Following an Authentic Life.* New York: Three Rivers Press, Crown Publishers, 1997.

Marinoff, Lou. *Plato, Not Prozac! Applying Philosophy to Everyday Problems.* New York: HarperCollins, 1999. The dedication reads: "To those who always knew philosophy was good for something, but could never say exactly what."

Somé, Sobonfu E. *The Spirit of Intimacy: Ancient African Teachings in the Ways of Relationships.* New York: William Morrow and Company, 1997.

Talbot, Michael. *The Holographic Universe.* New York: HarperCollins, 1991.

Tarnas, Richard. *The Passion of the Western Mind: Understanding the Ideas That Have Shaped Our World View.* New York: Harmony Books, 1991.

Waterfield, Robin, trans. *Plato Republic.* New York: Barnes and Noble Books, 1993.

Spirituality and Healing

Bradshaw, John. *Creating Love: The Next Great Stage of Growth.* New York: Bantam Books, 1992.

Breggin, Peter R. *The Heart of Being Helpful: Empathy and the Creation of a Healing Presence.* New York: Springer Publishing Company, 1997.

Breton, Denise, and Christopher Largent. *Love, Soul, and Freedom: Dancing with Rumi on the Mystic Path.* Center City, Minn.: Hazelden, 1998.

Carlson, Richard, and Benjamin Shield. *Healers on Healing.* Los Angeles: Jeremy P. Tarcher, Inc., 1989.

Carnes, Patrick. *A Gentle Path Through the Twelve Steps: The Classic Guide for All People in the Process of Recovery.* Minneapolis, Minn.: Compcare Publications, 1994.

Chödrön, Pema. *Start Where You Are: A Guide to Compassionate Living.* Boston: Shambhala Publications, Inc., 1994.

———. *When Things Fall Apart: Heart Advice for Difficult Times.* Boston: Shambhala Publications, Inc., 1997. If justice is about healing, then we need help dealing with pain, starting with our own. This Buddhist teacher's approach has been exceedingly helpful in showing us how to allow pain, neither running from nor reacting to it but staying with the process, whatever it is.

———. *The Wisdom of No Escape: And the Path of Loving-Kindness.* Boston: Shambhala Publications, Inc., 1991.

Cusumano, Joseph D. *Transforming Scrooge: Dickens' Blueprint for a Spiritual Awakening.* St. Paul, Minn.: Llewellyn Publications, 1996.

Dole, George F., ed. and trans. *A Thoughtful Soul: Reflections from Swedenborg.* West Chester, Pa.: Chrysalis Books, 1995.

Dossey, Larry. *Recovering the Soul: A Scientific and Spiritual Approach.* New York: Bantam, Doubleday, Dell Publishers, 1989.

Epstein, Mark. *Going to Pieces Without Falling Apart: A Buddhist Perspective on Wholeness.* New York: Broadway Books, 1998.

Gandhi, Mohandas Karamchand. *Autobiography: The Story of My Experiments with Truth.* Mineola, N.Y.: Dover Publications, 1983. Gandhi is the most exemplary anarchist and peacemaker.

Hallengren, Anders. *Gallery of Mirrors: Reflections of Swedenborgian Thought.* West Chester, Pa.: Swedenborg Foundation, 1998.

King, Serge Kahili. *Urban Shaman: A Handbook for Personal and Planetary Transformation Based on the Hawaiian Way of the Adventurer.* New York: Simon & Schuster, 1990.

Levine, Stephen. *Healing Into Life and Death.* New York: Anchor Books, Doubleday, 1987. Working from a Buddhist perspective, Levine shares what he has learned from terminal patients about healing responses to pain and grief.

Swedenborg, Emanuel. *Heaven and Hell: Drawn from Things Heard and Seen.* Trans. George F. Dole, The New Century Edition. West Chester, Pa.: Swedenborg Foundation, 2000. This new translation of Swedenborg's most famous work is a clear and powerful expression of his visions of a multidimensional universe.

Taylor, Jeremy. *Where People Fly and Water Runs Uphill: Using Dreams to Tap the Wisdom of the Unconscious.* New York: Warner Books, 1992. Chapter 5, "Dreams, Nonviolence, and Social Change" discusses how group dream work has been used to cut through, overcome, and heal racism.

Trungpa, Chogyam. *Shambhala: The Sacred Path of the Warrior.* Edited by Carolyn Rose. Boston: Shambhala Publications, 1988. The first task of the spiritual warrior is to make peace with ourselves, so we can live open and unarmed, without defensive thorns. The Tibetan tradition is devoted to this practice.

Tu Wei-Ming. *Centrality and Commonality: An Essay on Confucian Religiousness.* Albany, N.Y.: State University of New York Press, 1989.

———. *Confucian Thought: Selfhood as Creative Transformation.* Albany, N.Y.: State University of New York Press, 1985.

————. *Humanity and Self-Cultivation: Essays in Confucian Thought.* Berkeley, Calif.: Asian Humanities Press, 1979.

Van Dusen, Wilson. *The Country of Spirit: Selected Writings.* San Francisco: J. Appleseed & Co., 1992.

Native American

Barreiro, José, ed. *Indian Roots of American Democracy.* Ithaca, N.Y.: Akwe:kon Press, Cornell University, 1992.

Black Elk, Wallace H., and William S. Lyon. *Black Elk: The Sacred Ways of a Lakota.* Reprint, San Francisco: HarperSanFrancisco, 1991.

Bopp, Judie; Michael Bopp; Lee Brown; and Phil Lane, Jr. *The Sacred Tree: Reflections on Native American Spirituality.* Lethbridge, Alberta, Canada: Four Worlds International Institute, 1984.

Deloria Jr., Vine. *For This Land: Writings on Religion in America.* New York: Routledge, 1999.

————. *God Is Red: A Native View of Religion.* 2nd edition. Golden, Colo.: North American Press, 1994.

————. *Red Earth, White Lies: Native Americans and the Myth of Scientific Fact.* New York: Scribner's, 1995.

Highwater, Jamake. *The Primal Mind: Vision and Reality in Indian America.* New York: Meridian, 1981.

Johansen, Bruce E. *Forgotten Founders: How the American Indian Helped Shape Democracy.* Boston: The Harvard Common Press, 1982.

Johansen, Bruce, with Donald A. Grinde Jr. and Barbara A. Mann. *Debating Democracy: Native American Legacy of Freedom.* Santa Fe, N. Mex.: Clear Light Publishers, 1998.

Laduke, Winona. *All Our Relations: Native Struggles for Land and Life.* Cambridge, Mass.: South End Press, 1999.

Lyons, Oren, et al. *Exiled in the Land of the Free: Democracy, Indian Nations, and the U.S. Constitution.* Santa Fe, N. Mex.: Clear Light Publishers, 1992.

Mails, Thomas E. *Fools Crow: Wisdom and Power.* Tulsa, Okla.: Council Oaks Distributions, 1991.

Ross, Rupert. *Returning to the Teachings: Exploring Aboriginal Justice.* Toronto, Ontario: Penguin Books Canada, 1996. This book, which unlocked so much for us in understanding an Aboriginal approach to justice, is not available in the United States but can be obtained from the Albert Britnell Book Shop, 100 Adelaide St. W., Ste. 908 Toronto, Ontario, Canada M5H 1S3. Tel. (416) 362-0022 or (800) 387-1417.

Ross, Rupert, and Basil Johnston. *Dancing with a Ghost: Exploring Indian Reality.* Markham, Ontario, Canada: Octopus Publishing Group, 1992.

Sams, Jamie. *Dancing the Dream: The Seven Sacred Paths of Human Transformation.* San Francisco: HarperCollins, 1998.

———. *Sacred Path Cards: The Discovery of Self Through Native Teachings.* San Francisco: HarperSanFrancisco, 1990.

Schaaf, Greg. *The Great Law of Peace and the Constitution of the United States of America.* Mohawk Nation via Akwesasne, N.Y.: Tree of Peace Society, n.d.

Storm, Hyemeyohsts. *Seven Arrows.* New York: Ballantine, Paperback reissue 1985.

Wallace, Paul. *White Roots of Peace: The Iroquois Book of Life.* Santa Fe, N. Mex.: Clear Light Publishers, 1994.

Weltfish, Gene. *The Lost Universe: Pawnee Life and Culture.* Lincoln, Nebr.: University of Nebraska Press, reprint, 1990.

Restorative Justice, Conflict Resolution, and Peacemaking

Baldwin, Christina. *Calling the Circle: The First and Future Culture.* New York: Bantam, Doubleday, Dell Publishing, 1998.

Bazemore, S. Gordon; Maria Schiff; and Gordon Bazemore. *Restorative Community Justice: Repairing Harm and Transforming Communities.* Cincinnati, Ohio: Anderson Publishing Company, 2001.

Bedi, Kiran. *It's Always Possible: Transforming One of the Largest Prisons in the World.* Briar Hill, VIC Australia: Indra Publishing, 1999. Available from www.amazon.com. This is the amazing story of a police woman in India who was appointed inspector general of Tihar Jail in 1993 and transformed it from prison squalor to a community healing ashram—restorative justice decades, hopefully not centuries, ahead of where we are now. See the *Resources* under Web sites.

Beer, Jennifer E., with Eileen Stief. *The Mediator's Handbook: Developed by Friends Conflict Resolution Programs.* Gabriola Island, British Columbia: New Society Publishers, 1997.

Braithwaite, John. *Crime, Shame and Reintegration.* Cambridge, UK: Cambridge University Press, 1989.

Breggin, Peter R. *Beyond Conflict: From Self-Help and Psychotherapy to Peacemaking.* New York: St. Martin's Press, 1992.

Consedine, Jim. *Restorative Justice: Healing the Effects of Crime.* Lyttelton, New Zealand: Ploughshares Publications, 1995. This book may be ordered directly from the publisher: P.O. Box 173, Lyttelton, New Zealand.

Fischer, Louis. *The Essential Gandhi: An Anthology of His Writings on His Life, Work and Ideas.* New York: Vintage Books, 1962.

Fisher, Roger; William Ury; and for second edition, Bruce Patton. *Getting to Yes: Negotiating Agreement Without Giving In.* New York: Houghton Mifflin Company,1981; second edition New York: Penguin Books, 1991.

Hadley, Michael L. *The Spiritual Roots of Restorative Justice*. Albany, N.Y.: SUNY Press, 2001.

Houston, Jean. *Manual for the Peacemaker: An Iroquois Legend to Heal Self and Society*. Wheaton, Ill.: Quest Books, 1995.

King Jr., Martin Luther. *A Call to Conscience: The Landmark Speeches of Dr. Martin Luther King, Jr.* Edited by Clayborne Carson and Kris Shephard. New York: Warner Books, 2001.

Lerner, Melvin. *The Belief in a Just World: A Fundamental Delusion*. New York: Plenum Press, 1980.

Lozoff, Bo. *We're All Doing Time: A Guide to Getting Free*. Durham, N.C.: Human Kindness Foundation, 1984. See "Resources" for further information.

McCold, Paul. *Restorative Justice: An Annotated Bibliography 1997*. Monsey, N.Y.: Criminal Justice Press, 1997.

Nader, Ralph, and Wesley J. Smith. *No Contest: Corporate Lawyers and the Perversion of Justice in America*. New York: Random House, 1999.

Rosenberg, Marshall B. *Nonviolent Communication: A Language of Compassion*. Del Mar, Calif.: PuddleDancer Press, 1999.

Snyder, T. Richard. *The Protestant Ethic and the Spirit of Punishment*. Grand Rapids, Mich.: William B. Erdmans Publishing Company, 2001.

Stone, Douglas; Bruce Patton; and Sheila Heen. *Difficult Conversations: How to Discuss What Matters Most*. New York: Viking Penguin, 1999.

Tannen, Deborah. *You Just Don't Understand: Women and Men in Conversation*. New York: Ballantine Books, 1991.

Umbreit, Mark. *The Handbook of Victim Offender Mediation: An Essential Guide to Practice and Research*. San Francisco: Jossey-Bass Publishers, 2000.

———. *Mediating Interpersonal Conflicts: A Pathway to Peace*. West Concord, Minn.: CPI Publications, 1995.

———. *Victim Meets Offender: The Impact of Restorative Justice and Mediation.* New York: Criminal Justice Press, 1994.

Ury, William. *Getting Past No: Negotiating Your Way from Confrontation to Cooperation.* New York: Bantam, Doubleday, Dell, 1993.

Van Ness, Daniel W., and Karen Heetderks Strong. *Restoring Justice.* Cincinnati, Ohio: Anderson Publishing Company, 1997.

Weeks, Dudley. *The Eight Essential Steps to Conflict Resolution: Preserving Relationships at Work, at Home, and in the Community.* Los Angeles: Jeremy P. Tarcher, 1992.

Wills, Maralys, and Mike Carona. *Save My Son: A Mother and a Sheriff Unite to Reclaim the Lives of Addicted Offenders.* Center City, Minn.: Hazelden, 2000.

Zehr, Howard. *Changing Lenses: A New Focus for Crime and Justice.* Scottdale, Pa.: Herald Press, 1990.

———. *Doing Life: Reflections of Men and Women Serving Life Sentences.* Intercourse, Pa.: Good Books, 1996.

———. *Transcending* (forthcoming). This book is about victims transcending the pain of crime.

Zimmerman, Jack, and Virginia Coyle. *The Way of Council.* Las Vegas: Bramble Books, 1996.

Social Criticism and Future Vision

Barker, Joel Arthur. *Paradigms: The Business of Discovering the Future.* New York: HarperBusiness, 1992.

Blanchard, Geral; Robert Freeman-Longo; and Euan Bear, eds. *Sexual Abuse in America: The Epidemic of the 21st Century.* Branton, VT.: Safer Society Press 1998.

Blanton, Brad. *Practicing Radical Honesty.* Stanley, Va.: Sparrowhawk Publications, 2000.

————. *Radical Honesty.* New York. Dell Publishing Company, 1996

Bradshaw, John. *Bradshaw on the Family.* Pompano Beach, Fla.: Health Communications, 1988.

————. *Family Secrets: The Path to Self-Acceptance and Reunion.* New York: Bantam Books, 1995.

————. *Homecoming: Reclaiming and Championing Your Inner Child.* New York: Bantam Books, 1990.

Breton, Denise, and Christopher Largent. *The Paradigm Conspiracy: Why Our Social Systems Violate Human Potential and How We Can Change Them.* Center City, Minn.: Hazelden, 1996.

————. *The Soul of Economies: Spiritual Evolution Goes to the Marketplace.* Wilmington, Del.: Idea House, 1991.

Breton, Mary Joy. *Women Pioneers for the Environment.* Boston: Northeastern University Press, 1998. This moving book covers the lives of over forty women from around the world who worked for environmental justice, faced conflicts, and sought to resolve them.

Carnes, Patrick *The Betrayal Bond: Breaking Free of Exploitive Relationships.* Deerfield Beach, Fla.: Health Communications, 1997.

Carnes, Patrick, with Joseph Moriarity. *Sexual Anorexia: Overcoming Sexual Self-Hatred.* Center City, Minn.: Hazelden Information and Education, 1997.

Coontz, Stephanie. *The Way We Never Were: American Families and the Nostalgia Trap.* New York: Basic Books, 1992. Plato and Socrates were critiquing the family structure 2500 years ago, and the dialogue continues. Family life touches us so deeply. Let the critiques spur us to forge deeper, more authentic, and openhearted levels of intimacy.

Eisler, Riane. *The Chalice and the Blade: Our History, Our Future.* San Francisco: Harper and Row, 1987.

Eisler, Riane, and David Loye. *The Partnership Way: New Tools for Living and Learning, Healing Our Families, Our Communities, and Our World.* San Francisco: HarperSanFrancisco, 1990.

Elgin, Duane. *Collective Consciousness and Cultural Healing: A Report to the Fetzer Institute.* San Anselmo, Calif.: Millennium Project, 1997.

————. *Promise Ahead: A Vision of Hope and Action for Humanity's Future.* New York.: Quill, 2001.

Garbarino, James. *Lost Boys: Why Our Sons Turn Violent and How We Can Save Them.* New York: The Free Press, 1999.

————. *Raising Children in a Socially Toxic Environment.* San Francisco: Jossey-Bass Publishers, 1995.

Garbarino, James, and Claire Bedard. *Parents under Siege: Why You Are the Solution, Not the Problem, in Your Child's Life.* New York: The Free Press, 2000.

Gilligan, Carol. *In a Different Voice: Psychological Theory and Women's Development.* Cambridge, Mass.: Harvard University Press, 1982.

Harman, Willis. *Global Mind Change.* Indianapolis, Ind.: Knowledge Systems, 1988.

Hite, Shere. *The Hite Report on the Family: Growing Up under Patriarchy.* London: Bloomsbury Publishing, 1994. Again, we won't move to more fulfilling models of intimate relationships until we're honest with ourselves about what does and doesn't work in our current ways of being a family.

Houston, Jean. *Jump Time: Shaping Your Future in a World of Radical Change.* Los Angeles: Jeremy Tarcher, 2000.

Hyman, Irwin, and Pamela A. Snook. *Dangerous Schools: What We Can Do About the Physical and Emotional Abuse of Our Children.* San Francisco: Jossey-Bass Publishers, 1999.

————. *Reading, Writing, and the Hickory Stick.* Lanham, Md.: Lexington Books, 1990.

Kohn, Alfie. *The Brighter Side of Human Nature: Altruism and Empathy in Everyday Life.* New York: Basic Books, 1990.

———. *No Contest: The Case Against Competition.* Boston: Houghton Mifflin, 1987.

———. *Punished by Rewards: The Trouble with Gold Stars, Incentive Plans, A's, Praise, and Other Bribes.* Boston and New York: Houghton Mifflin Company, 1993.

———. *What to Look for in a Classroom . . . and Other Essays.* San Francisco: Jossey-Bass Publishers, 1998.

Korten, David C. *The Post-Corporate World: Life after Capitalism.* San Francisco: Berrett-Koehler Publishers and West Hartford, Conn.: Kumarian Press, 1999.

———. *When Corporations Rule the World:* 2nd ed. West Hartford, Conn.: Kumarian Press, 2001.

Miller, Alice. *Banished Knowledge: Facing Childhood Injuries.* New York: Anchor Books, Doubleday, 1990.

———. *For Your Own Good: Hidden Cruelty in Child-Rearing and the Roots of Violence.* New York: Farrar, Straus, Giroux, 1983.

Ray, Paul, and Sherry Ruth Anderson. *The Cultural Creatives: How 50 Million People Are Changing the World.* New York: Harmony Books, 2000.

Senge, Peter M. *The Fifth Discipline: The Art and Practice of the Learning Organization.* New York: Doubleday/Currency, 1990.

Williamson, Marianne, ed. *Imagine: What America Could Be in the 21st Century.* Emmaus, Pa.: Daybreak, Rodale Press, 2000.

Zohar, Danah, and Ian Marshall. *The Quantum Society: Mind, Physics, and a New Social Vision.* New York: William Morrow and Company, 1994.

❧ *Resources*

THE RESTORATIVE JUSTICE MOVEMENT is exploding globally. Given the scope of the movement and the diversity of methods being explored, we can't begin to cover everything that's going on. What we give below is only a starting point. But what a great problem!

Many of the following resources sound "official" or "established" or "institutional," but they all began with individuals who confronted pain and sought a better way of dealing with it. In one case, a close relative's arrest and sentencing to forty years in prison propelled a husband and wife into decades of helping prisoners use their time for inner work, turning prisons into ashrams and monasteries. In another case, a '60s-activist-turned-professor sought to carry the spirit of activism to the daunting task of changing the justice system, so he started a center for studying restorative justice and training people in its methods. Or a nun was drawn to visit a prisoner on death row, allowed herself to be transformed by his experience, wrote a book about it, and the rest is history.

Each person seeking a truer experience of justice responds differently, and all our responses are needed. But whatever our response, it starts with a simple individual experience—with a heart moved by human suffering, whether one's own or another's, and with a desire for healing that won't give up. This is the kind of anarchy—an anarchy of following heart, conscience, and calling—that, for us, carries the hope for the future, for making real in each life what justice can be.

Directories

Beer, Jennifer E., with Eileen Stief. *The Mediator's Handbook: Developed by Friends Conflict Resolution Programs.* Gabriola Island, British Columbia: New Society Publishers, 1997. In addition to an excellent bibliography on mediation, this book includes lists of newsletters, journals, and national mediation organizations.

The Church Council on Justice and Corrections. *Satisfying Justice: A Compendium of Initiatives, Programs, and Legislative Measures.* This must be ordered directly from the CCJC, 507 Bank Street, Ottawa, Ontario, K2P 1Z5, Canada, tel. (613) 563-1688, fax. (613) 237-6129, e-mail: <ccjc@web.net>. This is a compendium of 100 different programs from around the world, but it is much more than a directory. It is a deep investigation into the restorative justice process, including many stories of individual cases. It also critiques programs that advocate restorative justice measures but try to make them fit within the existing retributive model. It is a fascinating account of how people around the world are struggling to make the paradigm shift from retributive to restorative justice, case by case. We couldn't put it down—it's that good.

Consortium on Peace Research, Education and Development (COPRED). *Global Directory of Peace Studies and Conflict Resolution Programs, 2000 Edition.* c/o ICAR MSN 4D4, GMU, Fairfax, VA 22030-4444, tel. (703) 993-2436, fax. (703) 993-2406, e-mail: <copred@gmu.edu>, Web site: www.evergreen.edu/user/copred>. This global directory lists 381 colleges and universities around the world that have one or multiple programs on peace and conflict resolution, describing over 500 programs in all. Since their 1995 directory, 100 colleges and universities have added these studies to their curriculum. With each listing is a substantive description of the program, its nature, focus, and direction.

Newsletters, Publications, and Information

Conciliation Quarterly. Kristin Reimer, editor. A publication of the MCC U.S., Mennonite Conciliation Service, 21 South 12th Street, P.O. Box 500, Akron, PA 17501-0500, tel. (717) 859-3889, fax.(717) 859-3875, e-mail <mcs@mccus.org>. The Mennonites have a long heritage of pacifism, conflict resolution, and peacemaking. They were among the first European-American religious groups to champion restorative justice programs in this country, actually starting with a group of Mennonites in Canada, and they remain leaders in the field today. Far from being overly religious or academic, this journal is an open, honest, practical exploration of the challenges of conflict resolution from a Christian, peacemaking perspective. It often discusses the struggles Mennonites have within themselves and within their churches and communities in practicing pacifism and nonviolence. For example, what is a healthy management of feelings of anger? If suppressing it in the name of peace doesn't work—healing hurts only slightly by saying, "Peace, peace, where there is no peace" (Jeremiah 6:14)—then what is a genuinely healing, peacemaking response?

Hinduism Today. Kauai's Hindu Monastery, 107 Kaholalele Road, Kapaa, HI 96746-9304, tel. (808) 822-7032, x238 or toll-free, (888) 464-1008, fax. (808) 822-4351, e-mail: <subscribe@hindu.org>, Web site: <www.hinduismtoday.com>. Next to indigenous traditions, Hindu philosophy is one of the oldest spiritual traditions to teach nonviolence, *ahimsa*, to all living beings. This is the tradition that inspired Gandhi's "Satyagraha Campaign" or nonviolent, noncooperation with oppression, expressing the firm force of Truth and Love in human affairs. This excellent magazine, also available online including back issues, carries on this tradition in reporting everything from world affairs to home life to the problem of elephants stepping on land mines in the course of logging work. The magazine ran a powerful series on child-rearing opposing corporal punishment and exploring nonviolent methods of discipline, and it also reported on Kiran Bedi's work at the Tihar Prison. We value not only its information but also the gentle, compassionate, tolerant, balanced, nondogmatic tone the writers use in their reporting.

Justice as Healing newsletter. A quarterly publication of the Native Law Center of the University of Saskatchewan, 101 Diefenbaker Place, Saskatoon SK S7N 5B8, Canada, tel. (306) 966-6189, fax. (306) 966-6207, e-mail: <wdm133@duke.usask.ca>, Web site for the Native Law Center: <www.usask.ca/nativelaw/index.html>, Web site for *Justice as Healing*: <www.usask.ca/nativelaw/jah.html>. This is a powerful resource for investigating the aboriginal, indigenous approach to justice and how it contrasts with the dominant, retributive model. Published since 1995, the site offers fifty articles on the subject. Along with First Nation philosophies come many stories and first-hand accounts. Subscriptions to the printed version are also available. This is a fabulous resource.

National Criminal Justice Reference Service (NCJRS). P.O. Box 6000, Rockville, MD 20849-6000, tel. (800) 851-3420 or (301) 519-5500, e-mail: for questions, <askncjrs@ncjrs.org> or to order publications, <pub-order@ncjrs.org>, Web site: <www.ncjrs.org>. A federally sponsored information clearinghouse under the Department of Justice—described as "the 411 for criminal justice"—the NCJRS is a mammoth source of information, both online and in printed form. Seven information specialists are available to help locate the publication that would be most helpful. To find what they have on restorative justice, go to their web site (www.ncjrs.org), on the left bar, click on "More issues in criminal justice," then scroll down the alphabetized list to "restorative justice." Many publications will come up, available in PDF files or in hard copy. Some of the publications we have found helpful include (the reading is more interesting than these catchy titles might suggest): *Guide for Implementing the Balanced and Restorative Justice Model; Guidelines for Victim-Sensitive Victim-Offender Mediation: Restorative Justice through Dialogue; National Survey of Victim-Offender Mediation Programs in the United States; Directory of Victim-Offender Mediation Programs in the United States; Family Group Conferencing: Implications for Crime Victims; Multicultural Implications of Restorative Justice: Potential Pitfalls and Dangers;* and *Victim-Offender Mediation and Dialogue in Crimes of Severe Violence.*

The World of Forgiveness. A periodical of the International Forgiveness Institute, P.O. Box 6153, Madison, WI 53716-0153 or Communications Center, 6313 Landfall Drive, Madison, WI 53705. Coming from a restorative justice perspective, this periodical goes to the heart of the issue in addressing the concept of forgiveness: can we have it even in the midst of great pain and long-standing hostilities? Forgiveness can't be forced, but how can we open the door to it? And what of self-forgiveness: is it a cop-out or essential to breaking the cycle of harm? This journal explores these tough issues openly and authentically, not from "shoulds" or "oughts," but from a real need to seek healing and to break recurring cycles of trauma and pain.

Yes! A Journal of Positive Futures. P.O. Box 10818 Bainbridge Island, WA 98110, tel. (206) 842- 0216, fax. (206) 8425208, e-mail: <yes@future-net.org>, subscriptions tel. (800) 937-4451, e-mail: <subs@future-net.org>, Web site: <www.yesmagazine.org>. Though this quarterly magazine is not devoted specifically to restorative justice, its themes are always related to justice in one way or another: for example, environmental or eco-justice, justice in national and international economic relations, justice in media coverage and ownership, or justice as peacemaking among political and ethnic factions. This magazine is devoted to showing justice at work in the larger picture and showing how all of us can contribute to making that happen.

Private and Nonprofit Programs

Alternatives to Violence Project. 821 Euclid Avenue, Syracuse, NY 13210, tel. (713) 747-9999, Web site: <avpusa.org>. Originally founded by New York State Quakers in 1975, the Alternatives to Violence Project started as an outreach program for prisoners but soon expanded to activist groups, churches, communities, schools, and the general public. Ninety percent of the prison population returns to society, but coming from prison, they return from an extremely violent, vicious world. The obvious need is to help heal the internalized trauma and violence that prisoners carry within. It soon became obvious, however, that many of us do violence to ourselves through self-abuse, self-criticism, and harsh judgment, and this inward-focused violence does harm that extends beyond us. The need to help find alternatives to violence within and without has now made this work an international project.

The Moratorium Campaign. P.O. Box 13727, New Orleans, LA 70185-3727, tel.(504) 864-1071, fax. (504) 864-1654, Web site: <www.moratorium2000.org>. See also: <www.prejean.org>. Supported by Pope John Paul II's 1998 call for a moratorium on the death penalty, Sister Helen

Prejean has initiated an international campaign to make this happen. On her website, she writes: "In truth, American leaders now stand in a very vulnerable position as they are calling for democratic ideals and human rights throughout the world as they continue to uphold the execution of their own citizens—including juveniles and the mentally impaired." The movement is starting with a worldwide petition, which more than 3.2 million people have now signed.

Prison-Ashram Project. Human Kindness Foundation, P.O. Box 61619, Durham, NC 27715, tel. (919) 304-2220; fax. (919) 304-3220. Their sister organization in the United Kingdom is: Prison Phoenix Trust, P.O. Box 328, Oxford OX1 1PJ, tel. 01865–512521, Web site: <www. humankindness.org/project.html>. Started in 1973 by Bo Lozoff and Ram Dass, and two years later joined by Bo's wife Sita, The Prison-Ashram Project has touched the lives of thousands of prisoners around the globe with a vision of using prison time for inner work, self-improvement, and community healing. The Human Kindness Foundation, which funds this work, sends free to any prisoner who wants it Bo Lozoff's book *We're All Doing Time: A Guide to Getting Free.* Considering that the prison population in America has jumped tenfold in thirty years from 200,000 to nearly two million, that 70 percent of all prisoners are serving time for nonviolent offenses, and that 61 percent of federal prison inmates are doing time for drug offenses, the Lozoffs' efforts at bringing inner healing into prisons is profoundly needed. And it all started for the Lozoffs when a close relative was arrested on their boat for drug smuggling and sentenced to forty years in prison.

Education, Research, and Training Programs and Professional Associations

Center for Restorative Justice and Peacemaking and *National Restorative Justice Training Institute.* Mark Umbreit, founding director, University of Minnesota, College of Human Ecology, School of Social Work, 105 Peters Hall, 1404 Gortner Avenue, St. Paul, MN 55108-6160, tel. (612) 624-4923, fax. (612) 624-3744, e-mail: <rjp@tlcmail.che.umn.edu>, Web site: <ssw.che.umn.edu/rjp>. Dr. Mark Umbreit, a prolific researcher and writer on restorative justice, has built up an extensive center for advancing the field by developing resources (videos, books, publications, research programs) as well as by offering a wide range of training programs. He is a professor, but unlike many academics, he actively integrates spiritual and healing perspectives into his work. He is the '60s activist of whom we wrote, and his activism now is on the cutting edge of consciousness change around justice and all its implications for our lives.

International Alliance of Holistic Lawyers (IAHL). P. O. Box 753, Middlebury, VT 05753, tel. (802) 388-7478, fax. (802) 388-4079, email: <iahl@vtlink.net>, Web site: <www.IAHL.org>. Lawyers are caught in the middle of our most oppressive and destructive notions of justice: the combat-zone atmosphere, the pressure to win, and the warping influence of money on justice. This nonprofit educational organization seeks to address these issues head-on by exploring a holistic approach to law. Founded in 1991 by William van Zyverden, Esq., IAHL engages its members, legal practitioners, and the public in a dialogue about what justice can be if we take a holistic approach. To this end, its Web site offers a host of insightful articles to spur a paradigm shift in how we think about law and justice. To facilitate the considerable job of putting these ideas into practice, IAHL hosts annual conferences (2001 will be its ninth) for networking and the free and informal exchange of ideas, stories, and experiences. IAHL is also compiling a directory of holistic lawyers. This is powerful work in the trenches of everyday legal life, working to rethink what justice is all about.

National Association of Drug Court Professionals (NADCP). 4900 Seminary Road, Ste. 320, Alexandria, VA 22314, tel. (703) 575-9400 or (800) 316-2327, fax. (703) 575-9402, Web site: <www.nadcp.org>. The NADCP is devoted to preventing future drug-related crimes by helping current drug-addicted offenders break their addictions and heal. To this end, drug courts use the full weight of intervenors (judges, prosecutors, defense counsel, treatment specialists, probation officers, law enforcement personnel, educational and vocational experts, as well as community leaders) to transform the courts so that they offer those who go through them a healing, addiction-recovery experience. The approach is nonadversarial, designed not to work against offenders for punishment but to work with them for change and recovery. Judge Jeffrey Tauber, former president of the NADCP, describes the model as "therapeutic jurisprudence." The professionals strive to create a therapeutic community operating on the premise that people will make mistakes and that that's when they need help the most. There are currently four hundred drug courts in the world, two hundred of which are in the United States. According to outcome studies, those who have gone through the program have radically reduced rates of recidivism. The NADCP holds annual conferences for training, research, networking, and support.

Real Justice. Ted Wachtel, Founding Director. P.O. Box 229, Bethlehem, PA 18016, tel. (610) 807-9221, fax. (610) 807-0423, e-mail: <usa@realjustice.org>; Web site: <www.realjustice.org>. This is an international organization with centers in Australia, Canada, Hungary, Netherlands, New Zealand, Sweden, and the United Kingdom. It evolved from the restorative justice practice known as "family group conferencing" which Police Sergeant Terry O'Connell, a former policeman in the Australian town of Wagga Wagga, New South Wales, developed to help reduce juvenile crime. The organization now offers conferences and training programs nationally and internationally, literature, a newsletter, and an extensive Web site to support the use of this scripted approach to the restorative justice practice of bringing together victim, offender, and the support families and communities of each.

Restorative Justice Initiative, Minnesota Department of Corrections. Kay Pranis, Restorative Justice Planner. 1450 Energy Park Drive, Suite 200, St. Paul, MN 55108-5219, tel. (651) 642-0329, fax. (651) 642-0457, e-mail: <kpranis@co.doc.state.mn.us>; Web site: <www.doc.state.mn.us/organization/commjuv/restorativejustice.htm>; or, you can go to <www.doc. state.mn.us>, which takes you to the Minnesota Department of Corrections web site, scroll down and under "Get Information," click on "Restorative Justice." Besides providing a highly informative web site with excellent links, the Restorative Justice Initiative offers information on restorative justice, both theory and practice, as well as extensive training programs, carried nationally, in peacemaking, community building, and, fundamental to all of it, circles. The Restorative Justice Initiative takes healing circle methods into schools, families, and communities, as well as into victim-offender mediation sessions. It is exciting and cutting-edge work to be coming from a state department of corrections.

Victim Offender Mediation Association (VOMA). 2344 Nicollet Avenue South, Suite 330, Minneapolis, MN 55404, tel. (612) 874-0570, fax. (612) 874-0253, e-mail: <voma@voma.org>, Web site: <www.voma.org>. voma, an international membership association, supports people and communities working at restorative models of justice. They do this by providing resources, training, and technical assistance in victim-offender mediation, conferencing, circles, and other restorative justice practices. They have been holding their "Annual International Training Institute and Conference" since 1984.

Web Sites (not already listed above)

Since new work is emerging all the time, searching for "restorative justice," "peacemaking," "vorp or victim offender reconciliation program," as well as "vomp or victim offender mediation program," "conflict resolution" "mediation," "dispute resolution," or "alternatives to violence" will yield many sources, from the home pages of mediation firms, university programs, nonprofit organizations, and professional associations to the work of individuals. To get started, a listing of over seventy-five sites pertaining to restorative justice is available on each of the following two Web sites: *The Center for Restorative Justice and Peacemaking*: <ssw.che.umn.edu/rjp/RJ-Sites.htm>, and *Victim Offender Mediation Association*: <www.voma.org/links.shtml>.

Other sites we've found of interest include:

Anarchy: <home.nvg.org/~rchg/anarchy/>. This is a fascinating site with more articles on anarchy than one could read in weeks, including what anarchy means, its history, misunderstandings of it, and how it sheds light on current problems. Being anarchists, they note the differing views of anarchists on all these issues. Forced unity is not a priority with these folks.

Conflict resolution: <www.igc.org>. ConflictNet is a news site and lists the latest postings about conflict resolution and peace work around the world. It also hosts the Web pages of organizations doing similar work.

Environmental justice: <www.webofcreation.org>. This is "an ecumenical site offering eco-justice resources to faith-based communities." It's designed to help churches get their congregations involved in "defending creation" through education, awareness, and action.

Global Renaissance Alliance: <www.renaissancealliance.org>. Co-founded by Marianne Williamson and Neale Donald Walsh, this site describes a citizen-based, international network of spiritual activists. Their mission is to take a stand in local and national communities for the role of spiritual principles in solving the problems of the world. The method is to create small groups of people who regularly come together to bring their lives, their concerns about society, and their idealism into a circle of spiritual seeking, from which right action can then flow. It is a very innovative approach to tapping the desire in all of us to help address the world's problems by creating communities of shared vision and meaning.

Prison transformation: <www.kiranbedi.com/igprisons.htm>. Kiran Bedi, the first woman to become a police officer in India, transformed Tihar Jail from shocking squalor to a vital therapeutic community devoted to correction through community participation, community meaning the prisoners themselves. Programs for self-improvement of every sort were instituted, including "de-addiction," meditation, and yoga, as well as job training, schooling, and apprenticeships. She made happen in six years what restorative justice pioneers here in America only dream of happening, namely, turning people's lives around, treating prisoners as human beings with potentials for change, and instituting every possible channel and support for making personal transformation within a prison environment a reality. Once hell on earth, Tihar Jail has become a place for deep personal change.

Restorative Justice: <www.restorativejustice.org>. This site is maintained by the Prison Fellowship International, a Christian ministry global association. It offers news on restorative justice conferences and activities, research, dialogues, as well as an online library. It inspires prisoners with the message that justice as healing can happen.

Swadhyay— "Study of the self" creating a silent revolution: <www.swadhyay.org>. This site explains the life's work of Rev. Pandurang Vaijnath Shastri Athavale, the 1997 recipient of the Templeton Prize for Progress in Religion. This man is an ideal anarchist, for he has inspired a revolution in India on five fronts: (1) a spiritual revolution to an increased awareness and acceptance of God within; (2) a psychological and emotional revolution of bringing people closer together in seeking an enhanced quality of life; (3) a social revolution that does away with social injustice, social inequity, mindless rituals, and exploitative customs; (4) an economic revolution in which villagers work together in harmony to create impersonal wealth to help the needy, and (5) a political revolution born of a greater awareness of people's rights, duties, and needs, which enables people to settle issues and find solutions to problems by meeting together on a common platform. The logic behind these revolutions is simple: "God exists; God is indwelling within me hence within others as well; this makes me divine and worthy of self-respect; and it makes others divine and worthy of respect too; God exists within the whole universe, so everything within the universe is divine and worthy of reverence; I am thereby related to everything in the universe, which motivates me to care for others and the universe and not to damage them." The site explains how this philosophy translates into action in socially, economically, and politically innovative ways (community orchards, fishing cooperatives, childcare programs, youth programs, etc.), all designed to create a just society. First, it honors individuals and supports their good on every level, so that people can move from poverty to self-sufficiency. Then, once they're on their feet, it gives individuals an opportunity to give back to those in need through all sorts of community channels.

Tribal Court Clearinghouse: <www.tribal-institute.org>. This Web site provides an extensive source of information to people working in Native American tribal courts. The site is created by the Tribal Law and Policy Institute, 8235 Santa Monica Boulevard, Suite 205, West Hollywood, CA 90046, tel. (323) 650-5467, fax. (323) 650-8149. It presents a wealth of information not only about tribal courts but also about First Nations in general—their diversity, their history, their culture, and their understanding of law and justice, based on the Creator, natural law, and the path of healing that humans take in community, together.

ᘒ Index

Aboriginal approach, 48–54, 70–72, 76–78, 188–92, 205–207, 219, 224. *See also* First Nations, Haudenosaunee, indigenous cultures, Native Americans

abstract thinking: about deserving, 239; as ignoring connectedness, 97; about justice, 13, 182–83, 193, 195; and legal precedents, 187

Adams, Abigail and John, 260–61

addiction, 20–21; and drug courts, 120–21; around money and power, 130; prevention of, 216; social structures create, 157; and trauma, 90

adversarial model, 21–22; and "might makes right," 22; from model of separate individualities, 128; and rights, xi; vs. holistic approach, 50–51

African Americans: exclusion from Constitution, 185; and leading reformers, 217; slavery and injustices imposed on, 15, 232, 258

African spirituality, 116

anarchy (nasty): and changing the model causing it, 261–62; as consequence of departing from reality's order, 97–98; fear of, 84; from "might makes right," 257–61; psychological and emotional, 258; two opposite meanings of, 255–57

anarchy (visionary), 255–56, 273: based on who we are, 268–69; idealistic, 255–56, 262, 273; and not

adopting bad anarchy's methods, 263; as opposing control by force, 262–63; as subversive to control model, 263, 273; two opposite meanings of, 255–57; views chaos as model-created, 273

animal: abuse, 23; testing, 243–45

archetypal processes, 74, 178; we're connected to, 267

Asian philosophies, 125; on open vs. closed systems, 145-46; on wholeness, 97–99

assumptions: about human nature, 83–88; about use of trauma for control, 87–90

astrology, 108, 177

atomistic methods, 103

authorities: role of in current model, 15, 21

autonomy: and intrinsic motivation, 77; and process of learning, 172

Bacon, Francis, 223

balance: of gender perspectives, 188–201; in managing the seen, 235–36; and moderation, 204; pain as signs of systems out of, 115–21; among parts within whole, 102–103, 135; as quality of systems, 49–50; in resolving conflicts, 241–42; and scales of justice, 239; of seen and unseen, 212, 219–27, 241–42; using ritual to restore, 53. *See also* imbalance, the seen and the unseen